The Political Logic of Poverty Relief

Poverty relief programs are shaped by politics. The particular design that social programs take is to a large extent determined by the existing institutional constraints and politicians' imperative to win elections. *The Political Logic of Poverty Relief* places elections and institutional design at the core of poverty alleviation. The authors develop a theory with applications to Mexico about how elections shape social programs aimed at aiding the poor. Would political parties possess incentives to target the poor with transfers aimed at poverty alleviation or would they instead give these to their supporters? Would politicians rely on the distribution of particularistic benefits rather than public goods? The authors assess the welfare effects of social programs in Mexico and whether voters reward politicians for targeted poverty alleviation programs. The book provides a new interpretation of the role of cash transfers and poverty relief assistance in the development of welfare state institutions.

Alberto Diaz-Cayeros is Senior Fellow at the Center on Democracy, Development, and the Rule of Law at Stanford University.

Federico Estévez is Professor of Political Science at the Instituto Tecnológico Autónomo de México (ITAM).

Beatriz Magaloni is Associate Professor at the Department of Political Science and Senior Fellow at the Freeman Spogli Institute for International Studies at Stanford University.

Cambridge Studies in Comparative Politics

General Editors
Kathleen Thelen *Massachusetts Institute of Technology*
Erik Wibbels *Duke University*

Associate Editors
Robert H. Bates *Harvard University*
Gary Cox *Stanford University*
Thad Dunning *University of California, Berkeley*
Anna Grzymala-Busse *University of Michigan, Ann Arbor*
Stephen Hanson *The College of William and Mary*
Torben Iversen *Harvard University*
Stathis Kalyvas *Yale University*
Margaret Levi *Stanford University*
Peter Lange *Duke University*
Helen Milner *Princeton University*
Frances Rosenbluth *Yale University*
Susan Stokes *Yale University*

Other Books in the Series
Michael Albertus, *Autocracy and Redistribution: The Politics of Land Reform*
Ben W. Ansell, *From the Ballot to the Blackboard: The Redistributive Political Economy of Education*
Leonardo R. Arriola, *Multi-Ethnic Coalitions in Africa, Business Financing of Opposition Election Campaigns*
David Austen-Smith, Jeffry A. Frieden, Miriam A. Golden, Karl Ove Moene, and Adam Przeworski, eds., *Selected Works of Michael Wallerstein: The Political Economy of Inequality, Unions, and Social Democracy*
Andy Baker, *The Market and the Masses in Latin America: Policy Reform and Consumption in Liberalizing Economies*
Lisa Baldez, *Why Women Protest? Women's Movements in Chile*
Kate Baldwin, *The Paradox of Traditional Chiefs in Democratic Africa*
Stefano Bartolini, *The Political Mobilization of the European Left, 1860-1980: The Class Cleavage*
Robert Bates, *When Things Fell Apart: State Failure in Late-Century Africa*
Mark Beissinger, *Nationalist Mobilization and the Collapse of the Soviet State*
Nancy Bermeo, ed., *Unemployment in the New Europe*
Carles Boix, *Democracy and Redistribution*

continued after the Index

The Political Logic of Poverty Relief

Electoral Strategies and Social Policy in Mexico

ALBERTO DIAZ-CAYEROS
Stanford University

FEDERICO ESTÉVEZ
Instituto Tecnológico Autónomo de México

BEATRIZ MAGALONI
Stanford University

CAMBRIDGE
UNIVERSITY PRESS

University Printing House, Cambridge CB2 8BS, United Kingdom

One Liberty Plaza, 20th Floor, New York, NY 10006, USA

477 Williamstown Road, Port Melbourne, VIC 3207, Australia

4843/24, 2nd Floor, Ansari Road, Daryaganj, Delhi - 110002, India

79 Anson Road, #06-04/06, Singapore 079906

Cambridge University Press is part of the University of Cambridge.

It furthers the University's mission by disseminating knowledge in the pursuit of education, learning and research at the highest international levels of excellence.

www.cambridge.org
Information on this title: www.cambridge.org/9781316505892

© Alberto Diaz-Cayeros, Federico Estévez and Beatriz Magaloni 2016

This publication is in copyright. Subject to statutory exception and to the provisions of relevant collective licensing agreements, no reproduction of any part may take place without the written permission of Cambridge University Press.

First published 2016
First paperback edition 2017

A catalogue record for this publication is available from the British Library

Library of Congress Cataloging in Publication data
Diaz-Cayeros, Alberto, author.
The political logic of poverty relief : electoral strategies and social policy in Mexico / Alberto Diaz-Cayeros, Federico Estévez, Beatriz Magaloni.
  pages cm.
Includes bibliographical references and index.
ISBN 978-1-107-14028-8 (hardback)
1. Public welfare – Political aspects – Mexico. 2. Poverty – Government policy – Mexico.
3. Human services – Political aspects – Mexico. 4. Politics, Practical – Mexico. 5. Public administration – Mexico. 6. Mexico – Politics and government. 7. Mexico – Social policy. I. Estévez, Federico, 1956– author II. Magaloni, Beatriz. III. Title.
HV113.D53   2016
362.5´5610972–dc23   2015029274

ISBN 978-1-107-14028-8 Hardback
ISBN 978-1-316-50589-2 Paperback

Cambridge University Press has no responsibility for the persistence or accuracy of URLs for external or third-party internet websites referred to in this publication, and does not guarantee that any content on such websites is, or will remain, accurate or appropriate.

Contents

List of Figures	*page* viii
List of Tables	ix
Acknowledgments	xi
List of Abbreviations	xv
Introduction	1
PART I STRATEGIES OF VOTE BUYING	23
1 Poverty Relief in Latin America	25
2 Poverty Relief in Mexico: A Geographic Approach	45
3 Political Machines and Vote Buying	67
4 Clientelism and the Political Manipulation of *Pronasol*	86
PART II THE CONSEQUENCES OF CLIENTELISM AND ENTITLEMENTS	113
5 Improving Communities: Transfers for Basic Public Services	119
6 Saving Lives: Social Programs and Infant Mortality Rates	144
7 Electoral Payoffs of Antipoverty Programs	158
8 Conclusion: The Politics of Entitled Social Protection	182
References	205
Index	233

Figures

I.1	Types of Antipoverty Programs	page 8
1.1	Social Protection in Latin America	27
2.1	Social Protection in Mexico	48
2.2	Share of Population Living under Nutritional Poverty Line (CONEVAL), 2002	52
2.3	The Geography of Poverty Relief Transfers in Mexico, 1989–2005	59
2.4	Electoral Geography	64
2.5	Municipal Democracy: Years since Party Alternation	65
3.1	A Model of Ongoing Vote Buying	76
4.1	PRI Core Voter Support	93
4.2	Correlation between Core Voter Support and Vote Erosion	95
4.3	Clientelism and Development	98
4.4	Simulated Effects of Municipal Electoral History on Private Goods	103
4.5	Mean Core Size and Trends by Level of Competition	106
4.6	Clientelism and Competition	109
4.7	Clientelism and Effective Competition	110
II.1	Partisan Identity of Municipal Government and Poverty-Alleviation Funds	114
5.1	Change in Public Good Coverage, 1990–2000	129
6.1	Geography of Infant Mortality Rate in 2000	151
7.1	Simulated Electoral Returns of Social Programs	171

Tables

2.1	Evolution of Poverty in Mexico	*page* 47
2.2	Geographic Correlates of Poverty in Mexican Municipalities	54
4.1	Centralist Logic of *Pronasol*: The Core Voter	100
4.2	Mean Municipal Party System Descriptives	106
4.3	Peripheral Logic of *Pronasol*: Facing Elections	108
5.1	Decentralized Allocations of Infrastructure Funds	134
5.2	Improvements in Public Goods Coverage, 1990–2000	139
5.3	Effects of Alternative Measures of Electoral Democracy	139
5.4	Alternation and Improvements in Public Goods Coverage, 1990–2000	141
5.5	Democracy Index and Improvements in Public Goods Coverage, 1990–2000	142
6.1	Determinants of Changes in IMR in Mexico, 1990–2000	154
6.2	Effect of Democracy on Changes in IMR in Mexico, 1990–2000	155
6.3	Quantile Regression of Infant Mortality Change, 1990–2000	156
7.1	Effects of Programs on Vote Swings (Instrumental Variables Estimations)	168
7.2	Percentage Voting for Major Candidates and Program Beneficiaries	175
7.3	First-stage Probits for Propensity Score Estimation	176
7.4	Effects of *Progresa* and *Oportunidades* on Vote Choice in 2000 and 2006	177

Acknowledgments

This book was born from a shared passion and an endearing friendship. When we embarked on an intellectual voyage more than a decade ago we did not know that this book would become such an integral part of our lives for the years to come. The project was nurtured by countless trips between California and Mexico to bring the authors together, and endless nights of pondering, hundreds of hours running statistical models, and countless meals sharing good food and even better conversation. Sometimes a trip would yield marginal improvements to the project, at times major breakthroughs. But every trip reaffirmed our commitment to not declare the book finished until we were thoroughly satisfied with it.

At the risk of failing to mention the numerous people who have generously shared their ideas, criticisms, and detailed comments, we want to thank, in alphabetical order: Felipe Auyero, Robert Bates, Rikhil Bhanvani, Valeria Brusco, Pradeep Chhibber, Gary Cox, Alain de Janvry, Ana de la O, Thad Dunning, Barbara Geddes, Andrew Gelman, Miriam Golden, Kristof Gosztonyi, Karen Jusko, Robert Kaufman, Phil Keefer, Stuti Khemani, Herbert Kitschelt, Eliana LaFerrara, David Laitin, Santiago Levy, John Londregan, Isabela Mares, Rohini Pande, Simona Piattoni, Dan Posner, James Robinson, Natan Sachs, Elisabeth Sadoulet, Andreas Schedler, Ken Scheve, Susan Stokes, Guido Tabellini, Andrea Vindigni, Leonard Wantchekon, Rebecca Weitz-Shapiro, Paul Wise, Steven Wilkinson, and Cesar Zucco. Over the years most of them have moved from admired colleagues to close friends.

Preliminary research on *Pronasol* was supported with funding from the World Bank. Additional funding was provided by the Center on Democracy, Development, and the Rule of Law, the Department of Political Science Munro Fund, and the Vice Provost for Undergraduate Education grant from Stanford University. We learned a lot about clientelism and distributive politics in a conference we organized at the Bellagio Center, supported by the Rockefeller

Foundation, in December 2005, and at a series of subsequent meetings of a loosely organized group for the study of distributive politics meeting over the years, thanks to the efforts of Gary Cox (UCSD), Frances Rosenbluth, and Ana de la O (Yale).

We also want to thank a number of people we encountered in our field work that allowed us to gain critical insight about how social programs affect the poor. In Los Altos de Chiapas, Enrique Bentzul and his team opened their doors to us and allowed us to observe at a close range the operation of *Oportunidades* during two field trips in 2011 and 2012. We also want to thank participants in two focus groups we held in Oaxaca in 2009, as well as in door-to-door interviews we held in 2010 in various towns in the Zapotec and Mixtec regions of that state. We want to thank numerous women from poor villages in the Lake Atitlán region of Guatemala who have generously opened their homes to us and our students to help us understand the burdens of poverty, hunger, malnutrition, and disease that plague their everyday lives and those of their children. The experiences of these women serve as a tragic illustration of the hardships of living in extreme poverty without a safety net and government action.

We want to express our profound admiration to Santiago Levi, a scholar and government official who transformed the lives of millions. We invited Santiago to Stanford to give a seminar and many of our students described him as "one of the most inspiring persons" they had met. We want to second these views in acknowledging him for the huge contribution he has made to remedy extreme poverty in Mexico and elsewhere. The adoption of Conditional Cash Transfers in almost every country in Latin America was certainly influenced by Mexico's success story with *Progresa*, which Levi skillfully innovated.

Invaluable research assistance was provided by Sandra Pineda, Marcela Gómez, Arianna Sánchez, Lorena Becerra, Jorge Bravo, Katherine Kelman, Ana Gardea, Emmerich Davis, Hamilton Ulmer, Rachel Brule, and Stephanie Gimenez. Elena Cryst proofread the text and prepared the final maps. Belinda Byrne edited the final manuscript. Chapters and fragments of the project were presented in many venues. Papers were presented at professional conferences, including the Midwest Political Science Association Meetings, the American Political Science Association Meetings, and the Latin American Studies Association Meetings. We thank participants in seminars at UCLA, Berkeley, the World Bank, Duke, Columbia, Yale, Chicago, Michigan, Princeton, and Stanford. We specially want to thank Susan Stokes, Margaret Levi, and Lew Bateman from Cambridge University Press for a "Seattle Seminar at Yale," where we discussed an early version of the manuscript. The book was hopefully improved by our honest effort to incorporate the thoughtful dissection and constructive criticisms we received there. Finally, three anonymous referees from Cambridge University Press challenged us with incisive criticisms we hope to have addressed in this final version. The shortcomings and errors

Acknowledgments

in the book are obviously our own, while the merits are to be shared with all of them.

Final thanks go to our families, in particular to Margie, Nicolas, Mateo, and Emilia, who have lived with this project for so many years. For their love the book is dedicated to them.

Abbreviations

AFDC	American Families with Dependent Children
CCT	Conditional Cash Transfer
CETES	*Certificados de la Tesorería*
CONAPO	*Consejo Nacional de Población*
CONEVAL	*Consejo Nacional de Evaluación de la Política de Desarrollo Social*
DHS	Demographic and Health Surveys
ELF	Ethno-Linguistic Fractionalization
ENADID	*Encuesta Nacional de Dinámica Demográfica*
FAISM	*Fondo de Aportaciones para la Infraestructura Social Municipal*
FDN	*Frente Democrático Nacional*
FDSM	*Fondo de Desarrollo Social Municipal*
FISM	*Fondo de Infraestructura Social Municipal*
FONCODES	*Fondo de Cooperación para el Desarrollo Social*
Fortamun	*Fondo para el Fortalecimiento de los Municipios y el Distrito Federal*
GIS	Geographic Information Systems
HDI	Human Development Index
IFE	*Instituto Federal Electoral*
IMR	Infant Mortality Rate
IMSS	*Instituto Mexicano del Seguro Social*
INEGI	*Instituto Nacional de Estadística y Geografía*
INFONAVIT	*Instituto Nacional del Fondo de Vivienda para los Trabajadores*
ISI	Import Substitution Industrialization
ISSSTE	*Instituto de Seguridad y Seguro Social para Trabajadores del Estado*

IV	Instrumental Variable
LCF	*Ley de Coordinación Fiscal*
MIFAPRO	*Mi Familia Progresa*
MUAP	Modifiable Unit Areal Problem
NAFTA	North American Free Trade Agreement
Oportunidades	*Programa de Desarrollo Humano Oportunidades*
PAN	*Partido Acción Nacional*
PASSPA	*Programa de Atención de Servicios de Salud para la Población Abierta*
PMT	Proxy Means Testing
PRD	*Partido de la Revolución Democrática*
PREP	*Programa de Resultados Electorales Preliminares*
PRI	*Partido Revolucionario Institucional*
Procampo	*Programa de Apoyos Directos al Campo*
Progresa	*Programa de Educación, Salud y Alimentación*
Pronasol	*Programa Nacional de Solidaridad*
Sedesol	*Secretaría de Desarrollo Social*
SSA	*Secretaría de Salud*
UNDP	United Nations Development Program (in Spanish PNUD)
UNICEF	United Nations Fund for Children
WHO	World Health Organization

Introduction

This book is about the political economy of poverty relief. Poverty alleviation requires active government involvement in the provision of public goods such as health services, education, roads, water, and sanitation, among others. Poverty relief also presupposes some degree of redistribution to individuals and families through income supplements, direct aid-in-kind, pensions, and tax subsidies. All too often, transfers and public services fail to reach the poor because of misaligned political incentives and poor governance, which is manifested in corruption, abuse of power, rent-seeking, and dysfunctional or weak public institutions. Although there is consensus on the importance of good governance for poverty alleviation, not enough is known about the conditions under which it comes about and how it can be replicated.

Applying scientific knowledge and technical expertise is a fundamental first step in the design of successful poverty-alleviation policies. However, the real challenge of poverty relief is not to devise technical solutions – scientific knowledge exists, for example, to prevent infectious disease with simple interventions such as vaccines, oral rehydration, and antibiotics, or to improve the safety of drinking water. The critical problem is to structure the political process with clear incentives for politicians and bureaucrats to aid the poor while restraining their own rent-seeking.

A growing body of research in political science emphasizes that democratic political institutions are better at improving well-being than autocratic ones.[1] Although empirical findings in this literature are controversial, there is growing consensus that in democracies politicians tend to be more responsive to the poor. The basic logic behind this observation is that of electoral competition.

---

[1] See Przeworski et al. (2000); Navia and Zweifel (2003); Zweifel and Navia (2000); Stasavage (2005); Kudamatsu (2012); McGuire (2010); Baum and Lake (2003); Gerring, Thacker and Moreno (2005).

Democracies produce strong incentives for politicians to choose policies that reflect what the median voter wants.

However, political democracy does not always generate effective poverty reduction. Politicians take opportunistic advantage of poverty-alleviation funds, redirecting money, jobs, and other benefits toward supporters and away from opponents, as well as diverting government resources for personal gain. Myriad are the complaints that political manipulation, corruption, and vote buying plague the delivery of social benefits to the poor.

In this book we place electoral politics and institutional design at the core of poverty alleviation. Government decisions about redistribution – who gets what, when, and how much – are shaped by electoral considerations. The particular design social programs take is to a large extent determined by politicians' imperative to win elections and the existing institutional constrains. This book develops a theory with applications to Mexico about how elections shape social programs aimed at aiding the poor. Our theory first asks about distributive politics. Would political parties ever possess incentives to target the poor with transfers aimed at poverty alleviation or would instead give these to their supporters? Would politicians rely on the distribution of particularistic benefits rather than public goods?

Second, we study the welfare impacts of social programs. We measure the welfare impacts of these transfers looking at tangible outcomes: access to water, sanitation, and electricity, and reduction in infant mortality. The latter metric provides a rather compelling indicator of well-being linked to development policies. As noted by Wise (2003), the failure to save children from preventable deaths is usually seen as a tragedy and a "shameful" outcome that forces us to reexamine our public and social responsibility. Although pathophysiological factors, such as dehydration, may ultimately lead to a child's death, it is social conditions that produce the circumstances in which mothers cannot nourish their children properly, protect them from water-borne infectious diseases or seek adequate medical interventions that might save their lives – circumstances that attest to failures in government policy and the overall social environment in which poor children live – and die.

The simple notion that societies should not let children die from preventable causes resonates strongly with Amartya Sen's (1999) view of "development as freedom" and Partha Dasgupta's (1993) assertion that development is ultimately about "the manner in which people are able to live and die." In fact, one of the greatest advancements in the human condition, as highlighted by Fogel (2004) and Deaton (2013), was the possibility for ordinary people to escape hunger and high mortality – originally in Europe and North America, but more recently in other areas of the world. The achievement of long life expectancy and low infant mortality, however, has yet to be replicated in much of the developing world.

Third, the book provides a systematic measure of the electoral payoffs of poverty relief transfers. How many more votes do discretionary particularistic transfers yield relative to entitlements? How many more votes are generated by expenditures on discretionary private goods as against public goods? These questions are central to distributive politics. Only by understanding the electoral consequences of various poverty relief strategies – how they shape voting behavior and electoral alignments – will we be able to comprehend why politicians execute the programs they do.

1.1 ABJECT POVERTY AND GOVERNMENT ACTION

Francisca, a forty-year-old Mayan woman, lived in a squatter village on a coffee plantation several hours' walk from the nearest town. The village lacked potable water, a sewage system, and electricity. Francisca walked more than one hour every day from her adobe hut to the nearest well to collect water and to wash her family's clothes. Only seven of Francisca's thirteen children survived past their fifth birthdays. Her youngest child suffered a severe bout of dehydration at seven months and died before Francisca was able to reach the nearest clinic. All of Francisca's daughters died, leaving her with seven sons and one adopted three-year-old orphan girl. If only a health clinic had been closer, or there were some ready cash to buy medicine, she might have saved her daughters from premature death. Francisca's story serves as a dramatic illustration of what it means to be trapped in poverty when better-targeted government action could have saved her children's lives.

Francisca's story is a common one throughout the developing world, where the rural poor have limited or no access to a social safety net and where their children suffer and die from mostly preventable diseases. The leader of the 1995 Zapatista uprising in the South of Mexico, *Subcomandante* Marcos, decried the tragedy of such poverty trap:

> Or shall we ask pardon from the dead, our dead, who died "natural" deaths of "natural causes" like measles, whooping cough, breakbone fever, cholera, typhus, mononucleosis, tetanus, pneumonia, malaria and other lovely gastrointestinal and pulmonary diseases? Our dead, so very dead, so democratically dead from sorrow because no one did anything, because the dead, our dead, went just like that, with no one keeping count, with no one saying, "ENOUGH!" (Marcos, 2001: 30)

The Zapatista rebellion, of course, erupted at the end of Mexican president Carlos Salinas' administration (1988–1994), which had promised to put an end to poverty and take Mexico to the "first" world. His government had initiated a major antipoverty program named *Programa Nacional de Solidaridad (Pronasol)*. Acclaimed by the international community, the program relied on government transfers for projects proposed by community organizations and municipal governments throughout the country. Despite an average annual allocation to this program of 1.18 percent of GDP, the Zapatista rebellion poignantly attests that poverty remained unabated by the end of Salinas' presidential term. As we show in this book, the program's goal of reducing poverty was thwarted by the diversion of its resources in line with the electoral needs of the ruling party.

Much has changed in Mexico since 1995. In 1997 the government created a conditional cash transfer (CCT) program called the *Programa de Educación, Salud y Alimentación (Progresa)*, now widely touted as one of the most successful poverty relief programs in the world. *Progresa* offered money to mothers within poor families in exchange for attending basic courses on preventive health care and hygiene, making regular visits to health clinics, and keeping their children in school. Beneficiaries become ineligible for the program only through failure to comply with these requirements.

To insulate *Progresa* from political influences, beneficiaries were selected on the basis of objective measures of social deprivation and poverty. Initially implemented in rural areas, the creation of *Progresa* represented a turning point in the design of social policy in Mexico (Levy, 2006; Levy and Rodríguez, 2005). After the *Partido Acción Nacional* (PAN) defeated the hegemonic *Partido Revolucionario Institucional* (PRI) in 2000, the new administration expanded the program to urban areas using similar criteria to select beneficiary families. Renamed *Programa de Desarrollo Humano Oportunidades*, the urban part of the program has evolved into a demand-driven structure where applicants for benefits self-select instead of the government identifying eligible recipients.

A second important transformation occurred in the late 1990s, following the Zapatista rebellion. During the Ernesto Zedillo administration (1994–2000), social infrastructure funding underwent reform with the creation of the *Fondo de Aportaciones para la Infraestructura Social Municipal* (FISM). FISM implemented a major reformulation of federal transfers for public works and social infrastructure projects distributed according to poverty-based formulas to the more than 2,430 municipalities in Mexico. With the introduction of FISM, the PRI reduced its discretion to manipulate social infrastructure investments. The poorest municipalities receive disproportionate funds, which are now transferred in regular and predictable fashion. Once the funds reach the municipalities, their mayors play the central role in deciding how these are distributed. Patterns of local electoral accountability, or lack thereof, as we will see in this book, have become essential in shaping the provision and distribution of local public goods.

Prior to FISM, the government also spent considerable amounts of money on social infrastructure projects. But there was substantial leakage. For example, in a personal interview with a high-ranking public official in charge of federal finance at the time, we were told that when the new administration tried to audit *Pronasol*, many of the public infrastructure projects that had been reported in the books were either abandoned without completion or did not even exist.

Fifteen years ago, poor communities all over Mexico had very limited or no access to many basic public services. With her toothless smile, Francisca says that things have "improved a lot during the last years" and that her "children no longer die and seldom get sick." Although clearly still impoverished, homes

1.1 Abject Poverty and Government Action

in her community now have access to water from a communal faucet (even if available only a few hours per day), proper sanitation, paved streets, and electricity. New roads also make the local health clinic more easily accessible. When her youngest child was recently sick with diarrhea, they were able to reach the clinic before he became dehydrated. Francisca now receives regular cash transfers from *Oportunidades*, which enables her to buy food, soap, and shoes for her previously barefooted children, and if there is spare cash, school supplies. This is a story repeated in thousands of villages and communities throughout the country. The contrast with Mexico's previous history of clientelistic relief for the poor could not be starker.

Mexico was infamous for the extreme forms of political manipulation of public funds and social programs under the formerly hegemonic party. A study of *Pronasol*'s wide-ranging operations and programs allows us systematically to understand what political scientists refer to as clientelism, a form of political exchange between politicians and the poor prevalent in the developing world. According to Kitschelt and Wilkinson (2007) a clientelistic relation is characterized by:

[First], a contingent direct exchange that concerns goods from which non-participants in the exchange can be excluded. Second, such exchanges become viable from the perspective of politicians, if voter constituencies respond in predictable fashion to clientelistic inducements without excessive opportunism and free riding. Third, short of constituencies' spontaneous and voluntary compliance with the clientelistic deal, politicians can invest in organizational structures to monitor and enforce clientelistic exchanges. (p. 76)

Changing the rules for the allocation of local public goods and social infrastructure projects in Mexico produced a major impact on poverty reduction. Our approach highlights three elements in the transformation of social policies during this period. First, social programs became more progressive and better targeted to the poor. Since the early 1940s, Mexico began to put in place social insurance schemes tied to participation in the formal labor market. A common feature in Latin America and the Caribbean, the restriction of social insurance to formal sector workers led to the characterization of the region's social insurance systems as "truncated welfare states" because the majority of the population, especially the poor, did not receive these benefits (Ferranti et al., 2004; Fiszbein, 2004; Rawlings et al., 2004). Recent decades have witnessed the emergence of parallel social protection schemes, including social investment funds such as *Pronasol* and FISM and, more recently, conditional cash transfers aimed at households in extreme poverty.[2]

Second, the new social programs also reduced government discretion in the administration of the funds. It is always difficult to ascertain how much leakage

---

[2] The World Bank keeps periodically updated information on both social funds and transfer programs in its Social Protection webpage at: http://www.worldbank.org/sp (accessed March 11, 2012).

bedevils antipoverty spending such that social welfare is not improved. This includes the possibility of mismanagement of public funds, as well as outright theft, corruption, and rent-seeking. The new social programs have reduced such leakages, although by no means eliminated them. Professional bureaucracies administer the programs, with a new emphasis on transparency. The use of poverty formulas along with technical measures to identify beneficiaries according to need has also limited politicians' inclinations to respond to electoral and partisan imperatives rather than to the goal of poverty alleviation.

Third, subnational governments have become increasingly involved in the provision of local public works, with funds for these projects coming from redistributive federal transfers. Under PRI rule Mexico had a long history of centralized control over public spending. Decisions about social infrastructure projects were made and funded in the nation's capital. This political equilibrium changed in the 1990s, as the opposition gained control of more subnational governments and the PRI lost majority control of the Chamber of Deputies along with exclusive control over the federal budget. New fiscal arrangements at the national level devolved decision-making power over the selection and funding of social infrastructure projects to states and municipalities.

Better targeting, less government discretion, and redistributive decentralization had profound effects on the poor's welfare in Mexico. The clientelistic linkage between politicians and the poor that was prevalent during the authoritarian era has shifted to a new entitlement-based social protection regime. In 2009, we interviewed beneficiaries of *Oportunidades* in forty-eight poor rural communities in Oaxaca and asked about how they evaluated the program, if they felt that they could lose their benefits depending on their partisan loyalties and vote choices, and if they worried about the coming presidential elections. Our interviewees unanimously agreed that their benefits were secure. A Oaxacan mother of five told us in an interview: "Before, you had to be with the PRI to get anything from the government." Another woman told us: "The governor controls everything in Oaxaca. However, here you can be *PRDísta (Partido de la Revolución Democrática)*, back the governor [from the PRI], and still get benefits from *Oportunidades*," even though the PAN controlled the federal government. "Although sometimes people who do not really need it get *Oportunidades*, it is less corrupt because benefits arrive regardless of the party you favor," a young Zapotec father of two told us. Overwhelmingly, beneficiaries of the program were satisfied, although there were some concerns about whether the transfers were being targeted to the poorest among them.

I.2 THE GOVERNANCE OF POVERTY RELIEF

This book asks why and when politicians choose one form of redistribution as against another; we quantify how they impact the poor's welfare; and we estimate the electoral payoffs of each of these strategies of poverty reduction.

I.2 *The Governance of Poverty Relief*

In the following sections we sketch our theory about strategic choice among different distributive strategies.

For analytical purposes we focus on two important dimensions in the design, implementation, and management of social policies. The first dimension reflects the process by which beneficiaries are selected into a program and considers the degree of government discretion to decide who gets a public transfer, how much it is worth, and who gets withdrawn from a program. Along this dimension we distinguish *discretionary programs* from *formula-based programs*.

Discretionary programs are what Dixit and Londregan (1996) refer to as "tactical redistribution," which should be distinguished from "programmatic redistribution" or welfare transfers that are embedded in laws written in abstract and general terms and administered by autonomous bureaucracies. Programs with little formal government discretion offer benefits that are assigned according to objective or programmatic eligibility criteria – for instance, persons over sixty-five, women with children, unemployed workers – and in theory should not be withdrawn unless a beneficiary fails to meet the defined criteria.

The second dimension considers the type of benefits delivered – whether a program delivers nonexcludable public goods or targeted transfers of private goods. Public infrastructure projects, including roads, street pavement, sewers, health clinics, schools, running water, public markets, lighting, garbage collection, and so on are aimed at communities. Particularistic transfers such as cash benefits, land titles, scholarships, nutritional supplements, construction materials, and subsidized credit can be targeted to individuals. The more indivisible a transfer is, the less incumbent parties can employ them to target their supporters and punish their opponents.[3] A second difference between public and private goods is their reversibility. Discretionary private transfers can be withdrawn at any point in time, such as when a voter supports a rival at the polls. Infrastructure projects are fixed investments that are less vulnerable to opportunism because everyone in a given district can enjoy them.

Figure I.1 classifies the types of social programs that will be analyzed in subsequent chapters of this book according to the two governance dimensions highlighted above. In the lower-right quadrant are discretionary programs targeted to individuals. These programs can be unambiguously administered through clientelistic networks. This form of electoral linkage, to be effective, needs an organizational structure of brokers or other intermediaries (e.g., bosses, caciques, or local notables) that help parties select voters according to their partisanship or other attributes (Stokes et al., 2013; Magaloni, 2006; Calvo and Murillo, 2013).

In the lower-left quadrant are nondiscretionary excludable transfers, or entitlements. A *sine qua non* for entitlement programs to work is that politicians are

---

[3] Some public goods, of course, exhibit elements of excludability, for example, on a territorial basis, which permits politicians to select political jurisdictions for the delivery of benefits on the basis of political criteria such as, for example, the partisan affiliation of local officials.

	Non-discretional	Discretional
Public	Formula-based Decentralized Transfers	Pork-barrel Projects
Private	Entitlements	Clientelism

FIGURE I.1. Types of antipoverty programs.

not able to select and deselect beneficiaries at will. As we discuss in Chapter 1, entitlements require an independent or depoliticized bureaucratic agency to be effective and to enforce the legal criteria for selecting beneficiaries.

Selection into these programs is frequently accomplished through means-testing so that only those with incomes below a certain threshold are eligible.[4] In the upper-right quadrant of Figure I.1 are discretionary social transfers spent on infrastructure, electrification, street pavement, road construction, and so on. This kind of discretionary public works funding is often referred to as "pork-barrel politics." Originated in the United States, the term refers to public works whose benefits are concentrated in a particular district but whose costs are spread among all taxpayers. A key difference between clientelism and the pork barrel is that within a given district politicians can't screen potential users with the latter instrument.

---

[4] However, Alatas et al. (2012) note that in many developing countries it is challenging to implement a conventional income-based means test because recipients lack verifiable records of their earnings. They identify two alternative strategies: proxy means testing (PMTs) used, for example, by Mexico's *Progresa/Oportunidades* and Colombia's *Familias en Acción*; and community-based targeting used, for example, by the Bangladeshi Food-for-Education program. In the former, the government collects information through the use of surveys and census data about assets and demographic characteristics and creates a "proxy" for income, which is then used for targeting. In the latter, the government allows the community or its local leaders to select the beneficiaries. The authors evaluate both methods through a randomized control trial in Indonesia and find that proxy-means tests perform better in identifying the poor, but there is greater satisfaction among beneficiaries with the method that uses community rankings for that purpose.

Public goods programs can be discretionary or, as in the upper-left quadrant, the funding transfers to subnational jurisdictions can be decentralized, allocated by formula. Highly relevant in federal systems, formulas for the distribution of public goods investments restrain discretion in the allocation of projects across jurisdictions and allow for some degree of redistribution.

Our book explains the choice among poverty relief strategies that fall in each of the quadrants of Figure I.1. It also measures how effective these types of distributive polices are at alleviating poverty, and we inquire into the electoral consequences of different poverty alleviation strategies. The programs we study represent significant budgetary allocations and, unlike campaign gifts and handouts,[5] they can make a critical difference for poverty alleviation. Our book is about the governance of social programs – how they are designed and their transfers delivered – and how it impacts the poor's well-being. The book compellingly demonstrates that effective poverty relief requires nondiscretionary and better-targeted poverty relief strategies. Yet perversely clientelistic and pork barreling transfers, we demonstrate with empirical evidence for the case of Mexico, yield significantly more votes while allowing politicians to extract more rents. Why clientelism is such a prevalent form of electoral exchange in developing societies, how it skews social policies aimed at the poor, and under what conditions it can be superseded by more democratic and accountable forms of exchange are some of the central questions this book addresses.

I.3 DISCRETIONARY REDISTRIBUTION AND A THEORY OF VOTE BUYING

The first element of our inquiry is to understand discretionary redistribution, corresponding to the social programs in the right quadrants of Figure I.1. When do politicians choose to buy votes with discretionary private goods and when with patronage over public goods provision? To what types of voters are these benefits targeted? How effective are private versus public goods at gaining votes? To answer these questions, we begin by developing a formal model of vote buying which is then evaluated drawing on extensive original data and statistical analysis. Our empirical focus is on subnational variation in Mexico, although our theory aims to be broadly applicable to distributive politics in other parts of the developing world.

The book develops a theory of vote buying based on a portfolio diversification logic driving the relative shares of discretionary private and public goods distributed in a given district. We build on distributive politics models and the core-swing debate (Cox and McCubbins, 1986; Dixit and Londregan, 1996; Stokes, 2005; Nichter, 2008). Our theory departs from these models in three fundamental ways. First, we assume that voters base their choices on material

---

[5] For studies focusing on campaign handouts see, for example, Stokes (2005) and Nichter (2008). Most chapters in Stokes et al. (2013) also focus on campaign gifts.

considerations alone, with ideology playing a secondary role at best. We ask how parties can construct long-lasting winning coalitions when ideology or other symbolic appeals are not effective to mobilize voters, either because these promises are not credible (Keefer and Vlaicu, 2008; Wantchekon, 2004), or because poor voters place a much higher utility to material considerations – for example, how to provide for the next meal, a job, medicine, or clothes. Second, most of the existing models of distributive politics focus on vote buying on the spot – the distribution of transfers during an election in exchange for votes or turnout (Nichter, 2008). Our model focuses on vote buying embedded in an ongoing relationship. Third, our model takes party loyalty as conditional, or endogenous, rather than fixed. Voters' partisan attachments are *constructed* through reciprocal material and symbolic exchanges, past, present, and future.

A key implication of our theory is that politicians will funnel jobs, patronage, and other excludable benefits to their core voters. Our model is in line with Cox and McCubbins (1986), for whom political parties favor the core voter strategy mainly due to aversion to electoral risk. In a more recent extension of that argument, Cox (2009) incorporates the importance of mobilization and elite coordination as objectives inducing investment in core voters. We move beyond these formulations, sustaining that political parties will favor core voters to solve three salient problems of vote buying prevailing particularly in developing societies: (1) sustain stable electoral coalitions over time in the absence of other anchors like ideology; (2) mitigate voter opportunism; and (3) parties are able to extract more rents because it is cheaper to buy off voters the party knows best. This informational advantage allows parties to know voters' "reservation values" and pay them the minimal amount necessary to buy their votes (Zarazaga, 2011). These claims, we hold, better capture the logic of machine politics.

Our predictions run counter to swing voter models that claim that parties should not waste scarce resources on loyal supporters and should rationally prefer to cater to swing voters whose choice might swing an election (Lindbeck and Weibull, 1986; Dixit and Londregan, 1996; Stokes, 2005).[6] Stokes et al. (2013) also predict that parties will favor core voters, although in their account this strategy is electorally inefficient and represents a waste of resources that stems from principal-agent problems between party elites and their brokers.

In our approach parties do not waste resources when they invest in core voters. In the absence of strong ideological attachments or other symbolic appeals, the ongoing buying of votes constitutes a primary way to sustain stable electoral coalitions. Nurturing voter loyalty through repeated exchange, in turn, allows political parties to simultaneously mitigate voter opportunism problems

---

[6] There are a number of important contributions that empirically deal with the core-swing debate: Dahlberg and Johansson (2002); Calvo and Murillo (2004); Stokes (2005); Brusco et al. (2004); Magaloni (2006); Golden and Picci (2008); Magaloni et al. (2007); Kasara (2007); among others.

and reduce the costs of vote buying. The alternative would be to buy votes on the spot market, a far more costly and risky strategy because voters who are not tied to a party by a sense of reciprocity can always take the transfer and walk away.

The ongoing contract between the party and its core base is enforced, in our approach, through reciprocal threats of punishment. If the party fails to deliver particularistic transfers to a core voter, he can threaten to become disloyal in future elections. If the core voter, for his part, fails to reciprocate with his ongoing electoral support, the party can threaten to remove him from the spoils system. For this threat to be credible, the party needs clientelistic networks to gain local knowledge about its voters' and enforce the "punishment regime" (Magaloni, 2006). Vote buying and clientelistic contracts between a party and its core base usually go hand-in-hand because the latter are necessary to mitigate commitment problems. The alternative is to buy votes on the spot market, a treacherous and onerous way to build winning electoral coalitions.

An important corollary of our theory is that not all core voters will receive an equal amount of transfers. First, core voters might not possess enough leverage to oblige their party to treat them well – for example, it could be argued that ethnicity or other *primordial* attachments make voters relatively less mobile across parties, as seems to be the case in some contexts in Africa. In these settings, political parties might be able to keep a loyal base of voters without having to distribute too many transfers. Degree of electoral completion is another relevant variables to consider. When a party holds a virtual electoral monopoly, as was the case in very poor districts in Mexico, core voters do not possess leverage to oblige their party to fulfill its part of the contract and might receive benign neglect. The PRI, in fact, disproportionately targeted discretionary particularistic transfers to loyal places where its core base was deteriorating at a faster rate than in poorer areas. These core places were favored over poorer voters, the book compellingly demonstrates, because they were better able to threaten to become disloyal if the PRI refused to grant them transfers.

One reason why social programs administered through clientelistic networks fail to alleviate poverty is that they are not necessarily targeted to the poor, as this book demonstrates. Another reason why this form of electoral exchange is not effective at alleviating poverty is that it traps voters into supporting a party that extracts rents from them. The dilemma is that of coordination: if a core voter defects in isolation, she or he will be punished. If all other voters reason likewise the machine is sustained in equilibrium (Magaloni, 2006; Diaz-Cayeros et al., 2001). Core voters support the party in part because it gives them particularistic transfers and in part because of the threat of punishment.

When would parties diversify their portfolio by investing in more welfare-enhancing public goods over particularistic transfers? We argue that when a party's core base of support is not sufficient to win elections, it will be compelled to mobilize support from other voter groups, including swing voters. This creates a dilemma analogous to the one described in Przeworski and Sprague (1986) regarding socialist parties' imperative to create multiclass coalitions to win elections. In their approach, socialist parties that needed to mobilize the support of middle-class allies alienated their working-class core, which became available for political mobilization by other political parties. We consider here an analogous dilemma: the political machine risks losing its core supporters if it delivers particularistic transfers to buy swing voters off.

Our theory and empirical evidence suggest that parties can employ particular portfolios of private versus public transfers to mobilize both core and swing voters. The distributive politics literature has tended to portray investments in core-versus-swing voters as an all-or-nothing strategy, overlooking the fact that political parties have at their disposal a basket of polices that includes particularistic and collective goods. Our main theoretical predictions regarding portfolio diversification is that the share of public goods over particularistic transfers in a given geographic area will increase as a party's core base proves insufficient to guarantee victory.

The book thus identifies welfare benefits to voters stemming from electoral competition. The logic is akin to Bueno de Mesquita et al. (2003), who argue that democracy is advantageous for the provision of public goods because leaders need to appeal to broader coalitions in order to remain in power and this is more easily accomplished through public goods provision than through private transfers. Persson and Tabellini (1999) present a similar logic holding that politicians who need to win elections by majority are more likely to deliver public goods to the electorate. Chhibber and Nooruddin (2004) apply these same insights in their study of India.

Although electoral competition sharpens incentives to supply public goods, the theory and empirical evidence presented in this book makes explicit why politicians continue to resort to the distribution of discretionary particularistic transfers, and even when buying voters one-on-one would appear to be more inefficient than the supply of public goods. The reason is that as vote-buying strategy, public goods provision is riskier, even when it is assumed to be more cost-effective. With a systematic analysis of a variety of social programs in Mexico during the past decades, we demonstrate that investments in public goods do not yield as many votes per peso spent as particularistic transfers. Electoral risk compels politicians to diversify to public goods transfers in order to appeal to a majority, but also to resort to clientelism as a risk-hedging device (Magaloni et al., 2007).

1.4 FORMULA-BASED POVERTY RELIEF

Despite the virtues of electoral competition, democracies in the developing world more often than not underprovide public goods. This book's framework argues that in the absence of institutional reforms that explicitly aim at restraining government discretion and insulating social programs from

I.4 Formula-Based Poverty Relief

political manipulation, public goods will continue to be underprovided and what is provided will suffer substantial leakage.

With the establishment of Progresa/Oportunidades and FISM, Mexico social polices shifted from discretionary to formula-based poverty relief. Although clientelism and pork-barreling politics were by no means abandoned, huge progress was made in that major poverty relief transfers began for the first time to be distributed according to formulas that privilege targeting to the poorest citizens.

How can countries transit from this suboptimal equilibrium where antipoverty policies are distorted? Why would politicians ever tie their hands reducing their discretion to administer social programs? We underscore three important processes encouraging the PRI to abandon *Pronasol* and to create formula-based poverty relief programs.

First, the Zapatista rebellion erupted in December of 1994. Mayan Indians took six municipalities in Los Altos de Chiapas by force and declared war on the government. The rebellion took place after six years of the antipoverty relief strategy and millions of pesos spent on social programs under the banner of *Pronasol*. The Zapatistas rebellion turned crystal-clear the corruption of the clientelistic social assistance regime and its incapacity to combat poverty in a meaningful way.

The Salinas and Zedillo administrations had reasons to believe that violence could spread much beyond Chiapas. As explained in Magaloni (2006) and Trejo (2012) the outbreak of the rebellion motivated the electoral reforms that paved the road to democracy in Mexico. The rebellion also was critical in convincing the Zedillo administration, the PRI, and the economic elites that it was critical to combat poverty in a meaningful manner if Mexico wanted to avoid the spread of social unrest among the poor. The threat of social unrest made politicians more tolerant of technocratic solutions that sought to redress poverty through new policy innovations.

Second, Mexican voters rebelled against the system of corruption. After the Peso crisis of 1994–1995, they voted against the PRI in one local election after another. Furthermore, during the mid-term elections of 1997, the PRI lost the majority in the Chamber of Deputies necessary to pass legislation unilaterally. Voters' rebellion versus the PRI triggered a major institutional transformation in Mexico. For the first time in the PRI's history, the budget had to be negotiated with the opposition and the government could not operate without its endorsement. The Zedillo presidency had to negotiate legislation with the PAN. It was during this period that *Progresa* (later *Oportunidades*) and FISM were established. For the first time, social policies and the distribution of federal transfers to municipalities and states were established through interparty bargaining, which clearly limited the powers of the PRI.

Third, after the wave of defeats in the local elections and the PRI's loss of the majority in the Lower Chamber of Deputies, governors, bureaucrats, party cadres, and politicians at all levels of government from this party had good reasons to believe that their party could lose the coming presidential elections of 2000.

Following the line of reasoning in Geddes' (1994) model regarding civil service reform, we argue that the PRI had incentives to restrain clientelism and pork barreling by creating an independent and professional bureaucracy because voters had collectively rebelled the PRI and this party reasonably anticipated it could lose power. Incentives to delegate power to an independent bureaucracy arose to prevent the PRI's opponents from conquering the state in the future to serve their own patronage ends. The line of argumentation is also consistent with Moe (1995), who stresses the importance of political uncertainty in creating incentives to separate politics from the administration. He argues that in a democracy politicians often can only "shut out their opponents by shutting themselves out too. In many cases then [politicians] create structures than even they cannot control" (p. 125).

1.5 STATE CAPACITY

Separating the governance of poverty relief from the PRI had a major impact on the poor's welfare. This book emphasizes two social programs, *Progresa/Oportunidades* and FISM, which represented a huge step at combating poverty in Mexico. In contrast to the public goods programs administered through Pronasol, the formula-driven FISM was more effective at delivering local public goods (sanitation, water, and electricity) to the poorest places. The CCT program, for its part, is the single most effective policy we analyze in this book that contributed to saving babies' lives from the killer diseases so sharply described by Subcomandante Marcos.

To be effective CCT, programs require impressive state capacity. Aside from vast informational resources and bureaucratic coordination at the national level, they require close and continuous supervision in the localities where they operate. These programs put women and children at the center of poverty reduction. Making sure that the money arrives and stays in women's hands and that these resources are directed at improving children's health, nutrition, and education requires dense state and organizational capabilities. Essential for the proper implementation of CCTs is that the program's officials on the ground keep the program insulated from illegitimate capture by local bosses, brokers, and political parties, and that they stay proximate to women's everyday lives to protect them from potential abuses by health providers, teachers, and their husbands.

The problem of implementation is a local one that in our opinion can be properly understood only through ethnographic work. Enrique Bentzul generously shared with us valuable insights about what it takes to operate *Oportunidades* on the ground and to keep the program insulated from political influence. Enrique was rightly described to us as an "icon of *Oportunidades* in Los Altos de Chiapas." He was born in San Juan Chamula and is fluent in

I.5 State Capacity

Tzotzil and Spanish. He began working for the program in 1998 shortly after *Progresa* was created. In one of his first visits to a village in the municipality of San Juan Chamula, the community could not understand what the program's officials were saying and Enrique decided to step forward to translate.

One of the first persons of his ethnic background to enjoy so much political authority in Chiapas, Enrique is now (as of 2012) the Coordinator of Regional Support of *Oportunidades* in Los Altos de Chiapas. He is in charge of administering the program in 18 municipalities covering more than 100,000 families, mostly indigenous. Our conversations with him, and numerous visits to villages in Oaxaca and Chiapas, have allowed us to understand that *Oportunidades* has become much more than its cash-transfers. It is a program that is fundamentally transforming local social structures in poor communities throughout Mexico.

"A program that puts women at the center stage necessarily causes a lot of trouble," Enrique explains. "Take, for example, San Juan Chamula, where men have for centuries excluded and oppressed women and where powerful *caciques* (local bosses) have always ruled unchecked. Only if you are a man, a PRIísta and a Catholic have you a voice in Chamula." In such settings, to safeguard *Oportunidades* state officials need constantly to negotiate on behalf of women. "This is a very violent and complicated region," Enrique tells us. "My job basically consists in solving conflicts."

In our interviews we were able to identify three generic forms of conflict. First is intrafamily conflict – most commonly, husbands taking the CCT money from their wives or physically abusing them. Because battered women normally are afraid to denounce such abuses, often the only way to detect intrafamily violence is through word of mouth. This is one way through which the women's networks created by the program can help. Enrique tells us that when *Oportunidades* officials find out that a woman is suffering abuse, they intervene by arbitrating the intrafamily conflict and restraining the husband by threatening to withdraw benefits from the family.[7]

A second form of conflict involves extortion by teachers and health providers. *Oportunidades* has transferred a great deal of power to health providers and teachers in thousands of villages and towns. They are charged with certifying whether beneficiaries comply with the program's conditions. Thus, these individuals have a lot of leverage that can be used to extort women. The most typical abuses involve bribes, although other more serious crimes, including sexual violence, are not uncommon.[8] These abuses, Enrique tells us, are

---

[7] Concerns regarding intrafamily conflicts prompted the evaluation of Progresa to include qualitative research carried out by a team of anthropologists led by Nahmad (1999).

[8] In one community in the municipality of Zinacantán, for example, the health provider asked for bribes from women who were afraid to undergo their Pap smear because they thought it could sterilize them. The health provider extorted women to give him money in exchange for falsely reporting they had performed the procedure. Women who refused to give him money, he threatened, would be reported as noncompliant. Enrique was able to detect this abuse and duly correct it.

difficult to detect because women are often reluctant to report them for fear of retaliation. Often these abuses are detected through the vigilant presence of *Oportunidades* officials in the villages. Enrique makes sure that in Los Altos de Chiapas the program is monitored in every village through well-selected community liaisons. Furthermore, the program has instituted a clever system of complaints that allow women to voice anonymous grievances either in writing (a "buzón de quejas") or by calls to special telephone lines.

A third generic type of conflict involves political parties, their local brokers, or *caciques* trying to politicize the program, and this is particularly pronounced when national or local elections are celebrated. Prior to the most recent presidential election, in 2012 it came to our attention that local *Oportunidades* promoters were offered 40,000 pesos (around 3,000 dollars) to campaign in the name of one or another political party, which is illegal. Efforts are made to temper these temptations in what is known as the electoral "shielding" (*blindaje*) of social programs: officials are not allowed to go into the field or enroll new beneficiaries for six months prior to the elections.

Preventing politicization of the program on the ground requires an optimal institutional design and constant oversight.[9] Crucial to the design of the CCT program is that local delegates such as Enrique and his operators are appointed, paid, and promoted by the federal bureaucracy rather than by local authorities; another important aspect is that these delegates control neither the selection of beneficiaries nor money transfers to them.

When a year later we interviewed Enrique again, prior to the 2012 federal elections, we learned that the traditional authorities in San Juan Chamula had recently incarcerated two *Oportunidades* officials. They were accused of allegially campaigning in Enrique's favor for the coming municipal election and conditioning funds in exchange for vote pledges. The accusations were bogus, since Enrique had no intention to run for public office. In the days following the incarceration of the *Oportunidades* officials, hundreds of women in San Juan Chamula took to the streets to demand the liberation of the jailed officials and defend the program's autonomy. In the end, the traditional authorities, mostly affiliated to the PRI, levied a large fine against those responsible for the false accusations.[10]

Despite numerous and continual challenges, the organizational structure of *Oportunidades* works most of the time. The CCT program is present in

---

[9] For example, in the municipality of Zinacantán, where the community is deeply divided along partisan lines and there is "even a Church for each political party," the communities have attempted to politicize the program by embedding parties within the program's structure – for example, establishing four *vocales* (local delegates) per party and segmenting meetings and health clinics for beneficiaries according to their partisan leanings. Enrique had to intervene through complex political negotiations to exclude the parties from the program's structure.

[10] Similar charges of political manipulation are voiced every time elections are held anywhere in the country. It is hard to know which are true. What is clear, however, is that important efforts have been made to provide safeguards to prevent abuse.

almost every village in Mexico in the form of cash disbursements, health clinics, and hospitals, public schools and assorted officials involved in much more than program administration. This dense network of the state has impacted for good the lives of millions of women and children across poor villages in Mexico. The similarly dense patron-client networks of the past were never able to accomplish much.

1.6 THE POOR'S WELFARE

Studies of distributive politics are often narrowly focused on the question of whether politicians target core or swing voters.[11] Such studies largely disregard the critical issue of how electoral investment strategies impact voters' well-being. This lack of attention to the welfare consequences of vote buying strategies opens a huge gap in the distributive politics literature. The gap is particularly worrisome in works on clientelism, which reveal the limits of democratic accountability in developing societies.

The failure of public service provision in developing countries can be attributed to both supply-side and demand-side problems. On the supply side, corrupted public institutions, unaccountable governments, and weak and dysfunctional states can be credited with poor provision of services. On the demand side, the scholarly literature has focused on issues such as ethnic fractionalization as a cause of free-riding and coordination obstacles and on lack of citizen information, among other factors.[12] In this book we focus on the supply side, asking how variation in the governance of poverty relief shapes welfare outcomes. Through comparison of the effects of clientelistic versus programmatic social protection policies, we provide direct and comparable measures of the welfare effects produced by different forms of "political linkage" (Kitschelt, 2000). The book integrates an analysis of the electoral returns of distributive politics with an analysis of their welfare consequences. It therefore goes beyond studies currently available.

At the onset of the Zapatista rebellion in 1994, *Subcomandante* Marcos denounced the tragic fate of indigenous women and men who powerlessly witnessed their children die from treatable diseases. The Chiapas uprising was a great surprise to many because it took place after massive expenditures for poverty alleviation under *Pronasol*. It is ironic to note that the hospital constructed with *Pronasol* funds during those years in the town of Guadalupe Tepeyac became one of the headquarters of the Zapatista rebellion and served as a prison for such high-level hostages as a former governor of Chiapas.

---

[11] Cox and McCubbins (1986); Lindbeck and Weibull (1986); Dixit and Londregan (1996); Calvo and Murillo (2004); Stokes (2005); Golden and Picci (2008); Nichter (2008); and Stokes et al. (2013) are notable examples.
[12] See Alesina et al. (1999); Banerjee and Somanthan (2007); Banerjee (2004); Chang et al. (2010); Habyarimanna et al. (2007 and 2009); Ferraz and Finan (2008); Reinikka and Svensson (2004); Keefer and Khemani (2014); Chong et al. (2012).

According to most accounts, the state-of-the-art facilities in the hospital never became functional for lack of staff and medical supplies.

Poverty is a multifaceted condition going beyond a lack of income. It can encompass precarious living standards, deficient health, malnutrition, underdeveloped cognitive skills, and lack of access to public services. In this book we restrict the analysis of welfare consequences to two facets of poverty: access to basic public services and the life-and-death prospects of the most vulnerable population, infants. Our goal is to compare the efficacy of different forms of anti-poverty policies – the clientelistic program *Pronasol* and the entitlement program *Progresa/Oportunidades*, the pork-barreling within *Pronasol* and the formula-based social infrastructure program FISM. We also seek to assess whether electoral democracy and electoral competition play a role in attenuating poverty.

Our book contributes to a vibrant debate within the political science literature about regime effects on infant mortality rates (IMR). Existing comparative studies focus on the life-saving effects of democracy.[13] The book departs from this literature in two main respects. First, rather than using cross-national data, we focus on subnational variation in IMR in a single country as it democratizes. Second, the chapter studies the effects of the design of public policies in the reduction of IMR. A general assumption among public health practitioners and scholars is that well-designed policy interventions contribute to the reduction of IMR (Sepúlveda et al., 2006). There is some evidence in the literature, albeit contested, suggesting that democracies may be better at reducing IMR than autocracies. But few studies have been able to specify the channels and mechanisms through which political regime or democratic change may affect public health. We focus on social programs aimed at alleviating poverty.

Antipoverty policies can affect infant mortality directly or indirectly. Governments can provide public works that impact collective well-being through the provision of public goods. Social infrastructure programs such as FISM or *Pronasol*'s public goods programs might have an indirect effect on infant mortality through their impact on sanitation, the construction of health clinics and roads. Clientelistic programs might have an indirect effect on infant mortality by increasing household income, allowing parents to access otherwise unaffordable emergency transportation, health services, and medicines. CCTs, for their part, might have both direct and indirect effects on infant health through three channels. The first is an indirect income channel going through households' increase in cash availability that facilitates access to health services and medicines. The second is the indirect channel of female empowerment in the household. The third is a more direct effect related to how the program conditions the cash transfer on regular health visits and targets women with health education workshops.

---

[13] See Przeworski et al. (2000); Navia and Zweifel (2003); Zweifel and Navia (2000); Ross (2006); Gerring et al. (2005); Lake and Baum (2001); Baum and Lake (2003); Kudamatsu (2012).

Our empirical analyses demonstrate that when transferring funds to individuals for political motives underscores the design of social policy, the developmental goal of poverty reduction is greatly distorted. Despite millions of dollars spent, our book demonstrates that *Pronasol* had marginal effects at improving provision of basic services such as water, sanitation, and electricity in the poorest municipalities. The program's particularistic transfers – including its cash transfers – were ineffective at reducing premature infant deaths. In contrast, the creation of better-designed policy targeted to poor women has had a decisive impact on saving children's lives. Moreover, improvements of basic public service delivery through FISM also contributed to reductions in infant mortality.

Hence, new social programs such as FISM and *Oportunidades* that came as a result of stronger checks and balances increased electoral competition and decentralization, improved the provision of municipal public goods, and allowed poor families greater access to health services. Our results also demonstrate some direct effects of local democracy on improvements in public service delivery and reductions in IMR. Municipalities that experienced partisan turnover in power are better at preserving infants' lives and providing basic services than municipalities that remained under one-party rule.

There are some painful lessons for Mexico to be drawn from the story our book recounts: thousands of children likely would remain alive had the reform of social policy occurred a few years earlier. *Subcomandante* Marcos was right in pointing out that children died from curable diseases and no one took notice. *Pronasol*'s claims about "putting an end to poverty" are judged against a clearly defined metric: was the program able to save the lives of the most vulnerable? Our results suggest that its effects were at best marginal. Some poverty alleviation took place, but it paled in comparison to what better-designed poverty relief policies achieved.

1.7 HOW VOTERS RESPOND TO POVERTY ALLEVIATION PROGRAMS

The last element of our analysis brings us to a fundamental question regarding electoral accountability in democratic societies. How did voters respond to these various poverty alleviation strategies? Recent scholarship has begun to explore in more systematic ways the electoral returns to government transfers and programs (Magaloni, 2006; Magaloni et al., 2007; De la O, 2011; Hsieh et al., 2011; Zucco, 2013; Becerra, 2012). These studies demonstrate that voters respond positively to government transfers, a finding that is hardly surprising. Our approach moves beyond this kind of work in that we systematically compare the electoral payoffs of various types of government transfers: discretionary versus nondiscretionary transfers delivering particularistic versus public goods.

Among the distributive politics scholarly work, Wantchekon's (2004) study stands out because it seeks to compare how voters respond to particularistic versus public goods. His study randomly assigns campaign statements to politicians in different localities in a real national election in Benin. The campaign statements are either phrased as promises to deliver particularistic payoffs or promises to deliver universalistic benefits. Wantchekon (2004) finds that in most localities voters tended to respond more positively to the particularistic campaign statement possibly because they found the public goods statement noncredible. The study is about the electoral returns of campaign promises but is not able to measure how voters respond to *actual* policies. By focusing on effective budgetary allocations rather than campaign promises, we are better prepared to measure the vote-buying potential of public versus private goods, delivered through discretionary versus nondiscretionary programs.

Our study employs both aggregate municipal-level electoral returns and individual-level survey evidence to assess the electoral consequences of two decades of antipoverty programs in Mexico. Our findings demonstrate unequivocally that discretionary particularistic transfers delivered through clientelistic networks exhibit the highest electoral returns. These transfers were not disproportionately targeted to the poorest citizens despite the fact that they supported the PRI but to wealthier voters who could more credibly threaten to defect this party in future elections. The perverse nature of clientelism, we compellingly demonstrate with empirical evidence, is that voters are bought off with an array of material inducements that are not welfare enhancing in the long run. Clientelism perpetuates poverty and keeps the poor trapped.

Our findings also demonstrate that discretionary particularistic transfers yield more votes than discretionary transfers for public goods delivery, several times over. More welfare enhancing, discretionary public goods, or pork-barreling projects are riskier investments since they are targeted to places with typically smaller cores where project beneficiaries include nonsupporters.[14]

Despite having uncovered remarkable electoral efficiency for clientelism, our results leave ample room for optimism. Our book compellingly demonstrates that poor voters in Mexico handsomely rewarded incumbents that were credited with establishing or expanding CCT programs. Fully consistent with democracy, voters respond positively to programmatic policies that can effectively alleviate poverty.

1.8 ROADMAP

In subsequent chapters we explore the challenges of poverty relief in the developing world. Through a careful analysis of social programs in Mexico during the past two decades, we hope to understand how politics, electoral incentives, and political institutions impact the fight against poverty.

The first chapter places Mexico in comparative perspective by analyzing the transformation of social policies in Latin America during the recent generation.

---

[14] This does not mean that voters mobilized through pork are not valuable: in tight races they may determine the outcome of the election.

I.8 Roadmap

Political democracy has not always translated into effective poverty alleviation. This chapter documents the expansion of social protection in the region, distinguishing four paths of welfare system development: (1) *clientelistic social protection*; (2) *entitled social protection*; (3) *universalistic social protection*; and (4) *failed social protection*. By discussing variation in welfare regimes in Latin American democracies, the chapter highlights a central dilemma of poverty reduction: elected politicians often take opportunistic advantage of poverty-alleviation funds at the expense of the poor. Understanding how it is that democracies can transit from this suboptimal equilibrium to one where there is effective antipoverty action is a central task of the chapter.

The second chapter introduces the Mexican case properly and advocates for a disaggregated geographic approach to the study of poverty-relief strategies. It outlines the basic spatial patterns of poverty in Mexico, the mapping of political power across the territory, and the geography of public expenditure. It justifies our use of the municipal level as the politically relevant jurisdiction and unit of analysis.

The third chapter develops our theory of vote buying, from which hypotheses are derived regarding the particular strategies politicians choose in order to ensure their survival when deciding discretionary allocations of public resources. In particular, the chapter presents a model of *conditional party loyalty* and elucidates why party machines should favor their core supporters. The chapter also presents the portfolio diversification approach in which politicians choose to invest in a mix of both private and public goods to different voter groups.

Chapter 4 puts to the test our predictions about the political logic driving the allocation of discretionary funds, focusing on *Pronasol* expenditures and using municipal-level data. The *Pronasol* program comprised more than twenty programs for the delivery of public works and particularistic benefits. Our analysis reveals that the PRI disproportionately used *Pronasol*'s funds to target its loyal voters, thus distorting and abusing the program's goal of combating poverty. Over time the program became increasingly clientelistic, allocating more and more resources to particularistic transfers rather than collective benefits. These transfers, we demonstrate, were initially used to lock core voters into the clientelistic contract, with politicians disproportionately targeting municipalities where PRI voter loyalties were more rapidly eroding.

Part II of the book accounts for the transformation of social policies in Mexico and their effect. The introduction to that part seeks to answer why the PRI chose to give up clientelistic social assistance setting up instead an entitled social assistance regime. We provide an account that while leaving ample room for agency on the part of the specific individuals and policymakers involved in crafting new institutional solutions to poverty relief, highlights the structural and institutional restraints under which they operated. It is clear that a threat of rebellion and voters' profound discontent with the PRI's system of corruption played a crucial role in the abandonment of clientelism.

The fifth and sixth chapters examine the welfare effects of the antipoverty policies. Chapter 5 focuses on how public goods expenditures within *Pronasol* and FISM improved social infrastructure or basic public services (water, sanitation, electricity) for poor localities. We also provide answers to the question of whether decentralization and local electoral democracy and accountability lead to improvements in the delivery of public services. Chapter 6 examines the impact of these same types of public expenditure on the indicator that is essential to progress in social welfare: the reduction of infant mortality rates.

Chapter 7 explores the impact of social programs on the political survival of politicians, accounting for their electoral effects in three presidential elections in Mexico, in 1994, 2000, and 2006. The analysis allows us to understand how voters respond to the different poverty relief programs explored in the book. Which strategy is better in generating political support – clientelism or entitlements, private or public goods? Chapter 8 answers the question by systematically comparing the electoral payoffs of various antipoverty programs, employing both aggregate municipal-level and individual-level data.

The book concludes with a summary of our findings and a prospective look into the future of social protection. We speculate that we are witnessing an important departure from the welfare state institutions characteristic of the twentieth century, to a new paradigm of social protection that requires strong state capacity and democratic institution building. The new regime is not predicated on solidarity and socialization of risk, but rather privileges individual targeting and local provision of public goods. We show that, for better or worse, these new approaches are embedded in an old Latin American tradition of fighting poverty through the piecemeal creation of poverty relief policies and self-reliance for the organization of social service delivery. This tradition is more in line with early modern policies of poor relief deployed before the rise of the welfare state.

PART I

STRATEGIES OF VOTE BUYING

1

Poverty Relief in Latin America

> Well-fed people can enhance their dignity, their health and their learning capacity. Putting resources into social programs is not expenditure. It is investment.
> Luiz Inácio Lula da Silva (61st Session, UN General Assembly, September 19, 2006)

This chapter analyzes the transformation of social policies in Latin America. The poor were traditionally excluded from public welfare. Social insurance policies – old age pensions, health insurance, housing support and disability, and maternity benefits – disproportionately benefited the middle classes, leaving the poor unprotected. In theory, funded by contributions, Latin America's "truncated welfare states"ended up paid by general taxation, which meant that the poor effectively transferred income to the rich, reinforcing and widening income inequality (Lindert et al., 2006).

The biggest social policy challenge during the democratic era has been to extend welfare benefits to those traditionally excluded from social insurance programs, which in most Latin American countries were set up by authoritarian regimes (Mares and Carnes, 2009). Democratization in Latin America was not accompanied by immediate improvements in social expenditures for poverty relief. Countries in the region transited to democracy during an era of economic crises and structural adjustment, which made fiscal contraction necessary (Haggard and Kaufman, 1995). As Latin American countries were able to regain economic growth – in part spurred by recent booms in commodity prices – diverse social programs involving food support, conditional cash transfers, financial support of education, noncontributory old-age pensions, and health insurance for the poor had begun to mushroom throughout the region.

This chapter documents the expansion of social protection in the region, distinguishing four paths of welfare system development:

- *Clientelistic social protection* in which most poverty relief programs are discretionary and administered through partisan or personal networks. Examples are Mexico's PRI prior to 1997, Fujimori in Peru, Hugo Chávez in Venezuela, Rafael Correa in Ecuador, and the Peronists in Argentina. Clientelism in social protection fosters corruption and rent-seeking and is not effective at alleviating poverty.
- *Entitled social protection* whereby expanded benefits to the poor are targeted according to means-testing criteria, which are also better insulated from political manipulation. This outcome characterizes Brazil after the *Partido dos Trabalhadores* won the presidential election in 2002, when *Bolsa Familia* was expanded to become the largest CCT program in the world, and Mexico after 1997 when *Progresa/Oportunidades* was launched. Colombia, Chile, Uruguay, and Costa Rica also fit this characterization. Although an array of clientelistic programs and practices persist in these countries, these coexist with CCTs and other means-tested poverty alleviation programs.
- *Universalistic social protection* in which poverty alleviation programs, including CCTs, are universalistic rather than targeted. Bolivia during the presidency of Evo Morales exemplifies this pattern. Universalism discourages clientelistic manipulation and entails lower administrative costs, but makes poverty alleviation much more expensive.
- *Failed social protection* is the last of the four trajectories. Guatemala is a stark case to consider, in which expansion of social assistance programs for the poor was frail and short-lived.

This chapter proceeds as follows. Section 1.1 maps Latin American social protection policies on our conceptual map that highlights the governance dimensions of antipoverty programs: universalism versus targeting and nondiscretionary versus discretionary. Section 1.2 argues that democratization and pressures from below propelled Latin American countries to expand truncated welfare states by creating an array of social programs directed at the poor. Section 1.3 discusses how real poverty relief requires moving away from clientelism toward nondiscretionary programs that target beneficiaries according to income rather than political criteria. Whether countries will endorse nondiscretionary social assistance depends on the existence of institutional constraints that effectively deter political manipulation of antipoverty programs. Section 1.4 maps Latin American countries along the four paths of welfare system development.

1.1 VARIETIES OF SOCIAL POLICIES

Throughout most of the twentieth century, the main redistributive efforts in the region went into starting the construction of welfare states. Unlike their European counterparts, these Latin American welfare regimes were limited because, whatever their nominal degree of universality, they only covered

1.1 Varieties of Social Policies

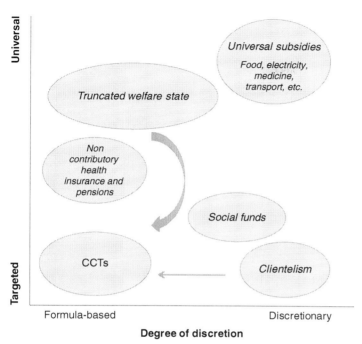

FIGURE 1.1. Social protection in Latin America.

persons with formal employment (Lindert et al., 2006). This restriction of social insurance to the formal sector has led to the characterization of the region's various social protection systems as "truncated welfare states" (De Ferranti et al., 2004; Fiszbein, 2004; Rawlings et al., 2004). Moreover, despite formal membership contributions, social insurance plans have run considerable deficits that must be financed through tax revenues.

Along these governance dimensions of poverty relief, Latin America's historical welfare regimes can be located in the upper left region of Figure 1.1, which maps social policies by degree of government discretion and the extent to which they are targeted or universal. Welfare polices benefited formal workers and state employees, who could not be withdrawn from the welfare regime on the basis of partisanship. Hence, according to our categorization, these traits make these social insurance programs nondiscretionary.

Latin American social insurance programs – maternity and family benefits, health insurance, old-age pensions, and disability benefits – typically began as emoluments meant for relatively small groups such as state employees, armed-forces personnel, and those working in certain favored industries (Mesa-Lago and Bertrabou, 1998). The welfare state's coverage gradually expanded throughout the twentieth century until most formal workers came under its umbrella (though formal employees in agriculture were rarely incorporated).

Nominally financed by contributions, most of these programs are in fact financed by general revenues. Because "the regressivity in social insurance schemes has not been helped by any significant progressivity in tax financing," these schemes foster a "reverse Robin Hood effect," in which the poor are made to pay for the benefit of the rich (Lindert et al., 2006). Latin American social policy, in other words, has mostly historically worked backward, making preexisting economic and social inequalities wider rather than narrower.

Another form of social policy commonly used in Latin America during the period of Import Substitution Industrialization (ISI) were price controls and universal subsidies – for food, gasoline, electricity, medicines, transport, among others. In Figure 1.1 these policies are mapped in the upper-right region. Many of these poorly targeted subsidies ended up benefiting in a disproportionate manner the middle and upper classes in the cities (Bates, 1981). Like social insurance benefits, these price controls and subsidies are poorly targeted, but they are also discretionary, since politicians can often start, stop, or modify them by decree. It is not uncommon, for example, to observe food, medical, and transport subsidies rise during electoral years and plummet once the election is over.

To expand benefits to the poor, especially once electoral democracy took root in the region in the early 1990s, Latin American countries began to introduce a series of social funds intended to improve social infrastructure and provision of public goods in poor communities (Rawlings et al., 2004). With its regressive urban bias, the era of ISI produced massive migration from the countryside to city slums on the outskirts of most major cities in Latin America. It also left thousands of towns and rural communities with no basic public services.

Two of the most well known of these social funds were Peru's *Fondo de Cooperación para el Desarrollo Social (FONCODES)* and Mexico's *Programa Nacional de Solidaridad (Pronasol)*. We map those social funds in Figure 1.1 as reflecting discretionary policies that deliver public goods to communities. Empirical evaluations of these social funds show mixed results. In principle, most of them assigned benefits in decentralized fashion in response to petitions from community organizations, while in practice politicians and bureaucrats at the center enjoyed wide discretion to choose beneficiaries.

Discretionary poverty alleviation programs such as FONCODES and *Pronasol* are particularly vulnerable to political interference, and as later chapters reveal, they do not alleviate poverty. Over the past decade Latin America has gradually begun to introduce nondiscretionary social protection programs to target the poor. Many social protection programs focus largely on helping raise the consumption levels of the destitute poor (Lindert et al., 2006). The best-known contemporary social assistance schemes are conditional cash transfers (CCTs). These programs are progressive in relative terms in that the average transfer represents a higher proportion of income (consumption) for those at the poorer end of the spectrum.

1.1 Varieties of Social Policies

Between 1997 and 2011, most Latin American countries introduced cash transfers granted to women conditional to their children's school attendance and health clinic visits. These programs may also require attending basic courses on preventive health care and hygiene and offer nutritional supplements. CCTs are meant to benefit the extreme poor.

Brazil implemented the first federal program in 2001 (after similar programs at the state level) and the first Lula da Silva administration (2003–2006) expanded *Bolsa Familia* to the entire country. Mexico implemented the first nationwide CCT program in 1997, Honduras in 1998, Nicaragua in 2000, Colombia and Jamaica in 2001, Chile in 2002, Ecuador in 2003, El Salvador and Dominican Republic in 2005, Guatemala in 2008 (Diaz-Cayeros and Magaloni, 2009; De la O, 2013). "By 2008 every Latin American country except Cuba, Haiti, and Venezuela had enacted a CCT program covering from 12 (El Salvador's *Red Solidaria*) to 100 percent (Ecuador's *Bono de Desarrollo Humano*) of its poor population" (McGuire, 2013: 3).

The largest CCT program is Brazil's *Bolsa Familia* followed by Mexico's *Oportunidades*. Both of these programs have been credited with reducing inequality (Soares et al., 2010). In general, evaluations reveal highly positive results from CCTs. Mexico's *Progresa*, which is arguably the most researched of all these programs, was found to be associated with increased food consumption, declines in school dropout rates, and increases in children's average height and weight, among other indicators (Levy, 2006; Gertler, 2004). Colombia's *Familias en Acción* boosted school enrollments and healthcare access, although it failed to show any effect on nutritional levels (Attanasio et al., 2005).

The process of diffusion of this policy innovation across Latin America is evident. But politics has played an important role in shaping the *timing* of adoption (Diaz-Cayeros and Magaloni, 2009) as well as the program's institutional details, including not only how beneficiaries are identified and selected, but also whether the program is properly insulated from political manipulation (De la O, 2012).

Democracy has generated a cycle of redistribution in the region, but whether this cycle ends up benefiting the poor over the long run depends on a country's institutions and on the design that social protection takes. CCTs vary significantly in their governance structures and implementation. Although in Figure 1.1 we have mapped these on the lower-left corner indicating nondiscretionary governance, there is variation across Latin America. De la O's (2015) evidence shows that in countries where the executive power's electoral strength was dominant, measured as undivided government, CCT program design is less strict. Hence, majority parties that rule unconstrained are more likely to attempt to direct CCTs for political gain. Further, CCTs are likely to be less effective in countries with limited state capacity in the provision of health services and education to the impoverished.

Mexico's *Oportunidades* and Brazil's *Bolsa Familia* are among the most professional and better insulated, and so is Colombia's *Familias en Acción*. But other countries have failed to enact CCTs that are free of political manipulation. Guatemala's *Mi Familia Progresa* (MIFAPRO) is perhaps one of the clearest examples of failure, driven by limited state capacity and defective design. As we further discuss, the program was terminated because of accusations of political manipulation by the former president, Alvaro Colom, and his electioneering wife, Sandra Torres.

Figure 1.1 shows a movement in social policy in Latin America from universalism to improved targeting. This movement is consistent with the current approach to poverty relief around the world, which has shifted away from universalism (Coady et al., 2004). How governments select or target the poor involves decisions about governance. To target the poor, governments can employ objective income criteria or they can resort to self-reporting; the latter can be done even through self-assessments of one's status or through community-based assessments (Alatas et al., 2012).

In Figure 1.1 effective poverty relief requires movements toward the lower-left region occupied by CCTs, or what we call *entitled* policies of *social protection*. These redistributive policies targeted to the poor are administered through professional bureaucracies. But expansion of social benefits to the poor can also take the form of *clientelistic social protection*, which we map on the lower-right region of Figure 1.1. Clientelism targets benefits to the poor through political criteria. In the section that follows, we discuss what propelled Latin American countries to expand welfare benefits to cover the poor and describe the particular form this expansion took place in various countries.

1.2 THE EXPANSION OF SOCIAL BENEFITS TO THE POOR

Despite important variations across Latin America, countries in the region have witnessed similar transformations in their welfare regimes. What drove the expansion of Latin American's welfare regimes? Why are poverty relief programs discretionary or nondiscretionary? The first question involves addressing movements along the vertical axis of Figure 1.1 from universal to targeted programs, and the second along the horizontal one from discretionary to nondiscretionary programs. In the pages that follow, we discuss each of these processes.

Moving beyond Truncated Welfare States

Changes in the mechanics of redistribution often result from pressures from below. Acemoglu and Robinson (2006) and Boix (2003) have made this claim for nineteenth-century Europe and the world in general. In their view, democracy and dictatorship are different equilibria of a game of redistribution between the rich and the poor. The elite can voluntarily extend democracy in order to prevent a violent revolution that ends by seizing their assets by force. Democracies are expected to arise in more egalitarian societies and, consistent

1.2 The Expansion of Social Benefits to the Poor

with the Meltzer and Richard's (1981) model, to lead to redistribution because electoral competition generates incentives to enact policies and a tax rate consistent with the median voter's preferences. If the median voter, rather than the elite, sets too high a tax rate, the elite can mount a coup against democracy, and a military regime will come to thwart demands for redistribution.

One of the challenges this view faces for the case of Latin America is that the creation of welfare states often took place under authoritarianism (Mares and Carnes, 2009). Dictators tended to privilege powerful interests such as labor and state employees over the mass of poor citizens. The poor were occasionally targeted with government transfers, yet it was often with highly discretionary policies, which were meant to control them. Land reform was a common form of social policy that was targeted to the poor to prevent revolt (Albertus, 2015).

Another lesser challenge to Meltzer and Richard's (1981) model predicting that democracy should lead to redistribution comes from the fact that in Latin America it took more than a decade for democracy to produce some meaningful redistribution. This is due to the fact that the shift to democracy in the 1980s and 1990s was accompanied by fiscal and state retrenchment as well as serious contractions of international financial flows, including public debt (Haggard and Kaufman, 1995). In many countries this period also witnessed episodes of hyperinflation and repeated but failed attempts at macroeconomic stabilization. In this context of hard times, governments on left and right converged on a set of policy initiatives (the so-called Washington Consensus) to confront these challenges. Hence, demands for redistribution by the mass of poor voters could not be promptly met with significant expansions of welfare benefits.

Although democracy did not have an immediate impact on redistribution, it did create an institutional space that gave more power to the poor. Kaufman and Segura-Ubiergo (2001) demonstrate that trade integration and openness to capital markets after the 1990s had a consistently negative effect on aggregate social spending. The authors then disaggregate spending into social security transfers and expenditures on health and education. They find that a shift to democracy led to increases in health and education spending. Similarly, Brown and Hunter (1999) investigate the effects of political regimes on social spending in Latin America, and they find that during times of economic crises, democracies, relative to autocracies, increased resources to social programs.

These studies do not contemplate other forms of social spending, including the enactment of social protection programs. Diaz-Cayeros and Magaloni (2009) employ a survival model to explain the *timing* of implementation of CCTs across the region. Their econometric findings suggest that democracy generated incentives to reach out to the poor with social benefits. The more years since the democratic transition, the larger the probability of adoption of a CCT. Their results also suggest that CCT adoption is not correlated with ideology: governments from the left and the right have sought to accommodate the poor with an expansion of social protection. The authors also show that inequality and poverty generate more pressures for the expansion of benefits to the poor. Finally, state capacity also seems to matter: CCTs are adopted more rapidly where public institutions are able to reach out to the poor, as measured by higher immunization levels that presupposed functioning clinics and health services.

From Clientelism to Entitlements

This chapter traces the evolution of Latin America's social policy in recent years, identifying two types of welfare regimes – *clientelistic* and *entitled social protection* – and argues that only the latter works to reduce poverty. Clientelism denies poverty relief to qualifying citizens on the basis of partisanship. That is why these policies often fail to improve the well-being of the poor. Entitled social protection programs instead target beneficiaries according to income, often through means-testing. Nondiscretionary programs are also harder to manipulate because politicians cannot deselect beneficiaries on the basis of political intent.

To account for movements along the axis of discretion, our approach emphasizes the political incentives to delegate the implementation of social protection to a professional bureaucracy. As argued by Geddes (1994), "bureaucratic inefficiency, patronage-induced overstaffing, and outright corruption retard economic development and reduce public well-being in developing countries" (p. 371). Proper bureaucratic insulation is necessary to restrain clientelism. Nevertheless, these types of administrative reforms often face severe obstacles to their enactment because politicians profit from manipulating social programs to better serve their prospects for remaining in power.

In her study of Latin American civil service reform, Geddes (1994) provides an insightful account of why and when politicians in developing countries are expected to adopt reforms that insulate bureaucracies from political manipulation. "No politician in competition with others engaged in trading jobs and favors for votes can afford unilaterally to eschew reliance on patronage. Some, however, might be willing to give up this resource if others did" (p. 375). Her game theoretic approach emphasizes the following factors as driving politicians' decisions to delegate power to independent bureaucratic agencies: (1) political parties are more likely to pass reform when patronage is evenly distributed among the strongest parties; (2) reforms are more likely to pass when the electoral weight of the top two parties remains relatively even and stable; (3) even when one party dominates, reforms are more likely to pass when the majority anticipates losing and seeks to tie the hands of its successors and prevent them from conquering the bureaucracy to serve their own patronage ends.

We extend this argument to understand the establishment of entitled social protection, which we claim is influenced by the balance of forces between political parties and their expectation to lose power in future elections. When a majority party dominates and there is no balance of power between competing parties, this party will seek to conquer the bureaucracy to administer social programs according to partisan goals.

An important implication of our theoretical approach is that effective poverty alleviation might paradoxically presuppose the presence of strong center-right parties that are necessary to restrain majoritarian left-wing coalitions in their attempt to conquer the state to serve their own partisan ends. A strong center-right political force is present in countries where we find entitled social protection regimes: Mexico, Brazil, Chile, Uruguay, Costa Rica, and Colombia. When center-right parties are weak, unable to build roots in society (often because of their ideological extremism as in Bolivia), or have a woeful record in power (as the Union Cívica Radical in Argentina or the AD and Christian Democratic parties in Venezuela), left-leaning parties or candidates will be better able to amass large electoral majorities and undermine the system of checks and balances to operate social programs and poverty reduction through clientelistic networks.

1.3 MAPPING SOCIAL PROTECTION IN LATIN AMERICA

Democratization in Latin America has contributed to the creation of new public programs aimed at poverty relief. Below we differentiate Latin American countries according to how they expanded welfare programs for the poor.

Clientelistic Social Protection

Clientelistic redistribution targets benefits to a party's support base. Poverty relief is given according to partisanship, and it is administered through clientelistic networks rather than professional bureaucratic agencies. Clientelistic redistribution hence presupposes that an incumbent party captures the bureaucracy to distribute jobs, government programs and transfers, and other benefits to its supporters.

We distinguish two different forms of clientelistic redistribution in Latin America, a "personalistic" and a "partisan" one. In the first, neopopulist leaders from outside the established party system use clientelistic redistribution to solidify their grip on power. In many of these cases, neopopulist leaders have also undermined democratic political institutions. Where established party systems failed to accommodate the poor with more expansive social policies, they became more vulnerable to the emergence of neopopulist leaders (Weyland et al., 2010; Cleary, 2006). Alberto Fujimori in Peru, Hugo Chávez in Venezuela, and Rafael Correa in Ecuador are notable examples.

Clientelistic redistribution can also be administered by established dominant parties, like Mexico's PRI and the PJ in Argentina. In both the cases, populist parties were able to amass electoral support by administering social programs and patronage through their partisan networks (Levitsky, 2003; Calvo and

Murillo, 2004; Magaloni, 2006; Molinar and Weldon, 1994). Partisan biases in fiscal and electoral institutions reinforced these parties' incumbency advantage. In line with Geddes' (1994) theory, these dominant parties possessed no incentives to delegate the administration of social programs to an independent bureaucracy.

Clientelism traps the poor in a perverse relationship: either you are with the government or you will not get government transfers. The problem is that poor voters under this type of "punishment regime" cannot sanction government corruption because individual defection is costly. Exiting the system requires the capacity of a voter to absorb the costs of not having access to the spoils system. These costs are formidable for the poor, who often depend on the machine's favors for basic survival.[1] In the following sections, we briefly discuss examples of personalism and partisan clientelism in social protection.

Peru

Peru witnessed one of the first episodes of neopopulism during the 1990s. An outsider and practically unknown candidate, Alberto Fujimori was elected in 1990 on a populist platform defeating rightist Mario Vargas Llosa. Upon assuming office, Alberto Fujimori switched his campaign promises and instituted wide-ranging neoliberal reforms, the so-called Fujishock (Stokes, 2001). Fujimori succeeded in stabilizing the economy and pacifying the country with the defeat of Sendero Luminoso. The fear of mounting social tension led him to enact a major expansion of poverty relief through the FONCODES.

The program provided public goods – clean water, roads, electricity, schools, clinics, and hospitals – as well as particularistic transfers, including nutritional supplements and food. Schady (2000) demonstrates that FONCODES funds were not assigned to reach the poor but to orchestrate Fujimori's reelection for a second term. Between 1991 and 1993, FONCODES expenditures favored his supporters. After a disappointing result in a national referendum held in 1993, however, Fujimori administration redirected resources in an attempt to "buy back the vote in turncoat provinces" (Schady, 2000: 291). FONCODES allowed Fujimori to bolster his popularity and political capital, enabling him to win the constitutional referendum to permit his reelection. He was also able to win the 1995 presidential election.

Fujimori resorted to increasingly authoritarian measures. In response to political deadlock, Fujimori decided to close Congress, suspended the constitution, and purged the judiciary with the support of the military – also known as the *autogolpe* (auto-coup). Fujimori ran for a third term, even though the constitution forbade this. His opponent Alejandro Toledo campaigned forcefully

---

[1] The problem is one of coordination: each voter acting alone has compelling reasons to remain loyal to the ruling party to avoid being excluded from the spoils system (Magaloni, 2006). And if most voters reason likewise, the machine will be sustained. It is a perverse equilibrium because everyone becomes an accomplice to the system, even though it is collectively detrimental.

1.3 Mapping Social Protection in Latin America 35

to have the election annulled. At this point, a corruption scandal involving Vladimiro Montesinos broke out (McMillan and Zoido, 2004). A cable television station broadcasted the footage of Montesinos bribing opposition congressman Alberto Kouri for his defection to Fujimori's *Perú 2000* party. Fujimori's support virtually collapsed. He left Peru in 2001 and eventually served jail time for using Montesinos to bribe and tap the phones of journalists, businessmen, and opposition politicians.

Since Fujimori left office, governments in Peru have not expanded social benefits to the poor in a substantial manner. Peru should hence be characterized today as a case of limited expansion of social protection; it spends less than most other Latin American countries in social policies. Only Guatemala and Ecuador spend less (Yamada and Castro, 2012).

Venezuela

Venezuela experienced a colossal challenge to its party system by a neopopulist outsider. The emergence of Hugo Chávez and the Movimiento Bolivariano can be traced to the collapse of Venezuela's two-party system, stable since the Punto Fijo Pact in 1958. Failed structural adjustment and neoliberal reform implemented by the administration of Carlos Andrés Pérez led to massive protests and looting. The president ordered the violent repression of the protests known as *Caracazo*, which left many people dead. The 1989 riots were the worst in Venezuelan history. The president decelerated a state of emergency. The crisis of government and economic collapse led to the impeachment of the president in 1993 (Weyland, 2004; Pérez–Liñal, 2007; Lupu, 2013).

Hugo Chávez began preparing for a military coup, and although he failed to grab power by force, he later won the presidential elections in 1998. The mass of poor voters supporting Chávez revolted against the domination of politics by Venezuelan oligarchy since 1958 and its two-party system, the Christian Democratic Party (Political Electoral Independent Organization [COPEI]) and Democratic Action Party (AD). Chávez was able to expand and solidify his power to a large extent because the Venezuelan oligarchy and the preexisting party system had failed to accommodate the poor, improve living standards for the vast majority, and curb corruption. In addition, ideological convergence between AD and COPEI led to a failure of representation (Seawright, 2012; Morgan, 2011).

He was able to amass power because he used money from the oil boom to expand social benefits. During his government, Chávez successfully mobilized support from the poor through a large expansion of programs such as *Las Misiones Bolivarianas*, which have entailed a massive expansion of antipoverty initiatives, including educational campaigns, construction of thousands of homes, enactment of food and housing subsidies, construction of clinics, expansion of medical protection, the granting of land titles, among others.

These programs are largely administered through clientelistic practices. In their seminal study, Hsieh et al. (2011) employ the well-known *Maisanta* list of several million voters who in 2003 signed a petition to remove Chávez from office and match it with household survey in order to measure the economic effects of being identified as Chávez political opponent. They find that voters who were identified as Chávez's opponents experienced a 5 percent drop in earnings and a 1.3 point drop in employment rates after the president released the list throughout the government bureaucracy. Hawkins et al. (2011) present a fascinating analysis of Las Misiones, showing that Chavez's control of the programs is strong and that the programs have been plagued with political manipulation and corruption. Stokes et al. (2013) also find that benefits in the *Misiones* social programs went to Chavez' supporters.

Similar to Fujimori, Chávez undermined democratic political institutions (Mainwaring, 2012; Levitsky and Way, 2010). When he was elected in February 1999, the legislative and judicial branches of the national government were controlled by opposition forces. Chávez diluted these checks and balances by rewriting the Venezuelan constitution and packing the new Supreme Court with judges he could control. After having been reelected trice, he died with large popular support in March 2013.

Argentina
The case of Argentina cannot be understood without taking into account the resilience of the Peronista Party (the *Partido Justicialista* or PJ) in both the provincial governments and the federal level since the return to democracy in 1983. The Peronista machines have traditionally mobilized voters in the city of Buenos Aires, its hinterland, and the other provinces by distributing food, medicines, or employment (Levitsky, 2003; Auyero, 2007; Szwarcberg, 2012; Giraudy, 2007; Weitz-Shapiro, 2012 and 2014).

After the transition to democracy in 1983, political power alternated between the Radical Civic Union (UCR) and the PJ. Argentina experienced a profound economic crisis and hyperinflation during the 1980s. President Menem campaigned as a populist but upon assuming office adopted a neoliberal agenda of economic reform (Stokes, 2001). The successful turnaround of the economy contributed to president Menem's popularity. After a political agreement with the UCR, he was able to modify the constitution to run for reelection in 1995. Menem's second term became tainted with accusations of corruption, and as a result his party suffered a massive defeat in the 1997 mid-term elections. He attempted to run for reelection a third time in 1999 but his attempt was ruled unconstitutional. UCR candidate Fernando de la Rua defeated Eduardo Duhalde of the PJ in those elections.

The pegging of the peso and mounting fiscal deficient made economic policies unsustainable. De la Rua enacted austerity measures and budget cuts. The financial crisis and the wave of capital flight led de la Rua to impose a freeze on cash withdrawals, which triggered popular protests and rioting. He was forced out of office with the cry "¡Que se vayan todos!" (Away with them all!) The riots toppled two presidents in the span of ten days. By the following

1.3 Mapping Social Protection in Latin America

legislative elections of 2005, his party virtually disappeared from the political scene (Lupu, 2013).

Little-known Peronist governor, Nestor Kirchner, won the presidential elections of 2003 after Menem withdrew from the run-off election. The country was bankrupt, with a depleted middle class and rising poverty. He was able to restructure Argentine debt first by announcing the cancelation of its foreign debt to the IMF and then offering a single payment. Upon assuming office, he declared social problems his first priority and expanded social programs. Nestor Kirchner "left office as the most popular outgoing president in modern Argentine history. After taking office in the aftermath of Argentina's worst-ever-recession, Kirchner presided over four years of export-led growth, rooted in a comparative exchange rate and soaring commodity prices.... Kirchner also pushed through a social security reform that extended access to unemployed and informal sector workers, thereby bringing more than a million new people into the system. Investment in public works increased more than a fivefold under Krichner, producing major expansion in housing and infrastructure" (Levitsky and Murillo, 2008: 17). Living standards improved and unemployment and poverty fell. Succeeding her husband, Cristina Kirschner won the 2007 election by a landslide and the PJ has been able to increasingly consolidate its dominance in power profiting from opposition weakness after the UCE collapse. The PJ remains virtually unchallenged in many peripheral provinces, although the major metropolitan areas are highly competitive.

Defying the trends throughout Latin America, Argentine leaders did not create a true CCT program, even though they had a large number of transfer programs in place, particularly related to unemployment, worker retraining and other labor issues. The character of the cash transfer programs in Argentina is consistent with the overall architecture of distributive politics in the country. Calvo and Murillo (2004) have provided strong evidence regarding the primacy of a partisan logic in the allocation of fiscal transfers and public employment opportunities in Argentina.[2] In the same vein, Giraudy (2007) shows that in the specific case of workfare programs (such as the *Plan Jefes y Jefas de Hogares Desocupados* created in 2002, following the *Plan Trabajar* launched in 1996 by President Menem) partisanship overrides criteria related to need or poverty. Within the framework of the social security system, Argentina has also created a universal child allowance program for uninsured workers in the informal sector. The program's targeting the poor is probably better than what was observed in *Trabajar* or *Jefes y Jefas*, and its coverage has been growing.

---

[2] Stokes (2005), Stokes et al. (2013), and Nichter (2008) study campaign handouts. Note that our object of inquiry in this book is not campaign handouts but the administration of *social programs* through clientelistic networks, which necessarily presupposes the conquering of the state apparatus by a party's machine. Vote buying through campaign handouts likely occurs in most elections in Latin America, whereas social program manipulation presupposes certain super-majoritarian institutional structure.

Networks of voters controlled or intermediated by political brokers (*punteros*) seem to play a key role in the way all these programs are designed and operated in Argentina. As noted by Stokes et al. (2013), those brokers may be at odds with the party leadership, but they are also necessary for voter mobilization on election day (Nichter, 2008). Political networks that mobilize support are not exclusive to the PJ, but are also present in other parties like the *Union Civica Radical* (UCR) (Calvo and Murillo, 2013).

A critical challenge Argentine social policies face today is rooted in politics and the absolute dominance of the PJ. After the collapse of the UCR, no new stable non-Peronist alternatives have emerged. "With the collapse of the UCR, the non-Peronist half of the party system has become a fragmented collection of personalistc vehicles, local patronage-based machines, and short-lived programmatic parties" (Levitsky and Murillo, 2008: 23). Without a strong opposition, the system of checks and balances is weak and the PJ has ample leeway to manipulate social policies and administer them through its clientelistic networks.

Entitled Social Protection

The establishment of entitled welfare regimes in Latin America has taken place in countries where systems of checks and balances operate more effectively to counterbalance majoritarian tendencies. Mexico and Brazil stand out for their capacity to reduce poverty and inequality through the implementation of effective social protection policies. Both counties have established welfare regimes based on entitlements rather than discretionary handouts. In 2010 the largest CCT programs in Latin America were Brazil's *Bolsa Família*, which served about 52 million people (compared to 53.3 million living on less than $4 per day), and Mexico's Oportunidades, which served about 24 million people (compared to 27.8 million living on less than US$4 per day) (McGuire, 2013). In both cases incumbent parties were constrained to administer social policies, and particularly CCTs. This does not mean no political returns accrued to their entitlement programs, but that they could not use partisan and governmental networks to skew program grants.

The Brazilian Social Democracy (PSDB), which has moved to the center-right after Fernando Cardoso forged an alliance with the Liberal Front Party and was elected president, played a fundamental role in creating the predecessor of Bolsa Familia. President Luiz Inacio Lula da Silva of the Workers Party must be credited for the dramatic reduction of income inequality taking place in Brazil during his administration because he massively expanded social benefits to the poor. But the presence of the PSDB and of Brazil's federal system of government have served as critical counterbalancing forces to restrain the Workers Party from administering Bolsa Familia and other social programs through clientelistic practices.[3]

---

[3] Chile has also witnessed the emergence of an entitled social protection regime. Entitlements are targeted according to means-testing criteria and administered through professional bureaucracies,

1.3 Mapping Social Protection in Latin America

Bolsa Familia had been originally pioneered in Brasilia and other municipalities and states had adopted it before Cardoso, and later adopted the program at the federal level. Upon assuming office, Lula chose moderation in economic policy and discourse (Campello, 2013). But he put social programs at the top of his agenda. In 2003 Lula formed Bolsa Familia by combining Bolsa Escola with other programs such as Bolsa Alimentação, Cartai Alimentação and Auxilio Gas. He also created a new Ministry of Social Development and War against Hunger and massively expanded the program to cover the poor all over Brazil. During Bolsa Família's first six years of operation (2003–2009) per capita public health care spending rose 70 percent.

As a redistributive program, Bolsa Familia depends on central local collaboration. Municipal governments act as the main agents of the federal government in the implementation of the program, although local authorities cannot claim credit or cut out beneficiaries. Hence, *Bolsa Familia* is embedded in a federal system of government that is strongly antimajoritarian. The program was mounted on Cardosso's successful fiscal reform that gave municipalities incentives to collaborate with the central government in fiscal stabilization.

The relative stability of Brazilian institutions and its party system created strong moderating incentives for president Lula's PT government (Hunter, 2010 and 2007). The president confronted multiple veto players and faced institutional constraints that would not have allowed him to design a discretionary welfare regime for the poor. Brazil has a strong federal system, and governors and municipal presidents are very powerful. State governors are able to constraint the central government. Subnational interests effectively get articulated within the Brazilian National Congress (Samuels, 2006).

The consolidation of the Brazilian party system was gradual, but it is with Lula's presidency (2003–2011) that the PT grew into a national party with widespread electoral appeal, to a large extent because of the expansion of social benefits and social policies to the poor, including through *Bolsa Familia*. Brazil's political parties were proscribed during the first part of the military dictatorship, but then they were allowed to compete from 1966 to 1979 into a legally enforced two-party political system: the National Renewal Alliance Party (ARENA) and the official opposition Brazilian Democratic Movement (MDB). When Brazil returned to democracy, a large amount of parties emerged and the system became very fragmented and inefficient (Mainwaring, 1999). The system has gradually consolidated into five stronger parties: the Workers party (PT), the Brazilian Social Democracy Party (PSBD), the Brazilian Democratic Movement (PMDB), and the Democrats (DEM). The PSBD is the strongest opposition to the PT. Although in its origins center-left in orientation, the party shifted to the right when Henrique Cardoso forged an alliance with the right-wing Liberal Front to run for the presidency. The PSBD was born as

rather than the Socialist Party's clientelistic networks. Like Chile, Uruguay, Colombia, and Costa Rica have center-right parties with strong roots in society that have played counterbalancing functions to restrain the clientelistic use of social programs.

part of the democratic opposition to the military regime and has a strong base of support.

Hunter and Sugiyama's (2009) study of clientelism and *Bolsa Família* in Brazil in 2009 found that the method of transfer (a debit card that cuts out the middleman) and provisions for voicing complains such as a toll-free number prevented *Bolsa Familia* from becoming a program easily manipulated by local officials for political gain. In his cross-sectional study of Brazil's 5,565 municipalities in 2008, Fried (2012) found no evidence of preferential targeting of *Bolsa Família* either to core government supporters or to swing voters. No doubt that Lula's government expanded eligibility for *Bolsa Família* with the aim of winning votes in the 2006 presidential election. "That might be interpreted as the politicization of a CCT program, but it is also a case of electoral incentives encouraging a policy that helps the poor" (McGuire, 2013: 10).

Universalistic Social Protection

Bolivia has embarked on a distinctive path in the expansion of its social programs. Universalism is the cornerstone of Bolivian social protection policies, including the recently instituted CCT programs, which constitutes a departure from the movement toward increased targeting taking place in most other Latin American countries.

Prior to the arrival of Evo Morales to the presidency in 2005, democracy in Bolivia had brought very little for the poor. During the 1980s, Bolivia experienced one of the deepest economic recessions in the region, with rampant inflation, massive job losses and a severe currency crisis. Austerity measures succeeded in curbing inflation but also widened the huge wealth gap between the white elite and the impoverished Indian population and generated social unrest (Madrid, 2012).

Bolivia introduced Latin America's first social investment fund, the Fondo Social de Emergencia, in 1986. The fund was demand-driven and gave cash transfers to successful proposals by community leaders. The funds were geared toward building or improving public facilities like health clinics, water and sewer lines, and roads. The most impoverished communities did not receive these funds because they did not have the capacity to submit successful proposals to the government (McGuire, 2013). The *Movimiento Nacional Revolucionario* (MNR) government of Gonzalo Sánchez de Lozada passed a decentralization law in 1994 that gave a much greater role to municipalities in designing and administering social services. Faguet (2004) demonstrates that these funds had a positive impact on improving investments in basic infrastructure for impoverished communities.

Sánchez de Lozada was forced to resign during his second term in office, after massive street protests related to the Bolivian gas conflict. Political instability continued after his resignation and in 2005 the new president, Carlos Mesa, also had to resign as a result of growing discontent and popular unrest.

1.3 Mapping Social Protection in Latin America 41

Massive protests and roadblocks made Congress to move the 2007 elections to 2005.

Evo Morales won with 53.7 percent of the vote. He became the country's first democratically elected president to win an absolute majority in the first round. His election represented a radical shift for his country. His victory was made possible by the systematic failure of the established political parties to enact policies to alleviate poverty and aid the country's indigenous majority. Until Evo Morales' victory, Bolivia had remained a country divided into two separate countries in which the indigenous majority was for the most part excluded (Madrid, 2012).

Social policies began to marginally expand under President Gonzalo Sánchez de Lozada. He introduced a universalistic *Bono de Solidaridad* (Bonosol) retirement pension, which gave every Bolivian age sixty-five or older an annual pension of about US $230. However, the triumph of Evo Morales brought a more fundamental transformation of the social protection regime.

During his first term, he increased state intervention in the economy by nationalizing oil, mines, gas, and communications. Thanks to revenue from the energy sector, he has been able to expand social programs, including through the introduction of a CCT program and the expansion of the noncontributory old-age pensions, renamed *Renta Dignidad*. A new state-owned committee was also established to distribute food at subsidized prices. Not only the *Bono Juancito Pinto* and the *Bono Juana Azurduy*, but also the noncontributory pension, *Renta Dignidad*, are funded by dividends from renationalized state corporations and by taxes on natural gas and mineral extraction (McGuire, 2013).

These social programs afforded Evo Morales huge electoral support. He was able to employ his popularity among the poor to win a referendum to enact a constitutional reform in 2009. After modifying the constitution, he was able to reelect himself for a second five-year term by a landslide victory of 64 percent of the vote in the 2009 presidential elections. Candidates from his party (Movement toward Socialism) have claimed large majorities in both Chambers of the National Congress and have won the majority of Bolivia's nine departments.

Extreme poverty and inequality remain pervasive in Bolivia. The government has emphasized the need to develop and expand social programs. Two CCTs have been enacted in Bolivia Bono Juancito Pinto (for schoolchildren) and Bono Juana Azurduy (for expectant and new mothers). According to McGuire (2013) careful analysis, they have not demonstrably reduced poverty and improved health. "One thing that distinguishes these programs is their universality. Bolivia has Latin America's only CCTs that are not targeted either to people below a certain income level, or to people living in particular impoverished regions" (p. 1). According to McGuire (2013), the lack of demonstrable program impact has to do more with problems in the public provision of health and education services, and low state capacity, than to the universality of these programs.

Indigenous peoples are clearly better off after Evo Morales came to power because now there are social programs aimed at assisting them. Moreover, his presidency has brought an important agenda of institutional reform that grants constitutional statue to indigenous traditions and governance. A dilemma Bolivia faces is that super-majoritarianism might work to undermine democracy. A related challenge is that without institutional constraints, the *Movimiento al Socialismo* has been able to conquer the state.

Aborted Expansion of Social Protection

Guatemala has traditionally excluded and oppressed the poor, mostly indigenous Mayans. Social and economic injustice and racial discrimination contributed to a long Civil War (1960–1996). The peace accords of 1996 ending the thirty-six-years violent conflict led to the establishment of electoral democracy. Guatemala experienced the first important expansion of social benefits to the poor during the presidency of Alvaro Colom, who was elected in 2007. He expanded social programs and access to health and education to the poor. Many of these programs, including the CCT MIFAPRO, were discredited because of alleged political manipulation. The incoming administration of Otto Perez Molina, of the right-wing Partido Patriota elected in 2012, reversed many of these social policies.

MIFAPRO constituted one of the first social protection schemes ever targeted to the poor in Guatemala. The program was created from a presidential initiative within the executive secretariat of the presidency. It was ascribed to the Ministry of Education. In addition, and most controversially, the execution and monitoring of the program was assigned to the *Consejo de Cohesión Social* (Council of Social Cohesion) and the *Oficina de la Primera Dama de la Nación* (Office of the First Lady). Hence Sandra Torres was in charge of orienting social investment and combating poverty during her husband's presidency. The program was ultimately discredited when there were rumors that Sandra Torres would divorce the president to overcome a constitutional impediment that forbade her to run for the presidential election of 2011. She wanted to run as the candidate of her party, the *Unidad Nacional de la Esperaza* (UNE). The Supreme Court ruled against her candidacy for the presidency on the grounds of a "serious intent to subvert the law" via divorce.

The accusations of political manipulation gave arguments to the right-wing Patriotic Party and the upper classes to reverse the expansion of social policies in Guatemala. MIFAPRO was one of the first social assistance schemes ever instituted in the country with the explicit aim to alleviate extreme poverty. According to the report by UNDP on MIFAPRO (UNDP, 2011), the Guatemalan CCT could have served as the foundation for a more ambitious social assistance regime in a country afflicted with extreme poverty. The report remarks that "even if the program is properly designed to insulate it from

1.3 Mapping Social Protection in Latin America

clientelistic practices and political manipulation, it is true that a better institutionalization would insulated it more effectively" (UNDP, 2011: 50).

Interviews collected by one of the authors in the summers of 2011 and 2012 with a large number of women in various rural communities in the region of Lake Atitlán made evident the difference the program was making for indigenous families to cope with child malnutrition and mortality from preventable illnesses. In several interviews it became clear how the cash given through MIFAPRO made the difference between life and death for the children of the impoverished communities. One woman reported using the cash to take her baby girl to a private doctor when she had a terrible attack of diarrhea that otherwise would have killed her. The little girl was now around three years old, and was playing with two of her brothers. The mother was clearly thankful to MIFAPRO for saving her only daughter's life. Other women reported using the cash to pay for transportation to reach the nearest hospital in an emergency. All of these women reported using the money to feed their children better – occasionally they could buy some meat, even if in small quantity. One woman was using the CCT cash to buy formula that allowed her to feed her baby after her breast milk dried out due to a postpartum infection. The alternative would have been feeding the baby "water and sugar", and most likely death due to extreme malnutrition.

In our interviews we learned about how frightened women were to talk about politics and about revealing their partisanship. Women hardly talked openly about the coming presidential elections, although we were able to gain insight from a few who were more outspoken. We learned about how terrified women were of the Patriotic Party and its candidate because they believed that if this party won MIFAPRO would be terminated. It was hence unsurprising that women did not want to talk about their partisanship openly for fear of being identified with the opposition in the event the candidate of the "Mano Dura" (strong hand) had won.

The critical importance of state capacity for proper implementation was evident in our interviews. In the communities we visited the last cash transfer scheduled to arrive in the spring never did. State officials had not returned since 2008 to collect new income information to be able to incorporate new deserving beneficiaries. More than political manipulation, many of the problems on the ground were clearly about implementation and lack of state capacity.

The program was terminated after the elections Otto Perez Molina won the presidential elections. When we returned the following summer to interview with families in the same communities, we encountered a sad panorama. The benefits from MIFAMPRO had been removed from the entire region, which was clearly supportive of the UNE in the presidential elections. As we were interviewing one woman who had recently delivered her sixth baby, we learned that she had been feeding the baby water with diluted corn maize because her breast milk had dried out after a postpartum infection. She had no cash to buy formula and the baby was literally dying in her desperate hands.[4] The optimism the CCT program had brought among the women had been replaced by stoic faces confronting, once again, the adversities of having to live in extreme poverty without a safety net.

1.4 CONCLUSION

This chapter has documented the expansion of social protection in the region, distinguishing four paths of welfare system development. Democratization and pressures from below propelled Latin American countries to expand truncated welfare states by creating an array of social programs to benefit the poor. We argued that effective poverty relief requires moving away from clientelism and establishing nondiscretionary programs that target beneficiaries according to income rather than partisanship or other political criteria. Democratic politicians will inevitably be tempted to manipulate social programs and poverty relief for electoral objectives. Hence nondiscretionary social assistance can come about only when there are effective institutional constraints to prevent incumbents from politicizing antipoverty programs.

---

[4] When we realized what was happening the baby was able to get formula from a group of health promoters with whom we were collecting the interviews.

2

Poverty Relief in Mexico: A Geographic Approach

> It is the variety of wants in different climates that first occasioned a difference in the manner of living, and this gave rise to a variety of laws.
>
> Montesquieu (1752)
> The Spirit of Laws, Book XIV, 10

Mexico provides a unique opportunity for the study of poverty relief strategies because of the fundamental transformation its social policies experienced over two decades, from 1988 to 2006. The clientelistic linkage between politicians and the poor that prevailed during the era of PRI dominance weakened with the emergence of an entitlement-based strategy of poverty relief. Clientelistic social protection was at the heart of the PRI's dominance by generating substantial electoral rewards. The ruling party spent billions of dollars on behalf of the poor but, as later chapters demonstrate, these resources had only a limited impact on poverty reduction.

This chapter lays the groundwork for the geographic approach that underlies our study of antipoverty policies. To understand poverty-alleviation strategies, we territorially disaggregate programs, policy interventions, and outcomes at the local level. In the next section we discuss poverty relief efforts, classifying the various Mexican social protection programs according to the scheme presented in the previous chapter. Section 2.2 discusses the geographic correlates of the spatial distribution of poverty across Mexican municipalities. Section 2.3 describes the overall strategies of public good provision and poverty alleviation in Mexico from a geographic perspective, and Section 2.4 recounts the changing patterns of political contestation in Mexico, also using a geographic approach.

2.1 MEXICO IN COMPARATIVE PERSPECTIVE

The poor in Mexico did not benefit much from the so-called economic miracle, when the country consistently grew at an average annual rate of around

6 percent from the 1930s until the early 1980s (Hansen, 1971). Despite revolutionary and propoor rhetoric, the PRI-led governments of the time failed to implement successful poverty-alleviation programs. Although many development indicators improved as the decades progressed (Wilkie, 1978), the improvements tended to disproportionately benefit the already wealthy regions, rather than the poorer areas, which lagged well behind (Medellin, 1974).[1] Despite overall growth, income distribution barely changed from 1958, when the first measurements were taken, to the 1980s, when Mexico plunged into economic turmoil.

With the debt crisis of 1982, prospects for the poor became even dimmer. Combating poverty with social programs in a low-growth economy was a daunting challenge. Employment and other income-generating activities grew sluggishly, while public resources for helping the poor became scarce. Real government expenditures suffered a dramatic cutback during the post-1982 period. At the same time, Mexico underwent a major economic restructuring involving privatization, trade policy, and fiscal reform. Income inequality is shown to have worsened during this period. Between 1984 and 1992 there was a "steep fall in the income of ninety percent of the population in favor of the wealthiest 10 percent" (Trejo and Jones, 1998). Despite prospects for recovery after the economic restructuring, the Peso Crisis of 1994–1995 delivered a massive setback to social programs. Poverty reached alarming levels.

Table 2.1 shows the evolution of Mexican poverty in rural areas and the country as a whole, according to estimates calculated by the National Council for the Evaluation of Social Policy (*Consejo Nacional de Evaluación de la Política de Desarrollo Social* [CONEVAL]).[2] The estimates use a common methodology to ensure comparable poverty lines based on data from household surveys.[3] The table report two types of poverty lines: one for nutritional status (caloric intake); and a second one for assets (possession of basic capacities plus other necessities, such as clothing, transportation, and shelter).

The table measures poverty using a headcount index: the percentage of persons falling below the poverty line. It also presents the standard errors of the estimates (in parenthesis) to better demonstrate how changes in the evolution of poverty through time are statistically significant. It is undeniable that

---

[1] It is important to note, however, that given high population growth, the per capita growth rates were more modest in the period.
[2] CONEVAL institutionalizes the work done by the Comite Técnico Para la Medición de la Pobreza (CTMP), an independent body created in 2002 for measuring the evolution of poverty. The technical committee was formed arguably by the foremost experts on poverty in Mexico, including Fernando Cortes (Colmex), Rodolfo de la Torre (UIA), Luis Felipe López Calva (ITESM), Graciela Teruel (UIA), Luis Rubalcava (CIDE), Enrique Hernández Laos (UAM), and John Scott (CIDE).
[3] The Encuesta Nacional de Ingresos de los Hogares (ENIGH), periodically done by the Mexican statistical office, the Instituto Nacional de Estadística, Geografía e Informática (INEGI).

2.1 Mexico in Comparative Perspective

TABLE 2.1. *Evolution of Poverty in Mexico (percent individuals below poverty line)*

Poverty Line	Rural Nutrition	Rural Assets	National Nutritional	National Assets
1992	34.0 (2.3)	66.5 (1.8)	21.4 (1.12)	53.1 (1.36)
1994	37.0 (1.8)	69.3 (1.7)	21.2 (0.82)	52.4 (1.22)
1996	53.5 (1.6)	80.7 (1.0)	37.4 (1.04)	69.0 (1.07)
1998	51.7 (2.2)	75.9 (1.8)	33.3 (0.93)	63.7 (0.94)
2000	42.4 (2.1)	69.2 (1.9)	24.1 (1.04)	53.6 (1.25)
2002	34.0 (2.0)	64.3 (2.3)	20.0 (0.93)	50.0 (1.11)
2004	28.0 (2.0)	57.4 (2.3)	17.4 (0.64)	47.2 (0.70)
2006	24.5 (1.7)	54.7 (1.8)	14.0 (0.73)	42.9 (0.83)
2008			18.6 (0.57)	47.8 (0.65)
2010			18.8 (0.55)	51.1 (0.63)
2012			19.7 (0.92)	52.3 (1.05)

Source: CONEVAL, 2007 and http://www.coneval.gob.mx/Medicion/EDP/Paginas/Evolucion-de-las-dimensiones-de-la-pobreza-1990-2014-.aspx accessed Oct 2, 2014.

Note: Information is not updated through 2014 for rural areas because CONEVAL introduced a multidimensional methodology for the calculation of poverty rates, that does not provide the breakdown. Poverty rates have witnessed moderate increases since 2008.

extreme poverty fell in Mexico after the introduction of the new social protection regime in 1997: Progresa and FISM. In 1996, 53 percent of the population were extremely poor according to CONEVAL's definition of nutritional poverty. This percentage fell to 24 in 2006.

The evolution of poverty is surely related to the historical policies followed by the federal government. Figure 2.1 maps Mexico's social policies during the twentieth century on the two dimensions of governance discussed in the previous chapter. Since the early 1940s, Mexico began to introduce social insurance schemes tied to participation in the formal labor market. Created in 1943, the *Instituto Mexicano del Seguro Social* (IMSS) provides insurance to non-government workers, including individual retirement funds, disability and life

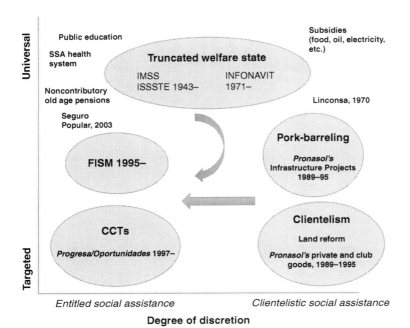

FIGURE 2.1. Social protection in Mexico.

insurance, health insurance, and health services.[4] The Instituto Nacional del Fondo de Vivienda para los Trabajadores (INFONAVIT) provides subsidized housing to private sector workers. Similar benefits are provided to state employees through the *Instituto de Seguridad y Seguro Social para Trabajadores del Estado* (ISSSTE), which also gives financial assistance from its housing fund (FOVISSSTE).

The poor remained without access to the formal social insurance system. In addition to investments in public education and health, land reform was surely the most important redistributive effort carried out by the PRI during the postrevolutionary period, up until 1991 when the era of agrarian reform was declared closed. Over the years, 60 percent of Mexico's territory was distributed. Owing to the clientelisitc implementation of land reform, the PRI was able to amass electoral support among peasants for many decades.

In 1988 the hitherto stable hegemonic party regime experienced an electoral shock that led to a shift in social policy. The electoral shock resulted from a combination of factors. A severe economic recession – low wages, high inflation, currency instability, and underemployment in the cities – led voters to

---

[4] The 1997 reforms transformed the pension fund in IMSS form a pay-as-you go system to a system where beneficiaries put their contributions into individualized accounts that are managed mostly by private companies (called AFORES, Associations for Retirement Funds).

defect to the opposition. Market-oriented reforms also restricted the availability of state resources that were traditionally used to buy off party factions and electoral support. The 1988 elections made it clear that the PRI had failed to build solid clientelistic networks with the growing masses of the urban poor.

President Carlos Salinas established *Pronasol* with the stated intent to combat poverty.[5] Instead, as we demonstrate in this book, *Pronasol* was designed as an instrument for reestablishing the PRI's electoral dominance. *Pronasol* sought to establish alternative party-society relationships that would go around the failing corporatist mechanisms and state bureaucracies. It soon became the cornerstone of the government's social policy. Its resources represented, on average, 1.18 percent of GDP each year.

A large proportion of *Pronasol* programs involved investments in sewerage, piped water, roads, and the construction of schools and health clinics. But *Pronasol* also included many programs that targeted discretionary private goods to individuals or small communities – subsidized credit, scholarships, wells, livestock, construction materials, and the like. The program's investments benefited the PRI's core supporters and were not properly targeted to the poor.

In the 1990s, as the process of democratization unfolded, a new social assistance regime came into place. Through the randomization of the first CCT program in Mexico, *Progresa*'s initial rollout from 1997 to 1999, scientific evaluations were made on the impact of the program on the welfare of the poor. The presidential administration of Vicente Fox became convinced that the program was effective; he decided to rename it and expand it into urban areas. We demonstrate in this book that beneficiaries of *Progresa* – and later *Oportunidades* – have generously rewarded incumbents at the polls.

After Vicente Fox's victory in 2000, the program was expanded in rural areas, and extended to urban and semiurban areas using parallel criteria to select beneficiary families. For the last phase, the program was also transformed into a demand-type scheme where eligible people were no longer identified by the government, but they self-select to apply. The scope of *Progresa/Oportunidades* is far-reaching. At the end of 1999, *Progresa* covered approximately 2.6 million families, and about 40 percent of all rural families. By 2005, *Oportunidades* covered 5 million families, almost 70 percent rural, and the rest semiurban and urban. This meant that by the end of 2005, more than half of Mexican families in extreme poverty were receiving *Oportunidades* funds. The program's budget has increased steadily since 1997, although transfers per beneficiary have decreased slightly.

---

[5] Salinas wrote his dissertation on the impact of government social infrastructure projects on political behavior in the state of Puebla (Salinas, 1982), arguing that increases in electoral support were short lived and needed local community organization to have new projects in the pipeline. Arguably this work constituted the intellectual seeds for the program he created as president.

Because of its progressive structure, *Progresa/Oportunidades* is the most propoor of all major Mexican social assistance programs. The World Bank has calculated in its public expenditure review for Mexico in 2005 that most public programs are regressive, and that public expenditure in general is slightly regressive (World Bank, 2004a). Other national programs that have been progressive are school spending (preschool, elementary and lower secondary), health clinics for the uninsured population through the ministry of health (SSA), and the Programa de Apoyos al Campo (*Procampo*) transfers to peasants.[6] *Procampo* replaced price supports for basic grains with direct cash payments. The most regressive programs have been those managed by the Public Employees Social Security Institute (ISSSTE) and support for public universities.

Despite enormous improvement in poverty alleviation under *Oportunidades*, the program still suffers limitations. For example, poor households are excluded from receiving transfers if there is no school or clinic in the community or within a reasonable distance, which is the case in some of Mexico's poorest localities. Second, the continuity of the program is always at stake when there is a change in federal administration and governments are tempted to water down its targeting. Third, the transfers themselves are not generous enough to place all households in the program above the poverty line, so a substantial population remains in poverty, even after the transfer. Finally, *Oportunidades* is not well integrated with other social assistance programs that seek to generate better quality services and to support income-generating activities (de Janvry, 2006).

Highly targeted programs may suffer important political limitations. As Pritchett (2005) explains: "If the budget for redistribution is politically determined, the impact of targeting on the poor cannot be determined by a technocratic evaluation of the hypothetical impact of a given targeting design alone; it must account for the effect of changes in the degree of targeting on the size of the budget available for redistribution. It is possible that 'more for the poor is less for the poor' and that the less targeted program will deliver fewer benefits for the poor" (p. 1).

CCTs can suffer underfunding. In fact, social spending is relatively low in Mexico at 9.1 percent of GDP in 2000.[7] Most of the spending goes to education and health (3.8 and 2.2 percent of GDP respectively). Social protection spending constitutes the remaining 3 percent. Around 72 percent of social protection spending is devoted to regressive programs (IMSS and ISSSTE), whereas only 27 percent (0.8 percent of GDP) goes to the better-targeted social

---

[6] *Procampo* was an unconditional cash transfer program that targeted peasants and provided subsidies proportional to the size of their land holdings.

[7] Social spending in Mexico is much lower than in Argentina, Brazil, Chile, and Uruguay where in 2000 governments spent 21, 12, 17, and 24 percent respectively of their domestic products in social transfers (Lindert et al., 2006).

assistance programs, including *Oportunidades* (Lindert and Allard, 2006).[8] Hailed as the most successful poverty alleviation program in Mexico's history, *Oportunidades* made only up 0.3 percent of GDP in 2000.

2.2 THE GEOGRAPHY OF POVERTY

Behind the national figures that exhibit some improvements, there are vast differences across the territorial landscape. Unpacking poverty in Mexico requires a better understanding of its relationship with geography. The central goal of our analysis is to understand the impact social programs have made on poor communities and the evolution of poverty. In the rest of this chapter, we outline the basic spatial patterns of poverty, the geography of public expenditure, and the distribution of political power across the territory.

Poverty in Mexico is highly correlated with specific topographic and climatic characteristics. A typical, extremely poor locality is generally isolated from main cities, roads, and highways. One of the most unequal countries in the world, Mexico's social disparities are reflected in its high incidence of poverty. The poor are concentrated in rural communities. The rural poor historically have lacked basic services such as drinking water, roads, and health care, and they have suffered from hunger, malnutrition, and preventable disease.

Figure 2.2 maps poverty across Mexico. The map uses the CONEVAL computation of nutritional poverty (i.e., a poverty line drawn at the minimum caloric intake necessary for survival) at the municipal level in 2000. It highlights the prevalence of extremely poor households across Mexico, with a spatial distribution showing that poverty is most concentrated in rural areas.

There is an undeniable statistical correlation between the patterns of poverty and destitution displayed by the map in Figure 2.1 and a set of geographic variables. The rural poor in Mexico tend to live in less accessible and hospitable places. Their settlement patterns usually reflect inherited and long-standing historical processes that have also generated the borders separating jurisdictions. The South is poorer than the North, and it also has the highest concentration of indigenous peoples. Southern states such as Chiapas, Yucantán, Oaxaca, Guerrero are among the poorest. Puebla, Michoacán, and areas of Veracruz also exhibit high incidence of poverty. In the North poverty is concentrated la Sierra Tarahumara, an area of the Sierra Madre Occidental inhabited by the Tarahumaras. Rural Western Central Mexico in Nayarit, Durango, Jalisco, and Zacatecas is also impoverished.

---

[8] Among the social assistance programs, *Oportunidades* and *Procampo* comprised half of the funds (28 and 19.6 percent respectively). The other half was made up of education programs (13.7), food-based programs such as *Liconsa*, *Diconsa*, DIF/FAM, and tortilla (8.9), health programs (8.6), labor programs such as Temporary Employment Program (PET at 6.4), and other small programs.

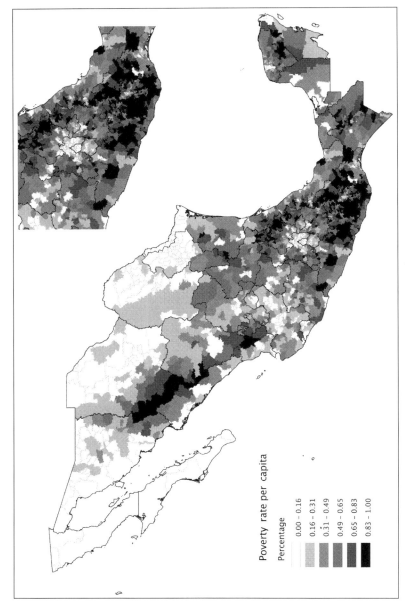

FIGURE 2.2. Share of population living under nutritional poverty line (CONEVAL), 2002.

2.2 The Geography of Poverty

Gallup et al. (2001, 2003) and Sachs (2005) have argued that geography plays a key role in development. For example, landlocked countries tend to grow at a slower rate than those with coastal access and navigable rivers. Across the world, it is well known that latitude is correlated with per capita GDP levels (Sachs, 2005). We know that institutional and historical processes also shape the evolution of well-being (Acemoglu and Robinson, 2006); and that geography is not destiny (Gallup et al., 2003). Yet poverty profiles are inevitably linked to the geographical characteristics of the territories where poor people live. This geographic relationship presents a methodological opportunity. Since human agency can only change geographic attributes at the margin (roads, bridges and tunnels can be built, swamps can be drained and rivers dammed, but mountains cannot be moved), geographic attributes are extremely good predictors of the spatial distribution of poverty.

The most striking aspect of Mexico's natural geography is its extreme variation. And those variations are highly correlated with poverty. Mexico provides a contrast to the findings by Gallup et al. (2001) that population and economic activity tend to concentrate on coasts and major waterways. The overwhelming majority of Mexican municipalities are landlocked and the population is not concentrated in coastal areas. The development of Mexico's transportation infrastructure since the nineteenth century has provided most municipalities with access to both railroads and major roads (within an average of twenty-three kilometers and five kilometers, respectively).

Table 2.2 presents an ordinary least squares (OLS) regression of several indicators of poverty and development on a selection of geographic variables.[9] The dependent variables are all normalized into z scores with a mean of 0 and a standard deviation of 1 to make it possible to compare the impact of various geographic features across regressions (although each of the indicators is constructed with different underlying data). To measure poverty, we employ three alternative indicators. The first indicator we use is the nutritional poverty headcount index presented in Figure 2.2. A second indicator measures the relative deprivation of municipalities in 1990. The index combines characteristics of households, including access to public services such as sewage systems, drinking water and electricity, access to housing construction materials, and individual traits such as literacy and earnings according to the 1990 census. The final dependent variable is the Human Development Index (HDI) calculated by UNDP on the basis of 2000 census data.[10]

---

[9] Previous efforts to study the geographical determinants of poverty include Esquivel (2000) and Blum and Diaz-Cayeros (2002). Those studies are carried out at the state level. For a municipal level analysis focusing on poverty and food security, see Bellon et al. (2004).

[10] The poverty headcount index comes from CONEVAL; the relative deprivation index is a widely used indicator produced by the Mexican population council (CONAPO) and based on factor analysis of census data; the HDI is constructed with an internationally shared methodology that combines indicators of income (measured as the municipal per capita GDP), education (literacy and school attendance), and health (infant mortality rates).

TABLE 2.2. *Geographic Correlates of Poverty in Mexican Municipalities*

	1	2	3	4	5	6
	Poverty headcount w/ Natural Geography	Poverty headcount w/ Human Geography	Marginality index w/ Natural Geography	Marginality index w/ Human Geography	HDI w/ Natural Geography	HDI w/ Human Geography
Spatial lag	0.265	0.169	0.174	0.117	0.123	0.06
	(0.054)**	(0.043)**	(0.057)**	(0.048)*	(0.062)*	(0.054)
North (Km/1000)	−0.963	−0.706	−0.97	−0.755	1.001	0.74
	(0.069)**	(0.070)**	(0.069)**	(0.071)**	(0.071)**	(0.072)**
East (Km/1000)	0.509	0.568	0.356	0.444	−0.275	−0.398
	(0.054)**	(0.051)**	(0.055)**	(0.053)**	(0.054)**	(0.054)**
Temperature (°C)	−0.014	−0.004	−0.015	−0.006	0.012	0.005
	(0.003)**	(0.002)	(0.003)**	(0.003)*	(0.003)**	(0.003)
Rainfall (Meters)	0.762	0.905	0.963	0.997	−0.813	−0.851
	(0.100)**	(0.081)**	(0.099)**	(0.085)**	(0.099)**	(0.084)**
Coastline (1 = coast/border)	−0.697	−0.504	−0.772	−0.643	0.84	0.678
	(0.073)**	(0.070)**	(0.074)**	(0.071)**	(0.070)**	(0.070)**
Rugged Terrain (st. dev. Km)	0.95	0.599	0.998	0.642	−0.814	−0.484
	(0.377)*	(0.292)*	(0.390)*	(0.291)*	(0.323)*	(0.249)
Altitude (km)	−0.893	−0.482	−1.067	−0.657	0.791	0.396
	(0.375)*	(0.291)	(0.388)**	(0.291)*	(0.322)*	(0.249)

Distance City		0.002		0.002		−0.003
(Km)		(0.000)**		(0.001)**		(0.000)**
Distance Rail		0.004		0.004		−0.005
(km)		(0.001)**		(0.001)**		(0.001)**
Distance Road		0.018		0.019		
(km)		(0.001)**		(0.002)**		(0.002)**
Population		−0.222		−0.14		0.159
(Log)		(0.012)**		(0.014)**		(0.014)**
Area		0.044		0.038		
($Km^2/1000$)		(0.010)**		(0.011)**		(0.009)**
Constant	−0.432	0.736	−0.041	0.405	−0.003	−0.504
	(0.160)**	(0.192)**	(0.163)	(0.215)	(0.163)	(0.221)*
Observations	2425	2375	2425	2375	2425	2375
R-squared	0.33	0.57	0.3	0.48	0.27	0.48

Note: Robust standard errors in parenthesis.

* Significant at the 5% level; ** significant at the 1% level.

The independent variables include a correction for spatial autocorrelation (poverty in neighboring municipalities) latitude, longitude, altitude, rainfall, and temperature. Mexico is a particularly mountainous country, so we calculated from the data on altitude the ruggedness of each municipality's terrain (measured as the standard deviation of altitude). This measure indicates how physically inaccessible a place is. We calculated the number of major rivers crossing a municipality and whether there was a major lake. The coastline variable detects access to the sea. Given the peculiarities of Mexico's highly permeable border with the United States, we coded municipalities on the northern border also as coastline.

The land area of the municipality reflects a measure of size, while population indicates the relative importance of municipalities. Population density combines both of these indicators, reflecting to a large extent the degree of urbanization. Finally we calculated four indicators reflecting accessibility to markets: distance to major highways, railroad tracks, cities of more than 100,000 inhabitants and Mexico City. All the distance variables were calculated, using a Euclidean metric, to the closest point on the border of the jurisdiction.

The table explicitly states in its headings that the coefficients should be read as suggestive of correlations to poverty, not of a causal relationship in which the geographic variables "explain" or produce specific outcomes of poverty and development.[11] Two estimations are reported for each index, one that includes only variables of natural or physical geography (latitude, longitude, temperature, rainfall, coastline, altitude and terrain ruggedness), and the other that includes what we call "human geography," indicating that the variables of distance, population and even land area are the product of demographic, socioeconomic, and political choices, accumulated over several decades and even centuries.

These results allow us to identify a distinctive geographic profile of poverty in Mexico. Estimations 1, 3, and 4 show that a third of the variance, as reflected by the R^2 statistic, is accounted for by natural geography variables alone. There is a powerful North-South divide that is evident in the latitude variable. The size of the effect is substantial. Using the coefficients from estimation 5, if we take municipalities with identical characteristics, except that one is located a thousand kilometers farther to the north, that sole difference would yield a change of one standard deviation in the HDI z score. The estimation also reveals an east-west cleavage. One thousand kilometers more to the east yields a poverty headcount index one-half a standard deviation larger.

Rainfall is statistically significant through all the estimations, including those with human geography variables, suggesting that places with more rainfall

---

[11] For good discussions of the limits to geography "explaining" development and the fascinating debate regarding the role of geographic versus institutional determinants of development, see Gallup et al. (2003); Acemoglu and Robinson (2002), Gallup, Sachs, and Mellinger (1998); Przeworski (2004); and Escobal and Torero (2003).

2.2 *The Geography of Poverty*

tend to be characterized by greater deprivation. Rugged terrain is significant at the 95 percent level, implying the presence of geographic poverty traps in areas made remote and difficult to access due to topography (Jalan and Ravaillon, 2002; Bloom et al., 2003). The poor in Mexican municipalities with inaccessible terrain have a hard time migrating out of those places or readily move their accumulated human capital or assets beyond a threshold that allows them to increase their productivity.[12]

Temperature and altitude are statistically significant only when variables linked to human geography are not included in the estimation, which suggests that the correlation of these environmental conditions with poverty is less pronounced in the presence of human activities that facilitate the movement of goods and people across a territory.

The inclusion of the human geography variables increases the power of the regressions significantly. More than half of the variance in the distribution of poverty is accounted for when human geography is taken into account, as indicated by the R^2 statistic. The equivalent statistics for the marginality index and the HDI are similar. The human geography variables are all significant in the expected direction. When a municipality is far from a large city, has no nearby railroad line and is not linked to the rest of the country through the highway network, its population is significantly poorer. Larger municipalities in terms of land area tend to be poorer, but more population is associated with less poverty, which in the end means that places with greater population density (i.e., more urban concentrations) exhibit less poverty.

When controlling for human geography, the variables related to the topography of the territory either cease to be statistically significant or reduce their association with poverty, which is consistent with the view that infrastructure and urbanization allow people to overcome poverty. Government action or inaction can hence have a large impact on poverty alleviation.

Among the human geography variables, the distance to railroads and the land size of municipalities have been virtually fixed over the past century. Most railroads were built in the nineteenth century (Coatsworth, 1976), and the municipal subdivision has only changed marginally since 1917 (Blum and Diaz-Cayeros, 2002). Most cities with more than 100,000 inhabitants were established as large urban concentrations in colonial times. According to Tanck de Estrada (2005) there were around twenty Spanish cities and "villas" in 1800, as distinct from the so-called Indian pueblos. Spanish cities were the centers of power and wealth in the colonial period. Although much has changed since

---

[12] Fearon and Laitin (2003) find that mountainous areas are likely to breed armed insurgency. In one of the few analyses using GIS to understand the determinants of social outcomes in Mexico, Villarreal (2002 and 2004) has shown that rugged terrain is an important determinant of crime rates across the country. Hence, rugged terrain is likely to be a reflection of a poverty trap in which destitution and violence are readily linked, although with the more recent eruption of drug-related violence, the geographic distribution of violence has changed, making Northern and less mountainous places the most dangerous.

then, today's large cities were established in the late colonial period, with the exception of cities on the northern border and some coastal ports that have blossomed as tourist centers in the past few decades.

On the contrary, other human geography variables have been changing rapidly during the past decades. Demographic patterns are not exogenous to the social, economic, or political processes of both the recent and the distant past. These sociopolitical processes include dislocations produced by social upheaval at the beginning of the twentieth century, massive urban migration since the 1960s, and the large-scale emigration to the United States since the 1980s.

National highway construction in Mexico began in the 1920s, and the new construction often followed old colonial routes (Ortiz Hernán, 1994). But there has been a steady expansion of road networks since the 1960s, with a recent boom in highway construction in the 1990s funded by joint private-public ventures. Among the geographical variables included in our estimations, highways are arguably the most reflective of recent government activity.

The location, climate, and terrain of a municipality are important predictors of poverty levels. Our results suggest that poverty is determined by a combination of human agency and geographic conditions, but is driven more by the latter. Again, the associations shown in these estimations are not necessarily causal. In fact, the social, economic, and political processes captured by the geographic variables, particularly the ones shaped by human agency, are very likely the consequence of poverty as much as the cause. Teasing out the links of causality goes beyond the scope of this chapter.

2.3 STRATEGIES FOR PUBLIC GOODS PROVISION AND POVERTY ALLEVIATION

The accumulated experience of two decades of poverty relief spending in Mexico affords a unique opportunity to compare and contrast poverty-alleviation efforts, particularly with regard to differences between discretionary and formula-based programs, targeted and universal approaches, and centralized and decentralized decision making. It also provides insights into the ways in which local politics influences the implementation and allocation of funds across households and political jurisdictions. This book compares social spending strategies in all of Mexico's municipalities that span three presidential terms.

Figure 2.3 shows the geographic distribution of the funds for *Pronasol*, FISM and *Progresa/Oportunidades* at the municipal level. The maps are organized into rows and columns corresponding to Figure I.1. The first two maps show nondiscretional or formula-based antipoverty funds distributed to municipalities while the maps in the next page discretional programs. The top map shows funds for localities (earmarked and block grants in the case of FISM and public goods constituting pork-barrel appropriations for *Pronasol*); while the bottom map depicts programs targeted to individuals (through entitlement-based

2.3 *Strategies for Public Goods Provision and Poverty Alleviation* 59

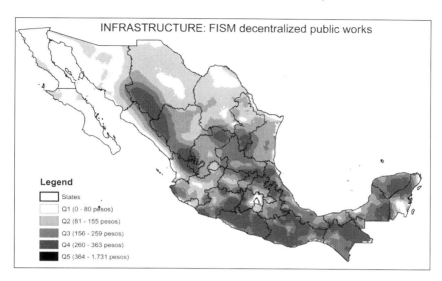

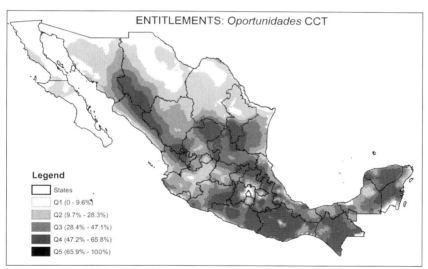

FIGURE 2.3. The geography of poverty relief transfers in Mexico, 1989–2005.
Note: Pronasol average data for 1989–1994; FISM data for 2000; Oportunidades coverage for 2005. All figures are per capita in real pesos of 1994 or share of population for *Oportunidades* (1 USD = 3.3 MXP).

transfers in the case of *Oportunidades* and in a clientelistic manner in the case of *Pronasol*).

The map in the bottom of the second page shows the mean per capita allocation of *Pronasol* funds for private goods, measured in 1994 pesos, for the

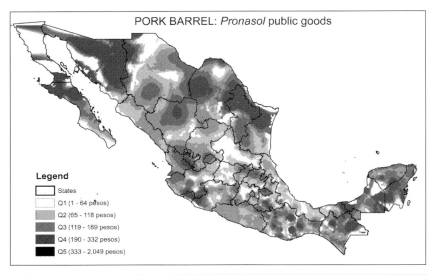

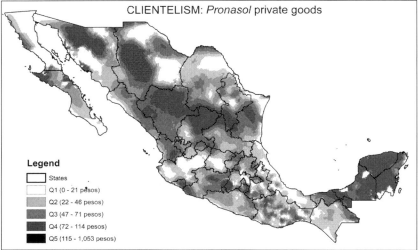

FIGURE 2.3 *(cont.)*

2,417 municipalities in Mexico at the time, during the six years of the program (1989–1994).[13] *Pronasol* was made up of more than twenty programs, which we reclassified into projects providing private goods and projects providing

---

[13] The database on *Pronasol* spending was painstakingly compiled by Marcela Gómez and Sandra Pineda (1999). The allocation of funds shown in the map in Figure 2.1 does not include contributions from beneficiaries and matching funds provided by state and municipal governments. The data does not report information for the boroughs of Mexico City.

2.3 Strategies for Public Goods Provision and Poverty Alleviation 61

public goods.[14] The map in the top row of that discretional column shows the public goods allocations of *Pronasol* for the same time period. The map in the top left cell shows the mean allocation of municipal social infrastructure funds (FDSM/FISM) from 1996 to 2000, also in real per capita terms.[15] The final map in the figure in the bottom left cell shows the mean per capita allocation of *Oportunidades* funds from 2001 to 2005.[16]

In order to render the visualization of highly disaggregated data more effective, the maps show smoothed surfaces of spending estimated in similar fashion to temperature or rainfall maps. This is created through a third degree spatial polynomial of spending over 30 neighboring municipalities in the territory (in the rainfall analogy, this is similar to having 2,430 weather stations, and the surface is generated by something similar to an average of their readings over the territory). The isolines shading the maps establish contours of territory with similar levels of funding, just like in a typical topographic map.

Despite their widely different levels of development, all municipalities in Mexico received at least some funds from each program. The different criteria for selecting beneficiaries are reflected in the geographic patterns observed in the figure. The magnitude of the funds involved in each program varies widely. *Pronasol* public goods comprised the largest appropriations, followed by FISM. *Oportunidades* funding is substantially smaller than the private goods component of *Pronasol*, which was less than half of the public goods allocation. The programs were different from one another in several respects: *Pronasol* included funding geared towards large infrastructure investment in highways, sizeable transfers devoted to financing local public goods and transfers to individuals and organized groups. FISM has a narrower scope, providing direct municipal financing for local public goods selected and administered by local governments. *Progresa* provided CCTs to individual households in rural areas only, while *Oportunidades* expanded the rural coverage of *Progresa* to urban beneficiaries using the same basic design of the CCT program.

The most notable feature to emerge from a visual comparison of the maps is the marked difference in the geographical distribution of funds. An even shading of any map would mean that funds were distributed in an equal per capita amount across municipalities, rather than targeted to poorest localities. Maps with contrasting dark and light shades indicate more unequal allocations or, in this context, better targeted allocations. Areas of the country with greater

---

[14] Analysis of individual programs can be found in Gershberg (1994) for the *Escuela Digna* program; Fox (1994) for Indian community development programs; Hiskey (2000) for electricity and potable water; and Magaloni, Estévez, and Diaz-Cayeros (2000) for potable water and sewage, road construction, and the *Fondos Municipales* program.
[15] Although there were some small changes adjustments in FISM after 2000, the formulas used for the municipal distribution of these funds have remained fixed since then.
[16] These allocations differ from *Progresa* allocations in the 1997–2000 period in that they incorporate more urban beneficiaries, as well as an expansion of the rural reach of the program.

concentrations of poor households should deservedly have more funds allocated to them than richer regions.

A comparison of the mapping of poverty and the distribution of social program outlays (Figures 2.2 and 2.3) suggests that the program that most closely matched poverty profiles across space is *Oportunidades*. FISM funds also show a remarkably similar distribution to the one found in a poverty headcount ratio. In contrast, private goods provision in the *Pronasol* program was concentrated in Northern Mexico and the Yucatán peninsula, not necessarily the poorest areas of the country. Very low allocations of those funds were observed in the state of Veracruz on the Gulf coast, and in the western highlands, particularly in the state of Jalisco. The distribution of *Pronasol* public goods is somewhat distinct: large amounts of funds were allocated in some Northern states, while smaller ones went to central areas, particularly the region North of Mexico City. An assessment of whether there is enough of a match between the territorial distribution of public funds and the mapping of poverty is developed in future chapters.

2.4 THE POLITICAL LANDSCAPE

Our focus in this book is on how social programs are shaped by political and electoral considerations, and how these programs impact welfare and voting decisions. In much of the analysis of the book we take into account the partisan identity of incumbents at the municipal level and the degree of competition they face. The complexity of capturing the political landscape of a country is reduced, to some extent, by the existence of relatively nationalized political parties. Through patterns of observed electoral support we are able to know something about the configuration of political preferences across the territory, which can be used as convenient shorthand for more complicated interactions between individual politicians, communities, and voters.

The first map shown in Figure 2.4 displays the support for the PRI in the 1994 federal elections, which yielded a PRI victory despite strong challenges from both the PAN and the PRD. The first thing to note is that, although the party no longer enjoyed the levels of electoral support it had grown accustomed to in the hegemonic era, it still commanded very large majorities in most municipalities in the country. Shaded in white are places where the PRI candidate Ernesto Zedillo received less than 42 percent of the vote; and in dark grey the municipalities where he got more than 50 percent of the vote. The municipal map visually exaggerates the importance of northern support due to the larger territorial size of municipalities in that region, but nevertheless it attests to widespread support for the PRI throughout the country, with the exception of greater Mexico City, the western highlands and parts of the south. A striking correlation is apparent between the geography of *Pronasol* expenditures displayed in Figure 2.3 and the geography of PRI support. This correlation will be systematically explored in subsequent chapters where we

2.4 *The Political Landscape*

will develop a measure of PRI core support using long-term electoral returns from 1970 until 1988 that are exogenous to later expenditures. The positive correlation between this measure of PRI core support and expenditures will be the subject of our statistical models in Chapter 4.

The second map shows the distribution of vote shares for the PAN in the 2000 elections, with the general shading indicating some regional contrasts in support. The highest vote shares for the PAN appear in the western highlands, the northern border and scattered municipalities in central Mexico. The party appears extremely weak, with vote shares below 10 percent, in the south, where most of the poor concentrate. In contrast to the PRI map above it, the levels of support for the PAN across municipalities were much lower than those enjoyed by the PRI, even in elections that the ruling party lost. A simple visual comparison between the poverty map in Figure 2.2 and the PAN's electoral returns in 2000 displayed in Figure 2.4 highlights its scant support among the rural poor when it won the presidency in 2000. In Chapter 8 it will become apparent how the PAN was able to increase its electoral base among the poor in the 2006 presidential elections, expanding *Oportunidades* during Vicente Fox's presidential term.

The third map shows levels of electoral support of the PRD in the 2006 elections, which candidate Andrés Manuel López Obrador lost by a small margin based on officially sanctioned results. We use 2006 to map the PRD's vote because that is the year of the left's strongest performance in national elections. In the Southern half of the country, PRD strength appears to be highly correlated with the distribution of poverty in Figure 2.3. In the Western highlands and the North, that is not the case.

Although the three maps reflect different presidential elections spanning twelve years, taken together the maps tell an important story about the character of electoral competition in Mexico. From the mid-1990s onward, partisan competition in federal elections has strengthened, but in clearly defined territorial patterns. The PRI is electorally competitive throughout the country, generally facing challenges from the PAN in the North and West and from the PRD in the South. The PAN and the PRD, however, rarely compete against each other in any particular municipality, state, or region. Truly three-party elections are mostly observed in the central region of the country, especially in greater Mexico City, and in some urban districts in the rest of the country.

While the federal electoral results provide a good overview of the conditions that make Mexican electoral politics so vibrant and competitive, it is important to note that democratization did not just come about as a national process. Local processes of alternation in political power, where the PRI had no other choice but to recognize its defeats in municipal and eventually state-level electoral contests preceded the transition to democracy. Figure 2.5 provides an indicator of the process of democratization from a local perspective, by showing the years since an alternation in mayoral races taking place in each of the municipalities.

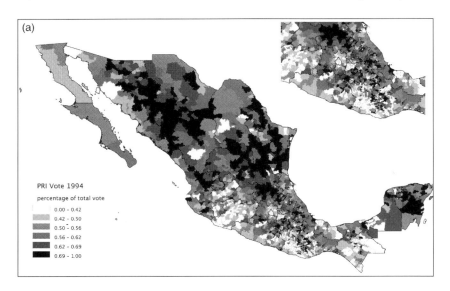

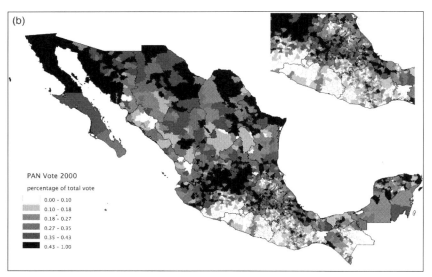

FIGURE 2.4. Electoral geography.

Alternation at the local level provides an unambiguous indicator that the PRI no longer held a monopoly of representation, even if voters may have decided to allow that party to return to political office in subsequent elections after its defeat. The general pattern displayed in the map shows, first, that virtually all municipalities have had some alternation by 2006. In this sense,

2.4 The Political Landscape

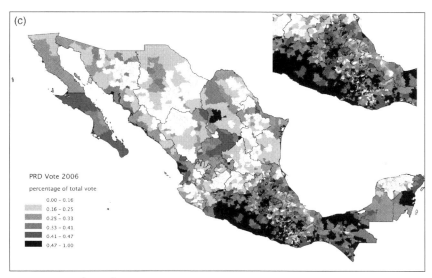

FIGURE 2.4 (*cont.*)

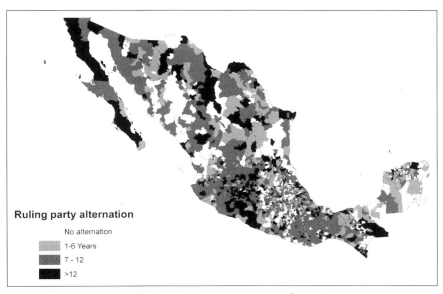

FIGURE 2.5. Municipal democracy: years since party alternation.

despite the deep entrenchment of party bosses and machines in various regions, democratization from below is undeniable.

Second, democratization from below does not seem to obey a particular territorial logic or be simply driven by modernization processes. While in the early 1990s capital cities in the states and relatively rich municipalities were more likely to vote against the PRI, as democratization advanced electoral victories of the opposition were observed throughout the country.

It is perhaps not so surprising, in the context of these electoral challenges, that PRI governments strategically used the distribution of poverty relief resources. The political imperative of the party was to remain in office, and prevent further erosion, in the face of vigorous competition by parties. The next chapter moves to the task of providing a theory of how politicians address electoral threats using the distribution of transfers to voters as a way to buy off political support; the chapter after that assesses the success of that strategy for the case of *Pronasol* during the Salinas years.

3

Political Machines and Vote Buying

> Core supporters will not long tolerate a
> party that delivers benefits to outsiders.
>
> Dixit and Londregan (1996: 1140)

3.1 INTRODUCTION

Poverty-stricken places are seldom transformed by growth- and welfare-enhancing policies steadfastly applied by government actors. Instead, politicians opt to target the poor with private, excludable benefits which tend to peak at election time. In many developing countries without a propoor bias in social spending, clientelism is often the only safety net available to them. In turn, they frequently reward political parties that engage in these practices. The poorer the voters are, the more they are trapped in this relationship of material dependence. Classic studies of political clientelism emphasize that this form of exchange thrives where voters are poor. For example, James Scott (1972a) argued that patron-client links are based on poverty and inequality and the fact that the "patron is in a position to supply unilaterally goods and services which the potential client and his family need for their survival and well-being" (p. 125).

This chapter provides a formal model of machine politics. We build on existing theories of distributive politics, originally developed for understanding the determinants of discretionary welfare transfers in consolidated democracies (Dixit and Londregan, 1996; Cox and McCubbins, 1986) and on more recent models of clientelism (Stokes, 2005; Nichter, 2010).

Most of these models focus on what Nichter (2010) calls short-term electoral clientelism. We define clientelism as the voluntary exchange of discretionary private transfers for votes, whose continuation is contingent upon demonstrable political support.[1] That transfers be discretionary is key to our

---

[1] Our understanding of clientelism is akin to Stokes (2007), who defines it as "*the proffering of material goods in return for electoral support, where the criterion of distribution that the patron*

definition of clientelism, making the allocation criteria explicitly political. Since most of a party's electoral investment strategies are embedded in ongoing relationships and programs that translate into accumulated benefits that accrue beyond elections, our theory is not focused on campaign handouts and vote buying on the spot market.

Our theory departs from the literature in two fundamental ways. First, we conceive of parties and voters as engaged in strategic interactions that extend indefinitely into the future. Second, we posit that partisan loyalties are conditional – a product of past political exchanges that are embedded in a relational network. Prior models of distributive politics rest on the assumption that a core or loyal voter's proximity to a party remains unaffected by the party's performance. Given this assumption, the loyal voter is captive, disposed to support her party *no matter what*, even after being cut off from the stream of patronage benefits (Stokes, 2005; Stokes et al., 2013).

This assumption is problematic. It implies that core voters are unresponsive to welfare benefits, which is particularly difficult to argue for developing societies. When voters are poor, they tend to base their decisions critically on material considerations – for example, what will provide for the next meal, a leak-free roof, medicine, or clothes and scholarships for their children. Ideology and other symbolic appeals are secondary considerations at best.

Our model posits that voters' partisan loyalties are *constructed* through a history of interaction with a party's brokers and organizational networks.[2] Material exchanges play a fundamental role in this relational history. Voter loyalty is also conditional on whether the party can credibly signal that these exchanges will continue into the future. This is one critical reason why particularistic transfers usually spike at election time, as we will empirically show in subsequent chapters.

The theory allows us to understand, for example, why the Peronist party in Argentina funnels jobs and patronage to its own supporters, why the rules-of-thumb for political machines in the United States were to "hold what you've got" and "take care of your own" (Holder, 1975, cited in Cox and McCubbins, 1986: 383), and why the PRI disproportionately delivered benefits to its loyal voters.

Our theoretical approach further answers some fundamental questions of strategy. When do politicians choose to buy votes with discretionary private goods and when with patronage for public goods provision? To what types of voters are these benefits targeted? The literature on distributive politics has for the most part ignored the fact that politicians have at their disposal a large

---

uses is simply: did you (will you) support me?" (emphasis in the original, p. 605) and with Kitschelt and Wilkinson (2007), who argue that "*clientelistic accountability represents a transaction, the direct exchange of a citizen's vote in return for direct payments or continuing access to goods and services*" (emphasis in the original, p. 2).

[2] Our notion of conditional partisan loyalty is akin to Fiorina's (1981) "running tally" of retrospective assessments of party performance.

3.1 Introduction

basket of potential transfers to build and mobilize electoral support. This chapter develops a theory and the next one provides empirical evidence for a portfolio diversification logic driving the relative shares of private and public goods distributed in a given district. We provide expectations of how voters should respond to the different strategies of vote buying – namely, how many votes do particularistic transfers provide compared to public goods provision. We thus provide a more comprehensive picture of electoral investment strategies than that available in most studies of distributive politics.

In our view, party machines deliver particularistic benefits to their core voters and public goods to the population at large. Machines favor the exchange of particularistic and excludable benefits to core voters because these can be targeted with precision, rewarding supporters and punishing opponents. The targeting is critical because it solves problems of voter opportunism and reduces the costs of vote buying, allowing the machine to appropriate more rents. The clientelistic contract further allows the machine to deter voter exit through a credible threat of punishment (Magaloni, 2006; Diaz-Cayeros et al., 2001). Clientelism is self-sustaining, in our theoretical claim, because party and voters expect to interact into the future and can sanction each other for breaking the contract.

But political machines also rely heavily on public goods or pork-barreling projects. Public infrastructure projects, we demonstrate, are employed for electoral purposes when the politician's base of electoral support falls below a certain threshold and the votes of a larger and more heterogeneous electorate are needed to win elections. Of course, there might be nonelectoral uses for both private and public goods transfers. In a classic article, Shepsle, Weingast, and Johnsen (1981) stress the private consumption gains that business or contract patronage entails for firms, labor, suppliers, and other interests, usually within the district but possibly outside it as well. Local public goods are rarely if ever "pure" public goods. We know that politicians and parties derive electoral benefits from pork-barrel spending, but our model provides an account of how it is used as a complementary strategy to clientelism in the face of stiffer electoral competition.

Our approach to machine politics is compatible with Calvo and Murillo (2011), who argue that voter-party linkages are not spot exchanges, but rather based on long-term interactions with partisan organizations and public officials. Machine politics is embedded in organizational networks where parties employ brokers, bosses, and patrons to acquire knowledge about local voters – their political predispositions, their reference groups and social networks, their patterns of political participation and their partisan affinities. Voters also develop distributive expectations as a result of their prior interactions with political networks (Calvo and Murillo, 2011). In their study, Stokes et al. (2013) also emphasize long-term linkages in their broker-centered account of machine politics.

This chapter unfolds as follows. The next section highlights the two dimensions of government transfers relevant for the study of distributive politics.

Section 3.3 places our theoretical approach within the core-versus-swing voter debate and studies of clientelism. Section 3.4 develops a formal model answering the core voter "puzzle": why do parties invest in voters that are already likely to support them? Section 3.5 develops our theory of portfolio diversification to account for public goods provision. Machines that are under pressure from competition are caught in a dilemma: sustaining their electoral coalitions over time by taking care of their core voters, or maximizing their chances of reelection by catering to swing voters. The latter strategy can be advantageous in the short term, but is destabilizing over time. To solve this dilemma, we argue that machines can diversify their portfolio of electoral investments by targeting discretionary private benefits to their core voters and spending on public goods to attract the support of a wider set of citizens.

3.2 DISCRETIONARY PRIVATE AND PUBLIC GOODS

We classify distributive policies conceived as "instruments of electoral investment" according to two dimensions: whether their benefits are private or public goods and the degree to which there is formal government discretion, or leeway, to decide who benefits, when transfers are given, and when they are withdrawn. Private goods can be targeted to individuals and exhibit excludability of consumption, whereas public goods can be targeted only to localities or districts and their consumption is generally nonexcludable. Instruments of electoral investment are nondiscretionary when the program defines *ex ante*, in legal and abstract terms, those who can receive benefits and under what conditions. This programmatic redistribution differs from discretionary transfers or what Dixit and Londregan (1996) call "tactical redistribution," which can take a variety of forms, including campaign handouts, subsidies, tariff protection, and pork-barreling projects. The focus here is on tactical redistribution – investments in discretionary private and public goods.

Discretionary private goods are excludable and reversible. Excludability allows parties to target benefits, rewarding and punishing voters according to their political loyalties. Many public works exhibit some degree of excludability because they are targeted to specific localities. Magaloni (2006) shows, for example, that *Pronasol*'s social infrastructure projects generally bypassed municipalities governed by opposition parties. Nevertheless, when a bridge is built or a public clinic or school constructed, it is not feasible to exclude opposition voters in that locality from consuming their benefits. Public goods cannot be targeted with precision to punish opponents.

The second fundamental difference is their reversibility. Discretionary private transfers can be made for any length of time and can be withdrawn when the politician so decides. In contrast, public goods once in place are harder to withdraw: infrastructure projects such as roads and highways, bridges and canals, sewage and irrigation systems, public service facilities and power plants are fixed investments. In some cases, however, politicians may intentionally choose to forego maintenance of fixed investments. For example, in their study of Peru, Paxton and Schady (2002) find that incumbents sometimes purposely neglect to maintain public infrastructure.

In the introduction we classified discretionary private goods as clientelistic transfers. Discretionary public goods transfers spent on infrastructure constitute what is often referred to in the literature as "pork-barrel" politics (Shepsle and Weingast, 1980; Ferejohn, 1974). Pork differs from clientelism in that its principal benefits cannot be targeted to the individual. Public goods, therefore, are subject to a commitment problem, since their benefits are widely shared, even by opposition backers. Yet public goods are more effective at reaching a larger share of the population and, consequently, building more encompassing electoral coalitions (Bueno de Mesquita et al., 2003; Chhibber and Noorudding, 2004; Magaloni et al., 2007).

3.3 CORE VERSUS SWING VOTERS

There are two opposed models of discretionary transfers that focus on what Dixit and Londregan (1996) call "tactical redistribution." The first model is the core-voter model, developed by Cox and McCubbins (1986), hereafter CM. Their theory begins by defining the conditions under which distributive politics will generate stable electoral coalitions. CM divide the electorate into three groups – core supporters, swing voters, and opposition backers – and ask which of these voting groups would reelection-minded politicians choose as the main beneficiaries of targeted transfers. These groups differ in what the authors call an "adherence dimension" – how responsive they are to transfers from a given party. In their model, core supporters are the most electorally responsive group because parties know their preferences and desires well, while swing voters and opposition backers are less well identified and less likely to be trustworthy. CM predict that risk-averse candidates trying to maximize electoral support will deliver redistributions first and foremost to their core voters.

The result of the CM model hinges on the assumption of risk-aversion on the part of politicians, on the one hand, and on the notion that core voters are less risky than other voters because politicians are in "frequent and intensive contact with them and have relatively precise and accurate ideas about how they will react" (Cox and McCubbins, 1986: 379). It has become commonplace to critique the core-voter model for this depiction of politicians investing scarce resources in a voter group that is likely to vote for them regardless. We will address this critique and its premises in the following sections.

A second set of models predict that politicians should benignly neglect loyal supporters and instead target swing voters, who can be decisive for election outcomes and for whom a benefit transfer may incline their vote choice in favor of the incumbent (Lindbeck and Weibull, 1987; Dixit and Londregan, 1996; Stokes, 2005 and 2006). The Dixit and Londregan (1996) model, hereafter DL, begins by asking whom politicians running for office would target with discretionary transfers. Voter utility is a function of issue positions and private consumption; the parties' issue positions are assumed to be fixed; and tactical reallocations of the budget are relatively flexible. Under the assumption that a politician's transfers are feasibly and equally targetable to all voters (i.e., the "leaky bucket" is the same for each voter group) and that any incumbent will seek to maximize his probabilities of reelection (the key premise also for Lindbeck and Weibull, 1987), the model predicts that politicians should favor swing voters, defined as those close to the point at which voters are ideologically indifferent to the alternatives.[3]

The literature has attempted by various means to identify swing-voter groups. One way is to employ surveys, as in Stokes' various contributions (2005, 2006, and 2013). The other is to use aggregate vote returns.[4] "Under some assumptions about the distribution functions (i.e., symmetry and single peakedness) and parties' objective functions, there will be a one-to-one correspondence between the density at the cutpoint and the closeness of the last election" (Dahlberg and Johansson, 2002: 30). This is the reason swing voters are commonly credited with deciding a tight race at the district level.

Stokes (2005) critiques these models for not taking commitment problems into account. "Both assume by caveat that the party will not renege on its offer of particularistic rewards once it has won the election. And they don't deal adequately with the fact that a voter once in the voting booth can also renege by voting his or her conscience or preference ignoring the reward he or she received" (p. 316). To deal with commitment problems, she proposes a repeated interaction game in which parties can monitor voters' actions and both sides foresee their interaction extending into the future. Her model builds on DL in that voters presumably are swayed by both the issue positions of the parties and the income and consumption transfers received from them. Stokes' model generates predictions akin to those of the swing voter model. Loyal voters do not extract private rewards because they cannot vote against the party. "Such a threat would lack credibility: the party knows that the loyal voter, even without rewards, is better off cooperating forever than defecting forever" (p. 320). Weakly opposed voters and indifferent voters are the target of vote buying because, in her approach, only they can credibly threaten to vote against the incumbent in the absence of a transfer.

Nichter (2008) departs from these approaches by arguing that parties buy turnout rather than votes. With the secret ballot, he asks, what prevents individuals from accepting rewards and then voting as they wish? He offers an alternative explanation, which he terms "turnout buying," suggesting that parties will reward supporters for showing up at the polls in order to activate their

---

[3] The DL model allows for a core voter result depending on the taxing technology. See also Londregan (2006).
[4] Some studies that use aggregate vote returns include Schady (2002); Dahlberg and Johansson (2002); Hiskey (2003); Calvo and Murillo (2004); Magaloni (2006); Magaloni et al. (2007).

3.3 Core versus Swing Voters

otherwise passive constituencies. Whereas Stokes's vote-buying model predicts that parties will target swing voters, Nichter's turnout-buying theory predicts that they will target strong supporters.

Stokes et al. (2013) provide an account of machine politics that stresses the importance of party brokers in targeting benefits to loyal voters. The model predicts that benefits will flow to core supporters because party brokers prefer to invest in them. Investment in the core can be very wasteful but generates opportunities for rent-seeking by brokers. The party leadership would prefer to direct investments to swing voters, an electorally more efficacious strategy, but cannot control their local agents nor their decisions over transfers. Thus, the core-voter model by this account is the product of misaligned incentives within parties that sustain strong agency losses. Investment in core supporters, in other words, is perverse.

The models discussed focus on short-term electoral clientelism and hence take party loyalty as exogenous. However, party's investment strategies are embedded in ongoing decisions whose benefits extend well beyond election time. Our approach departs from the existing literature by conceiving of parties and voters as engaged in *enduring* strategic interactions. We further distance ourselves by positing that partisan loyalties are *conditional* – a product of the history of political exchanges and tactical redistributions tying voters to parties.

Most theories of distributive politics rest on the assumption that a loyal voter's ideological proximity to a party remains unaffected by the retrospective tally of the party's behavior. Given this assumption, the loyal voter is captive. Even when cut off from the stream of patronage benefits, she is assumed to continue to vote for her party because her ideological proximity remains unaffected (Dixit and Londregan, 1996; Stokes, 2005; Stokes et al., 2013). This assumption is, at the very least, questionable. If the loyal voter is routinely ignored or disdained by her party, while other voter groups receive the party's discretionary favors, she may well begin to distrust the party, avoid turning out, and even consider switching support to an alternative.

The literature on core and swing voters ignores this strategic dilemma because it takes partisan loyalties as exogenous. A party that exclusively targets swing voters would not be viable in the long run. In their classic study on social democracy, Przeworski and Sprague (1986) emphasize this strategic dilemma. They argue that socialist parties that needed to mobilize the support of middle-class allies in order to win alienated their working-class core, which became available for political mobilization by other political parties on the basis of different political identities (religious or ethnic) or more extremist appeals (communist). The problem we consider here is analogous to the socialist party's dilemma: machines risk losing their core supporters when they attempt to build broader coalitions by delivering transfers to voter groups outside the core.

Partisan loyalties cannot be modeled independently from welfare transfers. CM put this idea succinctly: if a "politician's core supporters are those who will stick with him through thick and thin ... then core support groups will be totally unresponsive and will be given nothing (in pure redistributive terms)" (Cox and MCubbins, 1986: 380). However, as the authors note, "it seems irrational in the long-run for any group to be totally unresponsive to redistributions of welfare" (p. 382). Hence, swing-voter models generate the paradoxical result that core voters are unresponsive to welfare benefits and unmolested by their withdrawal.

Moreover, the common assumption that core voters will support a party *no matter what* is difficult to sustain in developing societies. Poor voters are typically more responsive to the delivery of pocketbook benefits. DL consider this possibility by positing a parameter that measures the relative importance of income and consumption gains to the voter. The higher the parameter, the more voters focus on transfers and the more "apolitical" they become (Weitz-Shapiro, 2014; Magaloni, 2006; Stokes et al., 2013).

The swing-voter model is hence unable to explain machine politics in developing societies and their residual survival in developed ones, because it seems disingenuous to think that a political party succeeds by ignoring its core base. This is particularly questionable when a party's core base is disproportionately composed of poor voters, as occurred with the PRI in Mexico and the PJ in Argentina and so many other party machines around the world.

Our working assumption diverges from these models. We posit that the poor's partisan loyalties are constructed through material inducements rather than symbolic or ideological appeals. It is not that poor voters in the developing world do not exhibit strong partisan loyalties. The argument is that their partisan identities are *constructed* through a history of interactions in which material exchanges play a fundamental role.

To put an example, it is evident that few voters can be thought of as PRIístas or Peronistas because of ideological or programmatic considerations or because of a personal attachment to caudillos like Lázaro Cárdenas and Juan Domingo Perón. These parties, in fact, have no sharp programmatic platform and draw support from many social groups, although disproportionately from the poor (Gibson, 1996; Magaloni, 2006; Calvo and Murillo, 2011). Moreover, most of their supporters were not alive when the caudillos held the stage.

Loyalty to these parties stems from the steady treatment of their loyal supporters as their core clienteles. This simply means that their supporters have repeatedly interacted with the party's brokers to collect favors and transfers in the past, and that they hold expectations to continue to benefit from its spoils system into the future. Party loyalty in these settings is the product of on-going relations between voters and brokers within the party's networks, in which the exchange of material benefits and political support plays a central role. In this context, loyalty reflects a voter's sense of belonging to the relational network rather than like-mindedness.

We hence model the strategic interaction between a core voter and her party as a dynamic game in which her attachment to the party is a function of their history of political exchanges. Partisan loyalties are anchored in that history. We call this *conditional party loyalty*. The corollary is that partisan loyalty is weakened when a party neglects its core constituencies and delivers benefits mainly to nonloyalists.

3.4 A THEORY OF VOTE BUYING WITH CONDITIONAL PARTISAN LOYALTY

To illustrate our theory of *conditional party loyalty*, consider the following game tree. A core voter must decide in the first period between voting for the machine or the opposition. The machine then decides to target side payments, rewarding or punishing voters according to their electoral choice. The core voter in the second period must decide whether to remain loyal to the party or change into a swing voter. The game results in eight possible outcomes, which we label a–h. The representation of the sequential game is presented in Figure 3.1.

This game is an extension of Magaloni's (2006) and Diaz-Cayeros et al.'s (2001) "punishment regime." Their game has only one subgame in which the machine moves last. If the game is not repeated, the machine possesses no incentives to reward the loyal voter. Hence, an important difference between the "punishment regime" model and this one is that voters here are given a second move at time t+1. After the machine rewards or punishes, the voter can opt to remain loyal or not. The model assumes that voters reciprocate a party with loyalty only when they are rewarded and otherwise they become swing voters. A swing voter is not attached to any political party either by personal reciprocity developed through a history of interaction or through ideology. Hence swing voters are open to political mobilization. By adding this last move to the punishment regime game, we can better uncover why a machine decides rationally to fulfill its part of the agreement by rewarding its core voters.

In the lower subgame, the core voter defects to the opposition and the machine needs to decide whether to reward or to punish her. Following the logic in the punishment regime game, we posit that the machine prefers to punish defectors because otherwise it would generate perverse incentives for disloyalty. Once the machine punishes, the voter must decide whether to recuperate her loyal status, and be rejected again, or remain disloyal. The off-the-path equilibrium outcome in the lower subgame is, hence, that the machine punishes the voter who will remain opportunistic thereafter. In other words, disloyal voters who defect are never "bought back."[5]

In the upper subgame, the machine needs to decide whether to reward a loyal core voter or to betray her. This choice has no bearing on the current election because the core voter has already voted. In line with the swing-voter logic, the machine still has incentives to disappoint core voters. Yet in our

---

[5] We provide empirical evidence for this claim in the next chapter.

76   Political Machines and Vote Buying

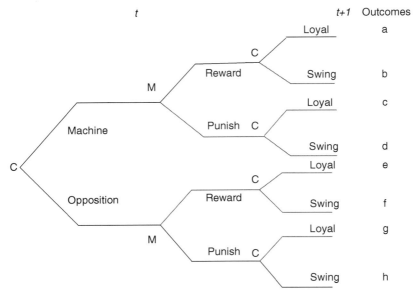

**The machine-loyal voter exchange
and the punishment regime**

FIGURE 3.1. A model of ongoing vote buying.

model there is a clear benefit in catering to the core because party opportunism undermines the strength of political loyalties in future contests (outcome d). Worse, reneging on loyal voters helps to create the conditions in which a buyer's market is changed into the opposite, a seller's market in which a vote inevitably grows more and more expensive.

Hence, the machine needs to compare the utility from outcomes *a* and *d* when making its choice in the upper subgame. If the machine continually delivers transfers to its core voters, this reflects its concern to preserve and strengthen political loyalty into the future. Just how valuable this reserve of voter loyalty is for the machine needs to be evaluated against the temptation to betray the core voter in this period and the expected value of buying swing voters in future elections. To answer this question, we develop an infinite game of vote buying that formalizes these intuitions, which is explained in the following pages in detail.

Consider this scenario: a voter must decide between supporting the incumbent or the opposition, and the incumbent must in turn decide to reward the voter with a transfer, $t > 0$, or to punish her $(t = 0)$. Stokes (2005) highlights the commitment problem in this interaction. She solves the dilemma by repeating the game infinitely and positing that the players follow a grim-trigger strategy: cooperate until the other player defects and then defect forever. However, in her approach, loyal voters do not get transfers at all because their ideological proximity remains unaffected should the incumbent renege on his promises in the previous move, in any number of times the game is repeated.

We propose a different formulation of the problem. In our view, partisan loyalties are defined as a function of the history of interactions. Imagine that the incumbent party has to decide whether to buy a particular voter through a monetary pay-off. This voter can be characterized either as a core or a swing voter. The core voter will vote for the incumbent party today, even if she does not get a transfer. But if her party shirks, she will become detached from her party and begin to act like a swing voter tomorrow. Hence, core-voter support is apparently unconditional today, but tomorrow it is conditioned by the changing history of tactical redistribution.

Core-voter loyalty translates into certain electoral support, so that the probability of voting for the machine is equal to 1. The risk of core-voter opportunism is negligible. This is because core voters, once at the ballot box, have no reason to renege on the contract after having accepted the patron's transfers. Money, transport, and other benefits might still be needed to mobilize core voters to the polls (Nichter, 2011),[6] but their vote choice is not in question. Swing voters are less proximate to the incumbent party and are not tied to it by a sense of obligation and mutual trust developed through a personalized history of exchanges. However, a transfer to a swing voter may convince her to support the incumbent according to a random variable s~[0,1]. The expected value of swing-voter support (E[s]) is less than the certain value of the core voter because swing voters are riskier investments and can behave opportunistically. They can renege without serious consequence and, thus, are the true source of commitment problems in vote buying.

Following CM, our model assumes that it is less costly to buy off core voters because they are more responsive to transfers, given that the party knows their needs and desires better than those of voters not tied to the party's organization. In other words, it is significantly less expensive to entice a voter to support you when he or she is personally tied to you, trusts you, and expects to interact with you into the future. Party brokers often know their core supporters by name, where they live, how many children they have, where they attend school, and what their needs and desires are. This informational advantage, Zarazaga (2011) claims, allows party brokers to be aware of voters' "reservation value," or opportunity cost, and accordingly pay core voters the minimal amount necessary. Less attached to the party and its brokers, swing voters need more expensive favors to be convinced to rally to the vote buyer.

Let the transfer for the core voter be denoted by t. The transfer used in the effort to buy off the swing voter is set at $\bar{t} > t$. This means that the core-voter

---

[6] According to Nichter (2011) vote buying is about turnout mobilization of core voters. His predictions are similar to ours in that core voters are targeted. But we claim that parties give transfers to core voters not only to bring them to the polls. As will become apparent in the following pages, parties reward their core voters looking forward, as a way to signal their commitment and keep them loyal over the long term.

strategy is less expensive, allowing party elites to capture some rents: $r = \bar{t} - \underline{t}$.[7]

The choice for the party is restricted to the allocation of funds to either the core or the swing voter.[8] Given our formulation of the problem, the party may be tempted to exploit core voters whose support is guaranteed in the current election in order to pursue swing voters. Note, however, that the swing-voter strategy entails the following costs: (1) it erodes core voters' loyalty for future rounds; (2) the party can appropriate fewer rents because it needs to spend more on transfers to buy swing voters; and 3) it is riskier due to the higher likelihood of swing-voter opportunism.

Suppose the party's utility function is simply the difference between a benefit measured in votes, minus the cost of the transfer used to induce the vote. The party cares about future elections, but at the discounted rate $0 > \delta > 1$:

$$U = (v_t - t_t) + \partial(v_{t+1} - t_{t+1}) + \delta^2(v_{t+2} - t_{t+2}) + \ldots \tag{1}$$

We can describe the value of catering to swing or core voters assuming that the party's decision in this election defines the stream of utility over time. To simplify, the party sticks to the same strategy – core or swing – in all subsequent rounds, and voters respond accordingly. This means that if the party chooses the swing-voter strategy, the core voter supports it in this election, but becomes a swing voter in all subsequent elections. If the party chooses the core-voter strategy, the party continues to deliver transfers to this voter and this voter remains loyal forever as she continues to receive transfers. The party's utility functions of following a swing strategy, U_s, and of following a core strategy, U_c, are given by:

$$U_s = 1 + E[s] - \bar{t} + \delta(E[s] - \bar{t}) + \delta^2(E[s] - \bar{t}) + \ldots \tag{2}$$

and

$$U_c = 1 - \underline{t} + \delta(1 - \underline{t}) + \delta^2(1 - \underline{t}) \tag{3}$$

The first utility function defines the benefits of betraying the core voter's loyalty in this election by giving the transfer to the swing voter. The swing-voter strategy clearly condemns the party to buying votes on the spot market every time elections are held, which is a far riskier, more costly, and very inefficient strategy over the long run.

The second one shows the steady support of the core voter that is obtained by delivering transfers to her. This strategy is significantly less costly over the

---

[7] These "savings" can also be invested in voters, either core or swing. But since core constituency needs have already been attended to, these disposable funds are freed for catering to swing voters if the machine so chooses. Later we discuss what happens when the party can diversify its electoral investments in both core and swing voters. For now the choice is binary in the sense that the money should be spent only on one voter type.
[8] We are not considering the case in which a party might choose not to engage in vote buying.

3.4 A Theory of Vote Buying with Conditional Partisan Loyalty

long run and entails a smaller amount of transfers to voters. The party will follow the swing-voter strategy if its utility is higher than what it obtains from favoring its core. Solving the infinite temporal horizon and substituting the transfers expressed as rents for the incumbent yields the following condition:

$$E[s] \geq \frac{\delta}{1-\delta}(1 - E[s]) + \frac{\delta}{1-\delta}r \qquad (4)$$

This basically states that the party will shirk its commitment to the core voter when the expected value of the swing voter (the left-hand side of the expression) is larger than the present value of two different opportunity costs. The first is the gap between the certain support of the core voter and the unreliable support of the swing voter. The larger this gap (i.e., the greater the likelihood the swing voter will behave opportunistically), the more likely the party will pursue the core-voter strategy. This gap is discounted from the second interaction or move onward.

The second opportunity cost, accruing over time, is the discounted value of the stream of rents that would be obtained from investing in buying the vote of the less expensive core voter. The larger the stream of rents, the stronger the party's incentive to choose the core-voter strategy. The core-voter strategy allows the machine to survive in office over the long run at lower expense. The machine, then, has strong and perduring incentives to construct and preserve partisan loyalties, generate rents, and minimize electoral risk. These are compelling reasons for parties to continue to invest in their loyal cores.

Clientelism entails a durable and stable relationship between a patron party and its core voters. When party and voter expect to interact into the future, it can be a self-sustaining contract. Loyal voters anticipate continued access to the spoils system and reciprocate the party with steadfast electoral support. Clientelism is also self-sustaining because both sides can sanction reneging on the contract: parties punish voters who defect and voters are unfaithful to parties that do not honor loyalty.

Robinson and Verdier (2003) argue that clientelism involves a strong commitment problem: what prevents individuals from accepting rewards and then voting as they wish? In their approach, the commitment problem is solved by privileging the distribution of jobs, which ties the political machine to the voter in a long-term relationship of mutual convenience. Voters will support the machine to protect their jobs, while the party will create and sustain jobs to keep its power over clients.

However, clientelism as a mode of vote buying encompasses many more transferable goods than job patronage. Politicians in the developing world often resort to the distribution of credit and cash handouts, production subsidies, food baskets, grain and livestock, fertilizer and other farming inputs, construction materials, household appliances, medicines, and so forth, because they are easy to distribute. Our explanation of how parties deal with the commitment problem is through repeated investment in established relationships with their core supporters.

The literature has overemphasized the violation of the secret ballot as a primary means of enforcing the patron-client relationship. Although direct observation of voting is advantageous, it is by no means necessary (Stokes, 2005; Magaloni, 2006; Nichter, 2008 and 2009). Clientelism can be self-sustaining even with the secret ballot. In our view, machines do not need to monitor votes on the day of the election, but they should distinguish allies from enemies by tracking voter loyalties *ex ante*, an effort that requires dense party organization.

Voters are loyal to the machine because they expect to receive benefits today *and* in the future, and because they need these to survive. Voter loyalty to a machine is, so to speak, a form of insurance for its core voters, a ticket to a continuous stream of benefits. Normally, at election time the machine signals with the transfer of particularistic benefits to its core supporters that the clientelistic contract remains valid. Although partisan loyalties may involve a moral sense of obligation (Greene and Lawson, 2011), these loyalties and the consequent sense of reciprocity (Finan, 2010) are essentially conditional. If the machine fails to dispense expected favors, core voters will soon cease to feel obliged to reciprocate.

The core voter strategy is an equilibrium strategy under certain conditions that we discuss in turn. First, political parties need to be long-lived organizations that expect to last into the future. This presupposes certain stability in the party system, or at least that parties able to compete and survive over the course of several elections.

Second, our approach presupposes that party loyalty is not anchored in ideology, affect or symbolic appeals, but is conditioned by personal exchanges of material inducements and support. The model could be extended to accommodate different "tolerance thresholds" on the part of core voters and these thresholds can be made to vary inversely with the strength of some *primordialist* basis of party identification or with a voter's ideology. The more captive the core voter is to ideology or to an affective source of partisan identification, the more parties can abuse them by catering to swing voters.

Third, the swing-voter strategy has one clear and undeniable advantage: it can make the difference in winning or losing the current election. The swing-voter strategy responds to short-term imperatives but is destabilizing over time because it undermines core-voter loyalties. Just how valuable those reserves of loyalty can be is clear when one considers that the alternative is to build more expensive, fickle, and uncertain electoral coalitions for every election and thus to encourage growing voter opportunism.

Finally, in the model the core-voter strategy is associated with higher rent extraction. Political machines capture more rents because core voters are presumed to be "cheaper" (or easily maintained), as long as they consistently receive the discretionary payments to which they have grown accustomed. Hence, the larger the price difference between swing voters and core, the stronger the

3.4 A Theory of Vote Buying with Conditional Partisan Loyalty

incentives to maintain a core base of loyal voters through the delivery of particularistic transfers.

This approach allows us to generate several empirical predictions to be tested in subsequent chapters. The central empirical proposition emerging from our model is that a party will target particularistic transfers mostly to its core base, here defined as voters who regularly support the party who are linked to the party organization and have access to the system of spoils. Hence we evaluate the following hypothesis:

Hypothesis 1: *Particularistic excludable transfers should be disproportionately directed to core voters.*

A further empirical implication of our approach relates to core-voter leverage. Machines in our model offer transfer to their core to prevent their disloyalty. Machines then should intensify their clientelistic practices or delivery of private goods to prevent their core from eroding. If core voters cannot credibly threaten to exit, they retain little leverage to entice their party to cater to them. In the presence of a credible alternative to the machine, core voters are more likely to receive attention from their party. From this argument we derive the following two hypotheses:

Hypothesis 2: *Higher levels of core erosion across electoral cycles should be associated with intensified efforts at retaining core-voter support through clientelism.*

Hypothesis 3: *If electoral markets are monopolistic, core voters may suffer benign neglect relative to places where electoral competition is stronger.*

With respect to the opposition, the machine must issue credible threats to punish defection. This involves avoiding all attempts to reward disloyalty by "buying back" former supporters who have defected to the opposition.

Hypothesis 4: *The machine should punish voters who defect to the opposition by withdrawing transfers from them.*

Finally, we also expect to find effects for the electoral cycle. The machine fulfills its part of the bargain when it rewards core voters whose support is certain; it does so in order to reaffirm its commitment to them into the future and to prevent erosion of party loyalties. We expect parties to increase particularistic transfers prior to elections as a way of signaling these commitments.[9]

Hypothesis 5: *Machines should increase particularistic transfers prior to elections.*

The temptation to buy swing votes on the spot necessarily increases in highly competitive elections when these votes can tilt the outcome. Machines under pressure from competition are hence caught in a dilemma. They can maximize their chances of victory by catering to swing voters, but at the cost

---

[9] This prediction is empirically equivalent to Nichter's (2011) turnout-buying.

of undermining core-voter loyalties. Machines can diversify their portfolio of electoral investments to solve this dilemma. We move now to the discussion of portfolio diversification and public goods provision.

3.5 PORTFOLIO DIVERSIFICATION AND PUBLIC GOODS PROVISION

The literature portrays the investment decision between core and swing voter as an either/or strategy. The empirical record is mixed at best (Londregan, 2007). There are empirical studies that support the swing-voter logic (Schady, 2000; Dahlberg and Johansson, 2002; Stokes, 2005); others are consistent with the core-voter logic (Calvo and Murillo, 2004; Hiskey, 2003; Levitt and Snyder, 1995; Nichter, 2008), and yet others who argue that not all core voters are alike and that machines target core voters in more competitive places while punishing the opposition (Magaloni, 2006). Many studies conflate private and public goods.[10]

Parties can devise strategies that allow them simultaneously to lock in their core and seek to expand their electoral coalitions beyond the core. Portfolio diversification, we contend, allows parties to accomplish this. Our approach is similar to Bueno de Mesquita et al. (2000) in that we argue that transfers for public goods can be used to expand the size of the coalition, while private goods can be employed to reward the core.

Most of the core-versus-swing voter debate has been conducted without paying much attention to broader patterns of political competition. Party systems, electoral rules, and levels of electoral competition shape incentives for engaging in vote buying. Some studies have examined these issues. Chhibber and Nooruddin (2004) investigate the impact of subnational party system configurations on the propensity of parties to invest in private or public goods provision in their study of India. Drawing on Bueno de Mesquita et al. (2000), they predict that the relative importance of private versus public goods will be a function of the effective number of political parties. Using data from Indian states from 1967 to 1997, they show that public goods are more important in bipartisan contexts, where a larger size of the electorate is needed to win elections. In contrast, private goods provision is more prevalent in multiparty systems because politicians can retain power by delivering particularistic benefits to a smaller group of supporters.

Our theory of portfolio diversification was developed in Magaloni et al. (2007). We summarize it here and use it to derive our hypotheses on public

[10] If the crucial distinction between private and public goods is introduced into earlier studies, the empirical validation of the swing-voter model is largely based on the discretionary distribution of public goods (the Peruvian and Swedish cases, for example). Stokes (2005) focuses on campaign handouts in Argentina, while Dixit and Londregan (1996) analyze tariff protection in the United States. These are the only examples of discretionary transfers of private and club goods to swing voters in the empirical literature.

3.5 Portfolio Diversification and Public Goods Provision

goods provision. Political parties must decide how to allocate a basket of discretionary transfers to voters that range from private, excludable outlays that can be individually targeted, to nonexcludable public goods that are targeted to districts and consumed by all voter groups. As instruments of electoral investment, these transfers differ in their relative budgetary cost, their expected electoral return defined as the number of voters they benefit, and their level of electoral risk.

Our theory of portfolio diversification assumes a positive correlation between expected yields and risks: risky investments yield higher expected electoral returns. Public goods are risky electoral investments, we claim, because they can't be targeted – everyone, including opposition backers, can enjoy them. Private, excludable transfers, if properly targeted to a party's core base, are risk-free but they may not yield the highest electoral return, since fewer voters can normally be targeted through clientelism. Moreover, governments face budget constraints, which means that they might not be able to buy every necessary vote with particularistic, excludable benefits.

The problem of finding the politically optimal allocation of public versus private transfers is determined by budget constraints, the size of the core base of support, and the incumbent's risk aversion. These conditions in turn depend on how cheap it is to buy votes from core constituencies. Hence, the central feature of the socioeconomic theory of clientelism, namely, the association between poverty and clientelism, is accounted for in this model by the demand-side assumption that it is cheap to buy votes from the poor.

A party's optimal strategy, then, is to diversify its allocation of funds between public and private goods, devoting a proportion of the budget to public goods, and the remainder to private ones. This mixed-basket strategy yields a higher overall return, taking advantage of the electoral opportunities afforded by public goods provision, while hedging risks through an optimal combination with the risk-free investment.

The proportion of public goods allocations will be higher:

1. The smaller the size of the party's core base.
2. The higher the costs of vote buying through clientelistic transfers.
3. The higher the vote threshold necessary to obtain victory.
4. The smaller the difference in yield between the two types of goods.
5. The lower the risk of the public good.
6. The less risk-averse the politician with respect to the risk-hedging function of clientelism within his investment portfolio.

Hence, we expect that political machines will diversify their portfolio of electoral investment and deliver public goods when the size of their core is not certain to sustain them in power. Public goods provision in our approach results from competitive pressures, pushing machines to cater to a wider set of voters. We evaluate the following hypothesis:

Hypothesis 6: *Machines should spend more in public goods when pressed by electoral competition.*

Machines diversify their portfolio of electoral investments to solve the perpetual dilemma of catering to core-versus-swing voters. Our approach highlights the virtues of political competition for the provision of public goods, but does not predict that clientelism will disappear with it. Clientelism can serve as a risk-hedging strategy under conditions of political competition and hence we do not expect politicians to abandon it altogether.

Finally, the expected yield of private goods provision varies inversely with income. It would be exceedingly costly to establish a solid base of core support on the basis of particularistic transfers when voters are wealthier. Politicians face budget constraints that compel them to find a combination of public and private goods that is electorally optimal and feasible. Moreover, rich voters are not likely to respond to particularistic transfers the way poor voters do.

Hypothesis 7: *Public goods provision should be higher at higher levels of development.*

3.6 CONCLUSION

Much of the extant theory on distributive politics has portrayed investments in core supporters as irrational. Yet strong empirical evidence in comparative studies points to the hard fact that parties target core constituencies. This chapter has developed a model of distributive politics that makes sense of this empirical regularity. Our argument that parties must invest in loyal voters is consistent with CM, although we derive these results from a different formulation of the problem that, we believe, better portrays the strategies of vote buying in the developing world.

Our model departs from the notion that partisan loyalty is exogenous. Where ideology and other symbolic appeals are but feeble sources of partisan identity, political parties are compelled to construct voter loyalty through relational networks and a history of exchange in which material inducements play a fundamental role. Partisan loyalty so constructed is essentially conditional.

Our conditional loyalty theory allows us to derive a logic of why machines devote a disproportionate amount of resources to their core supporters. We have claimed that machines target their core voters with particularistic, excludable transfers to keep them loyal over the long run. Our model demonstrates the benefits of owning a reserve of core voter loyalty. Voter loyalty serves to mitigate the perpetual risk of voter opportunism that vote buying on the spot entails.

Honoring core-voter loyalty also translates into clear material benefits for political machines. The core voter strategy allows the machine to appropriate rents because it can survive without having to transfer as many resources to core voters as it would in order to create new support coalitions with every election.

3.6 Conclusion

Although beneficial to each individual core voter, the clientelistic linkages trap them in a relationship based on material dependence and is sustained through a credible threat of punishment. Voters who defect to the opposition will be excluded from the stream of present and future benefits. This means that voters are loyal to the machine in part because of their access to a stream of welfare benefits, and in part because of fear of punishment. The dilemma is one of voter coordination. Each voter acting alone has powerful reasons to remain loyal to the machine because if she does not, she will be excluded from the spoils system. But if everyone reasons likewise, the machine can be sustained in equilibrium.

The following chapter will evaluate our empirical predictions through an analysis of the six-year duration of the *Pronasol* program in Mexico.

4

Clientelism and the Political Manipulation of *Pronasol*

> A political party may employ one of two basic strategies in its efforts to attract voters [...]. It may distribute divisible benefits – patronage of various sorts – to the individuals who support the party. Alternatively, it may distribute collective benefits or appeal to a collective interest.
>
> Martin Shefter (1994: 21)

4.1 INTRODUCTION

The *Pronasol* program was inaugurated in what today is known as Valle de Chalco Solidaridad, a municipality located in the State of Mexico, on the eastern outskirts of Mexico City. It split off from Chalco as a separate jurisdiction in 1994 and was renamed *Chalco Solidaridad* after *Pronasol*. At the end of the 1970s, Chalco was a rapidly expanding shantytown, as people began migrating out of Mexico City in search of land. By the 1980s, the valley was occupied by nearly a quarter million people living without potable water, paved streets, medical services, schools, or electricity. In the 1988 presidential elections, the people of Chalco voted two to one against the PRI. The PRI was so unpopular that the prospect of a visit from recently elected President Salinas filled officials with fear.

Salinas' team carefully planned a magical spectacle for his visit to Chalco, where it was decided that he would announce his strategy to "put an end to poverty." He invited more than thirty intellectuals and public opinion leaders to accompany him and spread publicity about the visit. They spent the night hosted in the humble homes of local families to gain perspective on the impact of Salinas' new poverty-reduction strategy. For his first act, as President Salinas walked down the dark, dirty streets, the newly installed public lighting turned on for the first time, illuminating the faces of a still-skeptical audience. Salinas then came to a raised podium where he opened a public faucet to release a gushing flow of potable water. As Chalco inhabitants shouted in unison "*ciérrale,*

4.1 Introduction

ciérrale" ("turn it off, turn it off," repeating a public campaign slogan against wasting water), Salinas told them that he wanted to make very clear that this time "government promises were for real," and that the new public services were here to stay. The hope was that after witnessing what some residents still remember as a "miracle," Chalco voters would handsomely reward the PRI in future elections.

Impressive as it sounded, the program over the long run did not do much to reduce the number of Mexicans living in poverty. Salinas devoted more than $15 billion in federal funds to the program. State officials, governors, municipal authorities, local party brokers, and community leaders were all branded with its symbolic ribbon: a red, white, and green braid that represented Mexicans working in solidarity. The emblem was placed on every project across the country. There was also continuous government propaganda, such as TV ads that showed touching scenes of women, children, peasants, old people, and farm laborers, all being helped out of poverty by the program. In the aggregate, public infrastructure projects covered 72 percent of all expenditures. A large share of these resources was spent on the construction of interstate highways that were not particularly beneficial to poor citizens without automobiles. Particularistic transfers (construction materials, credit to small businesses, tractors, scholarships, etc.) accounted for 28 percent of all *Pronasol* expenditures. Yet with the passing of time the program's portfolio changed. By 1994, close to 40 percent of the funds were devoted to clientelistic transfers.[1]

In this chapter we perform a systematic analysis of the political logic of *Pronasol*'s vast operations. We test our predictions about the political factors shaping politicians' decisions to invest in core versus swing voters and to transfer private versus public goods to buy votes. By modeling these logics, we will demonstrate with systematic evidence that *Pronasol* was driven by the PRI's inescapable need to sustain its core constituencies, staunch the erosion of its dominant-party status, punish and deter further exit to the opposition by municipal electorates, and to claim credit for reversing six years of deteriorating social and economic conditions in the wake of the financial collapse of 1982.

We focus on *Pronasol* for three main reasons. First, our theory of vote buying is about discretionary transfers, and political and bureaucratic discretion was the touchstone of *Pronasol*. The program was characterized by the discretionary selection of projects and beneficiaries, with input from voluntary "solidarity committees" at the community level (Kaufman and Trejo, 1997). However, in virtually all cases, it was organized at the top and run initially from the Office of the President and later from the Ministry of Social Development (*Sedesol*) (Bailey, 1994). Equally centralized was its system of financial control and coordination, with the Finance Ministry directly routing

---

[1] Exactly how the government managed to reallocate funds such that vote-buying took precedence over poverty relief is not at all clear in other studies of the program.

federal transfers to localities as well as earmarking revenue-sharing grants for state governments.[2]

Second, we are interested in understanding what makes poverty-alleviation programs effective or ineffective. *Pronasol* was ostensibly designed to alleviate poverty and the program became the cornerstone of government social policy. However, as we will demonstrate in later chapters, the program's results were disappointing. Results in this chapter suggest that *Pronasol* failed to help the poor because the program was administered with the overarching goal of sustaining the PRI's electoral hegemony by locking in voters through clientelism rather than seeking to reduce poverty.

Third, *Pronasol* distributed excludable private transfers as well as public goods, which allows us to assess our thesis of portfolio diversification. *Pronasol* was a large umbrella, comprising twenty subsidiary programs that involved a wide range of benefits delivered over six years to every municipality in the country. These included private goods – such as student scholarships, worker retraining grants, and temporary employment schemes – and club goods for producer groups, especially cheap credit and financial and managerial support for a privileged network of small businesses (known as *empresas de solidaridad*) as well as rural infrastructure for *ejidos*, the semicollective peasant farms still tied organizationally to one of the PRI's corporatist pillars. *Pronasol* also included a broad list of small-scale social and economic infrastructure projects as well as a very large program of municipal block grants for public works and maintenance.[3] Finally, there were two special programs that dedicated funds to the construction of regional hospitals and state and interstate highways, spanning numerous municipalities and states.

In order to discern the motives beneath *Pronasol*'s vast operations, we model the per capita allocations for each municipality over six years as total, private, and public goods, as well as the share of particularistic transfers in the total sum of allocations to every municipality during the Salinas administration. We

---

[2] The only exception to this pattern of centralized coordination was that presented by the state of Baja California. Governor Ernesto Ruffo, the first opposition member to win gubernatorial office, in 1989, refused to kowtow to the Salinas government on project selection and to sign the *Convenios Únicos de Desarrollo* through which the Ministry of Finance tied state funds to *Pronasol* projects (Flamand, 2004). Baja California's resistance, however, was mostly irrelevant, affecting only the fortunes of its five municipalities, out of a national total nearing 2,400 at the time.

[3] The Municipal Funds program is hard to justify in its entirety as transfers for exclusively collective goods. No doubt many maintenance projects were merely forms of job patronage and some public works were disguised corruption favoring local officeholders and their cronies. The impact on the statistical analysis of these misclassifications, almost impossible to disentangle from legitimate public goods provision in the official record of project funding for *Pronasol*, is that they bias estimates for clientelism *downward* and those for pork *upward*. As will be clear from the regression analysis in this chapter, these distortions in effect cut against the grain of our theoretical expectations rather than supporting them.

4.1 Introduction

equate particularistic transfers, as explained in the introduction, with clientelism and discretionary public goods projects with pork-barreling.

We proceed in two steps. The first is to model total municipal-level allocations from 1989 until 1994 without taking into account how municipal elections held between those dates might have changed yearly allocations. We call this the "centralist" logic of the program, designed with the overarching goal of sustaining the PRI's electoral dominance at the national level. Although *Pronasol* was a highly centralized program largely engineered out of the office of the president, it was operated by a vast network of state governors, municipal presidents, and local party brokers. The second step is to model the extent to which *Pronasol*'s allocations responded to the short-term dynamics of local elections, including the timing of municipal elections, their level of competitiveness, partisan divisions in the local electorate, and the partisan identity of municipal government. We call this the "peripheral logic" of the program.

Our overriding hypothesis is that the bulk of *Pronasol*'s allocations, for both private and public goods, should favor the PRI's core constituencies. Yet our *conditional party loyalty* model generates more nuanced predictions than simply claiming that more transfers are conferred upon hegemonic bastions. This is because not all loyal municipalities are alike. In some places, the PRI had a virtual electoral monopoly with no opposition presence; elsewhere, loyal voters had credible exit options. Our theory leads us to expect that the PRI would target more particularistic transfers to loyal municipalities whose support is expected to weaken in upcoming elections if the party fails to deliver benefits. We operationalize our notion of *conditional party loyalty* by looking at the dynamics of party loyalty over time. In particular, we expect the PRI to increase its clientelistic practices in loyal municipalities where voters' partisan attachments are eroding.

Our theoretical approach argues that party machines will diversify their portfolio of electoral investments, targeting the party's core with particularistic benefits while delivering public goods where the party's core is not strong enough to win elections. Our expectation is that politicians should emphasize public over private goods provision when they need to attract more heterogeneous voter groups to win an election.

A substantial amount of research has already accumulated on *Pronasol*, but we depart from this body of work in several respects. Many studies employ state-level data for specific years (Molinar and Weldon, 1994; Bruhn, 1996) or, when looking at municipalities, focus on limited samples (Hiskey, 2003). Only Magaloni (2006) and the present study cover all Mexican municipalities over the lifespan of the program.[4] Molinar and Weldon claim that *Pronasol* funds poured into communities where the PRI had its poorest showing in the 1988 presidential elections. Taking our Chalco example as emblematic, this is the

---

[4] While using a full data set on *Pronasol*, Cleary (2004) and Kurtz (2004) do not study the determinants of *Pronasol* allocations but use its financial transfers as an independent variable.

so-called buy-back strategy, meant to persuade localities that bolted in 1988 to return to the fold. Using municipal-level data for two states, Hiskey (2003) claims that *Pronasol* money went to hegemonic bastions where the PRI won with the largest margins of victory. Critiquing these results for their strong endogeneity problems and using municipal-level data for the entire life of the program, Magaloni (2006) shows that the PRI followed an "entry-deterrence" strategy in which opposition-controlled municipalities were systematically punished with fewer funds while loyal municipalities in more competitive contexts were rewarded by the PRI. Our results here are consistent with Magaloni (2006) in that the bulk of *Pronasol*'s programs were targeted to hegemonic places where loyalties were eroding, as opposed to the most secure bastions. But our analysis diverges when we dissect *Pronasol*'s allocations for targeted particularistic goods versus public goods. We build upon the theory of *conditional party loyalty*, which dissects the PRI's strategic decisions better.

Furthermore, whereas previous studies have mostly focused on one or two programs (see articles in Cornelius, Fox and Craig, 1994), our work encompasses all of *Pronasol*'s programs. In order to assess the welfare effects of *Pronasol* (discussed in Chapters 5 and 6) as well as its political logic, we have classified programs into the general categories of private and public goods provision.

This chapter is organized as follows. The next section proposes a new approach to the measurement of core size. The third section is dedicated to the overarching logic that informs *Pronasol* by offering support for our claims that core municipalities received disproportionately larger transfers and that hegemonic decline spurred intensified clientelism. This section also discusses the relationship between economic development at the municipal level and the distribution of clientelism and pork within *Pronasol*, questioning the conventional view that clientelism is endemic to settings of poverty and largely absent from wealthier regions. The last section explores the peripheral logic of *Pronasol*, gauging the effects of municipal elections and local partisan configurations on program transfers.

4.2 HOW TO MEASURE CORE SUPPORT

When focusing on aggregate electoral data, the conventional measure for core support of a party in Mexican electoral studies is its most recent vote share. But core support should not be measured using short-term indicators, for two reasons. The first relates to problems of endogeneity that stem from the fact that vote shares at time t are likely to be shaped by allocation decisions at time t and t-1. "Since there may well be serial correlation and an effect of expenditures on elections, studies that disregard the possibility of simultaneity must be treated with caution" (Schady, 2000: 298).[5]

---

[5] Hiskey's (1999 and 2003) analysis suffers from this problem – he infers *Pronasol* 's expenditures in the period 1989–1994 from vote shares in the same period.

4.2 How to Measure Core Support

But there is a second, theoretical reason why a party's core support should not be inferred from vote returns of a single election: partisan loyalties are long-term attachments. A party's core backers are those voter groups that honor partisan loyalties beyond one election, a form of stable support not readily captured by myopic measures of election results. Indicators like vote shares or victory margins in the preceding electoral cycle do not unambiguously reflect long-term attachments, and might be attributable to factors idiosyncratic to that election. Instead, underlying trends in the electoral history of local jurisdictions divulge more information about the dynamics of partisan loyalties than the vote returns of a single election.[6]

Students of Mexican electoral politics have long documented a clear modernization trend since the 1960s, in which the PRI gradually lost support across the country, especially in places exhibiting higher levels of development. Nevertheless, the PRI retained secure electorates in vast regions, often running uncontested for decades. After the devastating financial crisis of 1982, the process of dealignment from the hegemonic party became more pronounced, progressing at varying paces throughout the country, with some hegemonic bastions holding steady, others slowly drifting away, and still others showing rapidly deteriorating support for the PRI. During this time of contested hegemony, short-term electoral indicators fail to give an accurate picture of voter loyalties. In particular, conventional measures of party support – vote shares, the closeness of electoral races as measured by the margin of victory, electoral competitiveness reflected in the effective number of parties, and electoral volatility understood as net intertemporal vote swings – do not capture the deeply rooted partisan attachments that were crucial for building and sustaining hegemony over several decades.

Core support and stable partisan attachments, we contend, should be inferred from the long-term evolution in a party's vote shares. Thus, we focus on long-term voting trends in municipal elections. Long series of electoral returns summarize a great deal of information about the evolution of partisan loyalties and about the capacity of party cadres and brokers to deliver the vote for the PRI. Our theory leads us to predict that parties should target their core base with largesse, particularly when voter loyalty is conditional on the delivery of benefits.

In order to identify *conditional party loyalty* we calculate two variables that are distinct from vote shares, margins, competitiveness, and volatility. The first one measures the size of the PRI's core in each municipality. The second one captures the erosion of partisan attachments through time. This means that for

---

[6] Molinar and Weldon (1994) and Bruhn (1996), for example, focus exclusively on the PRI's vote share in the 1988 presidential elections to study state-level allocations within the Solidarity program. Although *Pronasol* came in part as a response to the party's deep split in 1987 and the consequent electoral debacle, the erosion of PRI support can also be traced to processes occurring over a much longer period of time.

each municipality our estimations describe not only the size of the PRI's core, but also the extent to which loyalties are stable, as measured by a time-sensitive level of erosion of core support.

The size of the core and the rate of erosion of loyalty in each municipality are calculated using data from 1970 to 1988. The data is truncated on both ends because there is no available compilation of municipal-level electoral data prior to 1970. After 1988, municipal electoral data suffer from an endogeneity problem given that *Pronasol* was enacted in December, 1988. To measure the size of the core, we borrow from asset-pricing analysis in the finance literature and regress the PRI's average vote share in the country as a whole (V_{Ni}) on its vote share in each individual municipality (V_{mi}). Hence for every municipality we estimate, across time i, the regression is:

$$V_{mi} = \alpha + \beta V_{Ni} + \varepsilon_i$$

The *alpha* parameter measures core support, namely, the predicted value of the PRI's vote share in a given municipality in the hypothetical scenario that the party receives no votes at the national level. *Alpha* conveniently captures the way in which local electorates behave independently of national electoral patterns in that it isolates the level of voter loyalty, as mediated by the local party organization and its brokers who mobilize electoral support for the party as a whole in that municipality.

In order to ensure that vote shares are bound between 0 and 1 we estimate the regressions in log-odds ratios. To understand better how *alpha* reflects the differential safety of each municipality, from the perspective of the PRI, one can express it in terms of an ordinary least squares framework:

$$\alpha = \bar{V}_m - \left(\frac{Cov[V_m, V_N]}{VAR[V_m]} \right) \bar{V}_n$$

Notice that *alpha* represents how much higher or lower the average vote share in a given municipality is with respect to the national average vote share gained in all municipal elections that same year, but corrected by risk (the term in brackets). In these calculations, the PRI's national vote share (V_N) is not its support in federal elections, but rather its aggregate electoral support in all municipal elections held in different states between 1970 and 1988. *Alpha* is thus the predicted value of every municipality's PRI vote, controlling for its national vote share in any given year in that period. The expected value of national vote shares is adjusted with the covariance between national and municipal electoral patterns divided by the variability of municipal elections.

By analogy with asset pricing, *alpha* measures the degree to which a municipality outperforms or underperforms the national market in municipal votes. "Excess returns" in elections, then, signal the skill or capacity of a municipal party, its office holders and cadres, brokers and candidates, organizational linkages and campaign strategies, in assuring relative support levels above the

4.2 How to Measure Core Support

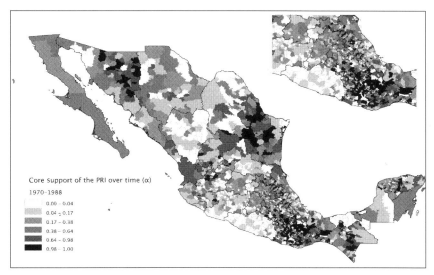

FIGURE 4.1. PRI core voter support.

national trend. Chronic underperformance, in contrast, implies that municipal parties are unable to stem losses in any given election and are therefore vulnerable to takeover. The *alpha* parameter, in short, tells us how many more or fewer votes the PRI receives in each municipality, according to its known behavior in the past.[7]

A useful illustration of the geography of *alpha* is provided in the municipal map in Figure 4.1. The darker zones have the highest *alpha* scores and include all municipalities in which the PRI held sway in uncontested elections or sustained its hegemony with at least 65 percent of the municipal vote since the onset of the series. The white zones are those with significant opposition presence, including several scores of municipalities won by opposition parties at least once between 1970 and 1988. The patent advantage of using log-odds ratios here is that they magnify opposition strength in a pattern spread throughout the country, when opposition presence was clearly marginal outside the big cities.

To measure the erosion of partisan attachments we use the linear trend in PRI municipal vote shares between 1970 and 1988. The trend is indicated by

---

[7] This means that *alpha* is similar in spirit to the calculation of electoral risk proposed by Wright (1974) in his seminal piece on the politics of social transfers during the New Deal in the United States, where he used the detrended standard deviation of electoral support for the Democratic Party in each state. But *alpha* incorporates more information, because it is related to both average levels of electoral support and to what is known in the capital-asset-pricing model as "beta risk," the sensitivity of portfolio returns to market returns. In the diversification logic of financial investments, fund managers seek to include assets in their portfolios with high rates of return, while keeping overall exposure to risk low.

the slope of a time series regression for each municipality on a time trend of the form:

$$V_{it} = a + slopeT_t, \qquad \text{where } T = 1, 2, \ldots t$$

Note that this is not a pooled time-series estimation, but rather the calculation of separate regressions, one for each municipality, where T reflects every year an election is celebrated. In federal elections, on average, the PRI suffered a yearly decline of 1.25 percent of its national vote from the peak year of hegemony in 1961, when it garnered 91 percent of the national total, to the national elections of 1994. In municipal elections, the decline averaged 1.5 percent per year since 1970 over aggregated three-year cycles. In the case of municipal trends, the variation across units is large, given that the accumulated impact of demographic change, modernization, political and economic events, and other election-relevant factors on the party's electoral fortunes was highly differentiated across the country's states and municipalities.

The slope of each of the regressions captures the erosion of the PRI's core support. Given the overall trend of decline for the PRI, this corresponds to the rate of dealignment from the party in every locality. As an analogy, the slope is the municipal trend in volatility specific to one party.[8] We term this variable *decline*. Higher negative numbers mean greater erosion of support over the years.

There is some overlap between erosion and the commonly used concept of volatility – more volatile municipalities do show more negative slopes for the PRI. But erosion and volatility are very different indicators. The conventional standard for measuring volatility in a party system is the Pederson index. However, this index suffers from the same deficiency as vote share in t-1 or first differences in consecutive election returns. Short-term volatility may simply not reveal sufficient information about the electoral dynamics of a jurisdiction. Instead, a long-term measure better reflects the cumulative effects of demographic change, geographical mobility, economic shocks, and political events in the historical dealignment from the PRI, as well as the slow but steady growth of opposition support in that period.

Figure 4.2 provides a scatter plot of our municipal measures of core size and its erosion. Naturally, there is a positive association between both variables, whereby higher levels of PRI core support correlate with lower levels of erosion over the years. Yet the figure shows that for any given level of core support on the horizontal axis, there are widely varying trends in electoral decline, on the vertical one. The average core value through 1988 was 0.47, while the average trend in dealignment was −0.29.

Our approach is to characterize each municipality by both core support and core erosion. Municipalities with high core support (large *alphas*) are loyal

---

[8] On the decomposition of electoral risk see Morgenstern and Potthoff (2005), who draw on Stokes (1965).

4.2 How to Measure Core Support

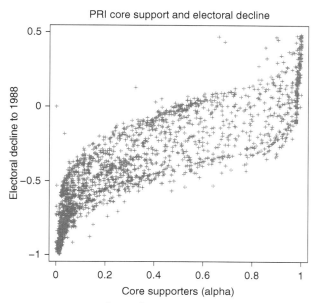

FIGURE 4.2. Correlation between core voter support and vote erosion (municipal level data using PRI vote shares from 1970 to 1988).

places. Loyal municipalities vote for the PRI in high numbers and remain reliable supporters even when other municipalities defect in response to economic recession, budget cutbacks, lack of jobs, currency devaluations, inflation, and so forth. Our theoretical expectations are that the PRI would invest resource transfers, for both private and public goods, in loyal places. But loyal voters are not all alike. Our core-voter model dissects loyalty according to levels of conditional core support. Some loyal municipalities exhibit little or no erosion of core voter support, while others have experienced a rapid deterioration over time. If core voters are not attended, they may defect and become swing voters in subsequent elections. This hypothesis leads us to expect that the PRI should concentrate its clientelistic practices in places where core size is shrinking in an attempt to lock-in still loyal voters.

With respect to municipalities with low core support (a small *alpha*), our theory leads us to predict an incumbent party's disinterest in vote-buying through particularistic transfers. These small-core municipalities are places where the local party organization and its brokers have failed to mobilize strong support in favor of the PRI in one election after another. It is possible that in those places the local party organization is too weak and disorganized to be able effectively to target benefits. Voters in these places are also likely to be distant from the PRI and perhaps wealthy enough to desist from selling their votes to a corrupt party machine. Even when we do not expect the party to target small-core places with particularistic transfers, our theoretical approach proposes that the incumbent party should increase public goods provision for the purpose of attracting swing voters and even opposition backers.

Our empirical predictions according to how core size and erosion, our two main independent variables, shape *Pronasol*'s investments are: first, the bulk of *Pronasol* transfers for both private and public goods should favor settings of high core support, meaning that *alpha* should be positively associated with allocations.

Second, consistent with our argument that partisan loyalties are conditional and that clientelism is used to lock-in a party's core backers, we expect private goods to be allocated preferentially to still loyal municipalities with higher rates of erosion (relative to those where erosion is negligible). Higher negative numbers mean higher erosions of core support; the effect of this variable should therefore be negative.

Third, we expect the PRI to allocate more public relative to private goods in small-core municipalities where the party must seek to build more encompassing electoral coalitions and cannot rely on its local agents to target benefits and carry the district. However, in line with the "punishment regime" approach, if the PRI has lost the municipality to the opposition in the past, we expect the PRI to punish these places with lower overall expenditures on public goods programs (Magaloni, 2006; Diaz-Cayeros et al., 2001).

4.3 MODELING *PRONASOL*'S CENTRALIST LOGIC

The model specification for our investigation of the *centralist* logic of *Pronasol* is exceedingly parsimonious. Aside from controls for population size and levels of development, our statistical model uses only three political variables: the measure of core size, the measure of core decline (both constructed with long-term municipal electoral data from 1970 to 1988), and the measure of electoral shock from the 1988 presidential election. We add this variable because there is consensus in the literature that this election led the PRI to enact *Pronasol* and influenced program expenditures.

The system shock in 1988 resulted from the split in the ruling party wrought by presidential contender Cuauhtémoc Cárdenas and his defeat in an election widely viewed as fraudulent. Cárdenas is the son of a former president, the revered Lázaro Cárdenas (president from 1934 to 1940). Cuauhtémoc split from the PRI, the party his father helped found, to form the group *Corriente Democratizadora* in 1987. The 1988 contest, by the official and much disputed count, saw the PRI lose almost a quarter of the national vote and created a strong and permanent opposition on the left. Following the bitter postelectoral conflict over the legitimacy of the vote count, president-elect Carlos Salinas promised a dramatic shift in social policy, aimed at poverty relief and social development after six years of a roller-coaster economy and stringent austerity in public finances. *Pronasol* mushroomed into being shortly thereafter. Apart

4.3 Modeling Pronasol's Centralist Logic

from the effort to mitigate protest, stifle discontent, shore up legitimacy for the new government, and marshal support for other parts of its reform agenda, *Pronasol* was an attempt to revive a ruling party reeling from the split and the electoral meltdown (Dresser, 1994; Cornelius, Craig, and Cook, 1994). Numerous studies of spending patterns have stressed the specter of the 1988 elections in the new government's effort to showcase its solidarity program, *Pronasol*. Specifically, this research highlights the purported attempt to buy back both the voters and the turncoat machines that defected to Cárdenas (Molinar and Weldon, 1994; Bruhn, 1996), finding evidence for a disproportional flow of transfers to states where support for Cárdenas was high.[9]

In addition to being part of the conventional wisdom about the motives and uses of *Pronasol*, the *buy-back* thesis merits our attention because it counters our expectations about the association between voter loyalty and party largesse. In effect, it is a variation on the swing-voter model. If the PRI targeted defectors from its ranks in 1988, then it rewarded partisan disloyalty. But if it did not, as Magaloni (2006) finds, our hypotheses about *conditional party loyalty* would be buttressed.

In order to gauge the accuracy of the buy-back claim, we include the controversial measure of the PRI's vote margins at the municipal level in the 1988 presidential race (*1988 margin*). This measure is controversial because the electoral data are incomplete. Electoral authorities at the time released the voting tallies for 29,999 precincts, out of a nationwide total of nearly 55,000, but never revealed the remainder's vote counts. Once these partial data are aggregated into municipal-level figures, precinct coverage ranges from almost 100 percent (in big cities) to just under 10 percent (in more outlying rural municipalities). While the bias of underreporting might be distributed along an expected continuum of high to low opposition support, as the precinct moves away from the cities, it is nonetheless the case that the geography of the Cárdenas vote in 1988 – cutting a swathe from east to west across the middle and heavily populated part of the country – does not seem to fit the conjecture. The 1988 vote margins reach only a correlation of 0.20 with the *alpha* measure of core support for the PRI, and one of 0.07 with the measure of core erosion. This dissociation between federal and local voting patterns should allow for a clean test of the impact on allocation decisions of the electoral shock from 1988.

Control variables in the model are straightforward. The creators of *Pronasol* pronounced it a program for poverty relief and social development. It is a reasonable assumption that the census-based measure of poverty or social marginality,

---

[9] Magaloni (2006) demonstrates, instead, that the larger part of *total* program transfers went to municipalities where the PRI had been strong in 1988 and Cárdenas weak. In the elections celebrated between 1988 and 1994, the PRI adjusted investments strategically by punishing municipalities controlled by the PRD and the PAN. As we will discuss further, her results are consistent with our findings here in that the PRI punished opposition districts while rewarding disproportionately its core supporters who had credible exit options.

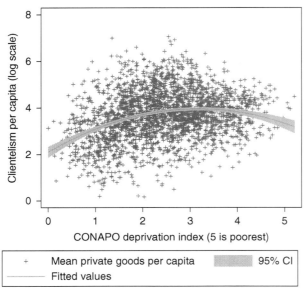

FIGURE 4.3. Clientelism and development.

known as the CONAPO index, guided the allocations made within the program over the course of its existence. Developed by the Mexican government, the CONAPO index calculates the level of social marginality per municipality, using a set of indicators that include the percentage of the employed population living below the minimum wage, illiteracy, housing without access to sewage, electricity, drinking water, and population engaged in rural activities.

In addition to the CONAPO index, we include its square value ($CONAPO^2$). In earlier work (Magaloni, Diaz-Cayeros, and Estévez, 2007), we found a curvilinear relationship between private goods provision and development levels, with more per capita funds going to municipalities at medium levels of development. Here, the reason for including the quadratic expression is to test for its impact on other categories of *Pronasol* expenditures that we use as dependent variables. Figure 4.3 shows the per capita allocation of private goods according to development levels as measured by the poverty index. Clientelism (measured by particularistic transfers) exhibits an inverted J-shape relationship with development, even without controlling for other variables, which is striking from the modernization point of view. As we will demonstrate, this relationship does not depend on political configurations as reflected by the measures of core support and core erosion (nor other conventional measures of political competition, such as the number of parties).

The finding that clientelism tends to decrease at the highest levels of development is consistent with the socioeconomic theory of linkage building, which

4.3 Modeling Pronasol's Centralist Logic

states that richer voters' preference for public goods provision over private transfers makes it too expensive for a party to attempt to buy them off through particularism (Kitschelt, 2000). Thus, clientelism tends to be greatly reduced, albeit never fully eradicated, at the highest level of development. Contrary to this theory, the Mexican case documents that clientelism is greatest at middle levels of development, not in the poorest localities.

The question arises as to whether core support, core erosion, and political variables in general respond to economic development. Our dataset allows us to separate the socioeconomic from the political processes that influence clientelism. In cross-national comparisons, development is correlated with political competition, and in Mexican studies, development levels usually show a strong inverse relation with PRI support (Klesner, 2000). Our long-term measures of municipal electoral behavior, on the contrary, are distinctly political. There is no correlation between the poverty index and the erosion of electoral support, as measured by our variable erosion (ρ = 0.05). Although poor localities tend to have larger shares of core voters, as one might expect, the correlation between the poverty index and *alpha* is modest at best (ρ = 0.24).

We also control for municipal size in the models, employing the natural log of population (logpop). To some extent, one should expect that large and more heterogeneous populations would be associated with higher development levels, but the Pearson's correlation between logpop and CONAPO is 0.40, indicating that these variables measure different municipal-level traits. In another order of calculation, in the event large cities are favored with per capita expenditures, one could surmise a political interest in those jurisdictions with large raw voting power.

The dependent variables for the central models of *Pronasol* are mean municipal-level expenditures from 1989 to 1994. We run four cross-sectional models. Model 1 considers total per capita expenditures. Models 2 and 3 look at per capita private and public goods, respectively. These three are all expressed in logarithmic terms. Model 4 tests the shares of private goods within total *Pronasol* transfers to each municipality. In order to ensure that the estimations do not suffer from spatially autocorrelated errors, a spatial lag is included. We have calculated a (queen) proximity matrix of order 2 in which both the contiguous and the contiguous-at-one-remove values in the dependent variable are taken into account. The spatial weights and the regressions including the spatial lag were all run on GeoDA. Results are provided in Table 4.1.

The initial result to highlight is that total per capita transfers averaged over six years show an extremely weak relationship to municipal welfare levels as measured by the CONAPO index (column 1). This is partially mitigated by a strongly negative relationship with municipal size, which rules out a big-district strategy for capturing large voter blocs. Thus, *Pronasol* funds, which were presumably intended to help the poor, were, in reality, spent with other priorities in mind.

TABLE 4.1. *Centralist Logic of Pronasol: The Core Voter*

	1 Total PC Expenditures	2 Private Goods PC	3 Public Goods PC	4 Share (Private/ Total)
Spatial lag	0.031	−0.032	0.051	0.060
	(0.037)	(0.055)	(0.041)	(0.058)
Constant	7.305	3.866	7.065	−0.057
	(0.257)**	(0.356)**	(0.274)**	(0.052)
Logpop	−0.272	−0.168	−0.251	0.011
	(0.012)**	(0.020)**	(0.013)**	(0.003)**
Conapo	0.014	0.804	−0.249	0.160
	(0.062)	(0.108)**	(0.069)**	(0.017)**
Conapo^2	−0.008	−0.132	0.037	−0.028
	(0.012)	(0.020)**	(0.013)**	(0.003)**
Alpha	0.319	0.395	0.162	0.035
	(0.076)**	(0.130)**	(0.083)*	(0.021)*
Decline	−0.233	−0.628	−0.048	−0.103
	(0.068)**	(0.119)**	(0.076)	(0.018)**
1988 Margin	0.192	0.033	0.250	−0.028
	(0.038)**	(0.066)	(.042)**	(0.012)*
N	2422	2422	2422	2422
R^2	0.310	0.125	0.220	0.073

Note: Coefficients from OLS cross-sectional regressions of municipal-level allocations (ln) from 1989 until 1994. Robust standard errors in parentheses.

* Significant at 5% level; ** significant at 1% level.

The strictly electoral variables are unambiguous in their impact. First, larger overall transfers are strongly associated with the PRI's traditional strongholds in municipal elections. The larger the core size for the party, as measured by *alpha*, the greater the total flow of per capita transfers. Second, the rate of vote loss over the long term affects allocations in the expected direction, with strong declines attracting higher levels of investment. Third, those localities staunchly loyal to the PRI in 1988 were favored with more transfers during the Salinas administration, while those that backed the opposition were punished, in relative terms. With respect to the overarching logic of *Pronasol*, a buy-back strategy aimed at voters who earlier had defected was not a systematic criterion in the geographical distribution of funds. Nor could it have been, since to bribe municipalities back into the fold would have established the wrong incentive by rewarding defection. In sum, the core-voter model and the notion of *conditional party loyalty* are strongly supported by these results with respect to total *Pronasol* transfers.

A more nuanced story about the core-voter strategy is told through the distinction made between the two basic types of electoral investment contained within *Pronasol* (columns 2 and 3). Our expectations are that core supporters will be preferentially targeted for benefits, in the form of both private and public goods. However, the objectives sought by the provision of private versus public goods will separate according to how threatening the core's defection is in any given municipality. Our *conditional party loyalty* theory claims that locking-in the core and halting core defection is a key motive of clientelism. Public goods are not the favored instruments for keeping the core loyal. These claims are strongly supported by the empirical evidence. Consistent with our *conditional party loyalty* theory, the PRI tried to halt the drift of its core base through the intensification of clientelistic transfers rather than through the provision of public goods. The variable *decline* is strongly significant in the expected direction in models 1, 2, and 4, but not in model 3. These results provide support to our claim that clientelism as an investment strategy is intended to preserve preexisting core constituencies that might otherwise defect.

From columns 2 and 3 it is clear that small municipalities as measured by population size (*logpop*) fare better than large ones for both categories of electoral investment. However, the poverty index and its squared value assume diametrically opposed associations with the two types of benefit outlay. With respect to clientelism, one observes an inverted J-shaped relationship with development level. Intermediate levels of development (or poverty) attract higher levels of private goods provision, while the polar opposites on the scale are less favored by particularistic transfers. In the case of public goods provision, the opposite relationship holds. It is the poorest and richest ends of the development continuum that receive larger transfers for collective goods, while the intermediate levels obtain fewer of these benefits. At the same time, the coefficients for the quadratic expression are much larger in the case of clientelism, indicating a pronounced differential in distribution. The curve for public goods is flatter and seems to indicate almost a buckshot strategy, if not quite a universalistic one, for the distribution of collective goods at all levels of development. In any case, the important result that *Pronasol* did not particularly favor the poorest municipalities continues to hold.

The last model in column 4 tests for the determinants of the share of clientelism within the complete basket of *Pronasol* transfers to each municipality. In our view, a critical difference with respect to the debate over core- versus swing-voters is that investment diversification entails obvious advantages for incumbent politicians with discretionary funds available. It is probably the case that the larger overall share of public goods provision within *Pronasol* (an average 72 percent over six years) and the intense media campaign that accompanied its expansion served to shield from public scrutiny the clientelism that lay within the program and that increased in proportion over time. The specific combination of these investments for each municipality, we posit, reflected to some degree the risk assessment the PRI devised for each locality and balanced the imperatives of catering to its long-term core constituencies while claiming credit for collective welfare benefits.

The results of the diversification model are presented in the last column of Table 4.1. The poverty index shows an inverted J-shaped curve, much like that of per capita private goods transfers. Municipalities at intermediate levels of development obtain the highest shares of private goods, but the poorest municipalities still receive almost double the share going to the richest. Population size is positively associated with the composition of the portfolio, with higher shares of clientelism going to larger municipalities, but this result reflects lower relative transfers for collective goods than for private ones.

The *alpha* parameter reflecting core size is positively related to shares of clientelism, as it was (more strongly) for private transfer amounts. These results are an indication that, per our predictions, the relative share of public goods in the portfolio increases where the PRI's core is smaller and the party faces stronger competitive pressures, a point that will become even more transparent when analyzing the peripheral logic of *Pronasol* with respect to local elections and local partisan configurations. Public goods provision is not as effective an instrument for the retention of partisan loyalties, but is used in places with low core support as a means of attracting non-core-voter groups. The measure for long-term electoral dealignment follows its earlier pattern, with intensified clientelism for those locations with higher rates of decline in PRI support.

Finally, the shock waves from 1988 skewed the distribution of total *Pronasol* funds in favor of districts loyal to the PRI in that watershed election. The results for public and private goods transfers within the program, however, reveal a differential impact of the 1988 elections. Most of the reward for loyalty in 1988 is concentrated in greater public goods provision, with disloyal districts assigned fewer funds for public works. Outlays for clientelism are unrelated to 1988 election returns.

To have a sense of the range of effects for our main explanatory variables *alpha* and *decline*, Figure 4.4 simulates the predicted values of per capita private goods provision or clientelism, according to varying electoral variables and with the socioeconomic controls and 1988 margins set at their means. Shown are three scenarios for *alpha*: a stronghold municipality at one standard deviation above the mean; another at the mean; and a third one at one standard deviation below the mean. The graph then plots the per capita transfers for private goods according to the rate of decline in party loyalty over time. The simulated effects for both variables are substantively important: a stronghold with stable support for the PRI receives a bonus of 8 pesos per capita over one with few core supporters; an unstable bastion obtains 20 pesos more per inhabitant than the amount going to the PRI's weakest districts. Moreover, when the PRI's rate of decline increases from the mean rate (−0.299) by one additional standard deviation (−0.682), per capita allocations grow by about 10 pesos; when it jumps two standard deviations (−1.164), the benefits almost double in value per head over those for municipalities at the average rate of dealignment.

On the basis of these general models of *Pronasol* allocations, the conclusion is inescapable. *Pronasol* was a program designed and operated on behalf

4.4 The Peripheral Logic of Pronasol

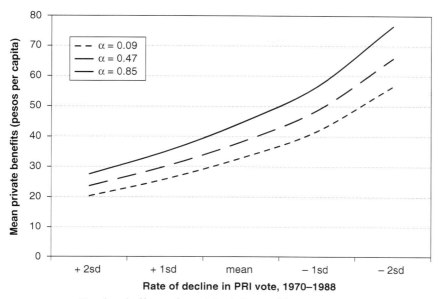

FIGURE 4.4. Simulated effects of municipal electoral history on private goods.

of the PRI's core constituencies throughout the country and its expenditures markedly benefited municipalities consistently loyal to the ruling party. There is scant evidence in these models of behavior approximating the party opportunism of the swing-voter model. We also uncover strategic behavior by the PRI that resulted in more clientelistic transfers disproportionately targeted to municipalities where core support was eroding more rapidly over time due to a multifaceted process of development. Consistent with our theory of *conditional party loyalty*, the PRI used clientelism primarily as an attempt to lock-in its core base. Finally, there is no evidence of a buy-back logic. Disloyal municipalities, and especially those that supported Cárdenas in 1988, were punished with fewer per capita transfers. Overall, *Pronasol*'s total per capita expenditures were not targeted to benefit the poor, but to sustain the PRI's electoral hegemony, to block if not destroy the embryonic party formation that resulted from the Cárdenas split, and to lock-in ruling party voters through intensified clientelism.

4.4 THE PERIPHERAL LOGIC OF *PRONASOL*

The partisan heart of *Pronasol* should beat just as strongly when faced with more immediate or short-term challenges such as election schedules, local party systems, and the party label of local incumbents. Our expectations are that the investment strategy adjusted to every municipality's political facts on the ground will reflect the dependence of the national incumbent on the party machines and operators who *reliably* turn out the vote and govern localities in alliance with party higher-ups.

To this point we have focused on *Pronasol*'s political motives as centrally devised, driven by national electoral imperatives, including safeguarding hegemony and maximizing electoral support across the board. But as we have emphasized, *Pronasol*'s operations on the ground were run through a vast network of politicians and officials, including state governors, municipal authorities, local party brokers and community leaders, as well as centrally designated *Pronasol* delegates. In this section we assess the extent to which local and regional politicians were able to shape *Pronasol*'s investment strategies to attend to their district's electoral needs. We ask in particular if *Pronasol*'s disbursements responded to municipal election schedules, local party system configurations, and the party label of local incumbents.

Our expectations are that the investment strategy adjusted to every municipality will continue to reflect a core-voter orientation. However, we expect to observe some tinkering of *Pronasol* according to local election calendars and expectations about the competitiveness of coming municipal elections.

Municipalities, of course, range widely in terms of their levels of electoral competitiveness and their party system configurations. Small cores in one set of localities translate into lower vote shares, tighter electoral margins, and a larger effective number of competitors within the municipal party system. In such places, it is unlikely that mere cultivation of the core constituency will produce victory in any upcoming election. Electoral competition, then, should oblige incumbent politicians to appeal to segmented electorates beyond their normal constituencies through policies and promises that entail a broadly cast net of welfare benefits generated by public goods provision – thus, the imperative of diversification in the choice of electoral investments.

In addition to previously used socioeconomic controls and the lagged values of the dependent variables, the peripheral models respecify the political and electoral variables used earlier. In the peripheral logic models, we are dealing with pooled-time series, where our dependent variables vary from year to year, rather than cross-sectional models. Here we include dummy indicators for election year, one for federal elections held in 1991 and 1994 (national election), and another for election years in the staggered municipal calendar (local election). It should be noted that in Mexico's busy election calendar, municipal elections take place in staggered three-year cycles, meaning that every year there are municipal elections taking place in different states. If national and local politicians took electoral dynamics into account in their allocation decisions, we expect both variables to be positively associated with our dependent variables.

Also included are electoral variables strongly related to the political measures specified for the previous models but which highlight more telltale

4.4 The Peripheral Logic of Pronasol

features of partisan control and competition during the years of the Salinas administration. We propose a typology of competitiveness from the perspective of the PRI, which incorporates the influence of the electoral legacy of the 1970s and 1980s and dissects its strength in the 1990s. The typology comprises four exclusive categories of municipal competition:

1. *Monopoly* is defined as a one-party municipality in which the PRI had an unbroken string of victories with at least 65 percent of the vote in every election since 1970, and ran uncontested (100 percent of the vote) during the Salinas administration.
2. *Hegemony* is defined as a municipality in which the PRI registered vote shares between 65 and 100 percent from the 1970s to the Salinas years, but faced opposition on the ballot.
3. *Marginals* is the label given to all other municipalities governed by the PRI, though they are not, strictly speaking, marginal districts, but rather competitive ones, in which an opposition party has sufficient strength to count as a viable contender in any local election.
4. *Opposition* refers to municipalities governed by any opposition party.

This simple typology of competitive challenges faced by the PRI at the municipal level is defined in terms of mean *alpha* and *decline* scores (Figure 4.5). Predictably, the categories of monopoly and hegemony exhibit much larger mean cores than competitive municipalities. But only monopoly provides a stable electoral trend over time. The municipalities corresponding to opposition and marginals are practically indistinguishable in terms of their electoral legacies.

In line with the results from the central models in Table 4.1, we expect in these peripheral models that the highest per capital funding levels should go to hegemonic municipalities where *alpha* is large but, in contrast to monopolistic electoral markets, strong erosion of PRI support over time has occurred. Although PRI marginals and opposition municipalities possess very similar electoral legacies, they should receive very different treatments, the latter being unambiguously out of favor, consistent with the notion of a punishment regime. Once again, this punishment strategy is inconceivable within the swing-voter model.

More conventional indicators of competitiveness also differentiate these categories in predictable ways. Table 4.2 describes the Laakso-Taagepera index of the effective number of parties (N), as well as the mean absolute margin of victory in municipal elections held from 1989 to 1994 for the four categories. While the PRI's monopolistic and hegemonic municipalities could endure the loss of one standard deviation in votes, or the entry of 0.5 competitors as measured by the Laakso-Taagepera index, without facing high odds of losing the municipality, the same was not true for competitive municipalities. If the ruling party had staked its interests in winning competitive municipalities, logically it should be expected to invest more heavily in

TABLE 4.2. *Mean Municipal Party System Descriptives*

	Effective N	(sd)	Margin of Victory	(sd)
Monopoly	1.224	(.401)	0.807	(.308)
Hegemony	1.585	(.516)	0.518	(.264)
PRI Marginals	1.825	(.785)	0.276	(.242)
Opposition	1.437	(.980)	0.288	(.266)

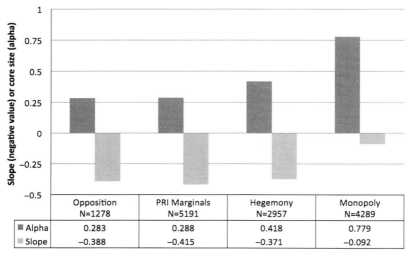

FIGURE 4.5. Mean core size and trends by level of competition.

them, following the imperatives of the swing-voter model. Our theory holds, instead, that core constituencies should continue to reap the benefits of electoral investment.

There are two strategic exceptions to this general expectation. First, monopolistic or noncompetitive elections in which the ruling party runs uncontested do not require a high ratio of clientelism-to-pork transfers because core supporters have no credible exit option. Second, we claim that the PRI should diversify its spending by investing in higher shares of public goods in competitive or high-N municipalities, which, not coincidentally, are the municipalities with small PRI cores.

To explore this facet of investment diversification further, we include municipal-level N in the peripheral model, in line with Chhibber and Nooruddin (2004). However, since the local structure of competition during the period 1988–1994 is clearly affected by *Pronasol* expenditures, we instrument the

4.4 The Peripheral Logic of Pronasol

effective number of municipal parties with its value in $t-1$.[10] This instrumented measure of $\hat{N}$ captures, then, the effect of an expected competition structure in any municipality.

The results for the peripheral models are presented in Table 4.3. The first two models test for per capita allocations in private and public benefits, respectively, and the third for the relative share of private goods within the total basket of municipal funds. Since we explore the effects of local electoral politics on transfers over time, yearly observations are pooled, controlling for the time trend (year) and the lagged value of each dependent variable.

The behavior of the control variables is very similar to that observed in the earlier models. Clientelism is strongly curvilinear with development levels, while pork shows no relationship to the poverty index. Per capita transfers for private goods increase and for public goods decrease with municipal size. Importantly, recourse to clientelism increases strongly over the lifespan of the program.

Electoral cycles in spending are quite clearly present during the Salinas term, but specifically for federal elections in 1991 and 1994. Indeed, a national election always trumps local ones, indicating the dominance of the centralist strategy over six years of *Pronasol* operations. There is weak evidence that *Pronasol*'s particularistic transfers increased prior to municipal elections, but transfers for public goods paradoxically decrease quite dramatically. In other words, the local election calendar did not dictate disbursements among *Pronasol*'s social infrastructure projects. Credit-claiming by its municipal parties perhaps rested on the record of accumulated pork-barrel transfers, but was not based on opportunistic infusions of funds for public works and infrastructure projects. Nonetheless, the context of an upcoming municipal election modifies the investment strategy in favor of clientelism, albeit with its funding levels unchanged. This relative stability of clientelistic transfers with respect to local electoral cycles, in contrast to the erratic flows of resources for public goods, supports the core-voter model. Particularism, as expected, enjoys a steady and constant resource flow that confirms the primacy of delivering the goods to core voters.

Municipal competition types perform as expected. Clientelistic per capita transfers are highest in hegemonic municipalities, while monopolies and marginals receive almost equal treatment. Opposition-controlled municipalities, the base category for model comparisons, obtain the lowest amounts of particularistic transfers. In the case of per capita public goods transfers, one-party and hegemonic districts enjoy the highest allocations, while opposition districts and PRI marginals receive very similar treatment at lower levels of funding.

---

[10] In earlier research (2006) we have included an instrumented *margin* in order to capture the impact of expected vote returns in municipal elections. So does Magaloni (2006), who finds that more of *Pronasol*'s transfers went to municipalities that were expected to be won by smaller margins. N and *margin* are in any case strongly correlated.

TABLE 4.3. *Peripheral Logic of* Pronasol: *Facing Elections*

	1 Private Goods pc	2 Public Goods pc	3 Share (Private/Total)
N	−0.122 (0.064)*	0.363 (0.070)**	−0.057 (0.009)**
Monopoly	0.403 (0.096)**	0.269 (0.047)**	−0.015 (0.007)*
Hegemony	0.720 (0.089)**	0.262 (0.042)**	0.028 (0.008)**
Marginal	0.444 (0.077)**	−0.051 (0.039)	0.030 (0.007)**
Local Election	0.189 (0.102)	−0.737 (0.113)**	0.097 (0.014)**
National Election	0.285 (0.048)**	0.061 (0.024)**	−0.001 (0.004)
Logpop	0.154 (0.023)**	−0.175 (0.013)**	0.008 (0.002)**
Conapo	1.226 (0.112)**	−0.091 (0.062)	0.123 (0.010)**
Conapo^2	−0.194 (0.022)**	0.016 (0.011)	−0.021 (0.002)**
Year	0.421 (0.021)**	−0.005 (0.011)	0.034 (0.002)**
Private Goods $_{t-1}$	0.377 (0.010)**		
Public Goods $_{t-1}$		0.190 (0.009)**	
Private Share $_{t-1}$			0.319 (0.010)**
Constant	−40.363 (2.058)**	5.883 (1.044)**	−3.162 (0.164)**
N	11008	10995	10991
R^2	0.35	0.15	0.19

Note: Coefficients from OLS pooled time series regressions of municipal-level per capita allocations (ln) and shares. Robust standard errors in parentheses.
* Significant at 5% level; ** significant at 1% level.

The full measure of the core-centered logic of *Pronasol* can be appreciated in Figure 4.6, which maps clientelism for each category of competition against the poverty index. Particularistic transfers to hegemonic municipalities were double those received by opposition-held municipalities, at any level of development. Particularistic transfers destined for monopolies and marginals were about 50 percent higher than what opposition-held municipalities received. The largest breach in absolute terms comes at intermediate levels on the poverty index, as before, yet the poorest localities enjoy at least three times the

4.4 The Peripheral Logic of Pronasol

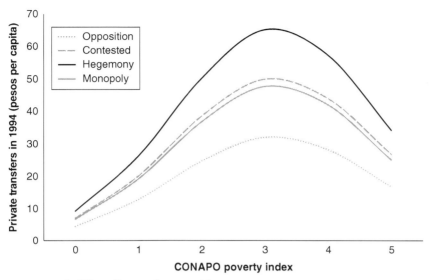

FIGURE 4.6. Clientelism and competition.

resources delivered to the richest. At the same time, one-party and competitive municipalities controlled by the PRI are assigned similar amounts of clientelism at all development levels.

From the perspective of the swing-voter model, this distribution of particularistic transfers would seem perverse; from that of the core-voter model, it reflects the centrality of partisan expectations and commitments to both voters and local party brokers. That is, private benefits that are selectively targeted should not be given to outsiders because they generate the wrong type of incentives by rewarding defection. Larger core constituencies take the greater slice of the pie, mitigated only by the lower incidence of private transfers in situations of monopoly where core voters have no credible exit option. This last finding is in accordance with Medina and Stokes (2006) who argue that monopolies suffer benign neglect by incumbents with respect to handouts. In competitive municipalities, with smaller cores, the party label of municipal government is decisive for allocation. Again, the swing-voter model would argue for similar treatment of all marginals, since a weak marginal municipality controlled by the opposition entails the same vote-buying potential as a weak marginal governed by the PRI. However, that claim devalues the comparative advantage of partisan organizations in control of government in local politics. Hence, our results indicate that opposition municipalities, even if lost by small margins, invariably get the short end of the stick.

However, what the swing-voter model fails to find in patterns of private transfers in the Mexican case can account for part of the distribution of pork

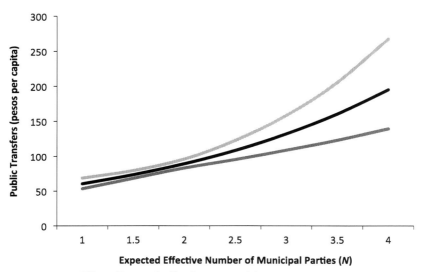

FIGURE 4.7. Clientelism and effective competition.

transfers across municipalities. The results reveal that more public goods are assigned to districts where the coming elections are expected to be competitive. This is measured by the predicted effective number of parties ($\hat{N}$) which has a positive and statistically significant sign for public goods allocations and a negative and statistically significant sign for private goods allocations and for the share of private goods within the municipal portfolio. The same results hold if we run the regressions with expected margin of victory, with higher public goods provision where upcoming municipal elections are expected to be close. These results support our claim that incumbent parties will diversify their portfolios by investing more in collective goods in competitive districts. We should emphasize that $\hat{N}$ is the expected competition structure for the very next election. This instrumented variable of competitiveness, unlike our party configuration typology, is constructed with short-term election results or returns from the previous municipal race. Thus, the effect of N conveniently captures the way in which politicians adjust investment decisions according to short-term election imperatives.

In Figure 4.7 we simulate the effects of $\hat{N}$ on the disbursement of collective benefits in local election years, holding other variables at their mean. The patent result is that per capita expenditures for collective goods increase rapidly as the expected effective number of parties grows. For the bipartisan and multipartisan competition mushrooming in Mexico in the 1990s, this corresponds to about double the per capita investment in pork assigned to low-N municipalities in an election year. As a result of the skew favoring core constituencies in the allocation of private transfers, the share of public goods within the *Pronasol* basket increases markedly for N in the competitive range.[11] The cost is hefty, since per capita transfers for pork are routinely two to three times the amount distributed as private transfers.

4.5 CONCLUSION

The *Pronasol* projects in Chalco Solidaridad had a lasting impact on improving the lives of the poor in that municipality. Many other *Pronasol* projects also contributed to improving welfare by bringing health clinics, schools, water systems, sewage systems, electrification, and more to previously impoverished localities. Unfortunately, this was not the overarching logic behind *Pronasol*'s vast operations. One of the central political motivations behind its public infrastructure projects, as our results suggest, was that the PRI could no longer count on core support sufficient to win elections and thus needed to legitimize itself through broader collective projects for which it could claim credit. For the most part, the poor were not actually targeted nor preferentially benefited by the program's array of particularistic and collective projects. Our results in this chapter demonstrate that clientelism was used to lock-in the PRI's core base of support. But, as we will demonstrate in subsequent chapters, clientelism contributed very little to improving the welfare of the poor. Although our results demonstrate that it paid to be loyal to the PRI, the logic of political linkages left the poor trapped in a long-term relationship of material dependence.

The results in this chapter provide robust empirical support for our main theoretical claims. The chapter has presented empirical evidence for our theory of *conditional party loyalty*. The theory departs from the core- versus swing-voter debate in viewing partisan loyalties as endogenous, shaped by the history of interactions and tactical redistributions. Voters' loyalties cannot be taken for granted, we argue, and this is especially true where voters respond weakly to ideological, programmatic, and other symbolic appeals, as is prevalent throughout the developing world.

We see politicians as motivated by both short- and long-term considerations. They seek to construct partisan coalitions that are stable over time and they want to win the current election as well. These goals often place parties in a strategic dilemma: if they appeal to swing voters to win the current election by delivering discretionary transfers to them, they risk alienating their core voters in future elections. Alienating the core can be quite self-destructive. One

---

[11] Chhibber and Nooruddin (2004) find evidence in Indian states for the greater incidence of private benefits (government salaries) and of lower public goods expenditures in multiparty environments than in two-party ones. Our findings for Mexico are exactly reversed and, in addition, extend to undercompetitive environments, which take the lion's share of both clientelistic transfers and pork outlays. Of course, the Mexican case is one of centralized control over *Pronasol* disbursements and of only one national incumbent party until the year 2000.

solution to this dilemma, we have argued, is to diversify the portfolio of electoral investments, targeting particularistic transfers to core supporters, while delivering collective benefits to electorates at large.

The strategy we uncover has a strong core-voter bias: parties should primarily target particularistic benefits to voters who have consistently supported them in the past. These voters are not only better known by local party brokers, but are also less risky as investments. Yet the more the core is willing to drift, given the presence of alternatives to the ruling party, the more we expect a machine to rely on clientelism to lock-in loyal voters. Our theory argues that discretionary private transfers are preferable to collective goods if one is to construct stable and durable electoral coalitions. This form of political exchange is what we, and others, have characterized as clientelism.

Our theory is also one of portfolio diversification. *Pronasol*'s strong bias in favor of core constituencies and districts under firm PRI control is undeniable with regard to discretionary transfers of private benefits. Clientelism was consistently used to reward core-voter groups, with politicians strongly intensifying this practice in municipalities that were experiencing higher core erosion over time. The strategy employed in the allocation of pork-barrel projects is less straightforward. Our results reveal that within *Pronasol*'s overarching strategy, public goods provision also emphatically favored core districts and punished opposition-controlled ones. However, local politicians modified their portfolios of electoral investment to increase the share of public goods over private goods in small core voter municipalities. Intended to attract support from broader and more heterogeneous coalitions, pork appears to be a second-best, though necessary, strategic choice for party machines facing rising competition.

Finally, the models accounting for the peripheral logic of *Pronasol* strongly suggest that politicians privileged and even intensified clientelistic practices prior to national and municipal elections alike. Local party organizations and brokers were able to adjust investment decisions to take their own short-term electoral needs into account. Overall, our empirical results demonstrate that poverty alleviation was, at best, a secondary objective. Expenditures did not systematically benefit the poorest municipalities. The entire program with its vast array of transfers and projects was administered with the goal of sustaining the PRI's electoral hegemony. *Pronasol* was highly successful at buying votes for the PRI, as we will demonstrate in later chapters, but extremely ineffective at combating poverty.

PART II

THE CONSEQUENCES OF CLIENTELISM AND ENTITLEMENTS

Pronasol embodied the social policy expression of the waning hegemonic political equilibrium of the PRI. The new social assistance and decentralized development funds that emerged in the late-1990s slashed the discretionary powers of the federal executive, creating a completely novel social program, based on conditional cash transfers. The CCT program included a notice printed in all communications and documents that read as follows:

> We remind you that your participation in Progresa [later renamed *Oportunidades*] and receipt of benefits are in no way subject to affiliation with any specific political party or to voting for any specific candidate running for public office. No candidate is authorized to grant or withhold benefits under the program. Eligible beneficiary families will receive support if they show up for their doctor's visits and health education talks and if their children attend school regularly.

This was a far cry from *Pronasol* that clearly discriminated against PAN- and PRD-affiliated municipalities. Figure II.1 shows the evolution of social development funds in Mexico over time, first within the *Pronasol* program, and after 1996 with the federal programs that replaced it, in the budgetary category for decentralized spending called Ramo 33. The graph breaks down the per capita allocation of funds according to the partisan affiliation of the municipal government.

Unsurprisingly, *Pronasol* shows a large gap between PRI municipalities and those governed by PAN and PRD. Funding falls precipitously in 1995 as a consequence of a deep financial crisis.[1] But after that year, as spending

---

[1] The finances of the federal government were in such disarray that year that we do not really know how much money was allocated to municipalities through the remaining *Pronasol* programs in 1995. But public documents suggest that the amount decentralized in 1996 was two-thirds of the funds, while one-third had been decentralized the prior year. The figure shows that year as a break in the lines.

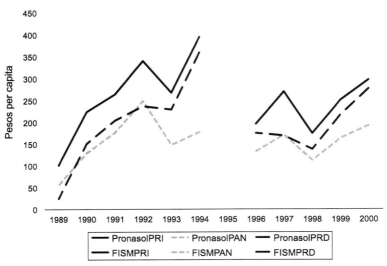

FIGURE 11.1. Partisan identity of municipal government and poverty-alleviation funds.

recovered, the partisan differences in funding for PRI and PRD statistically disappeared and became much smaller for PAN. The distribution of funds for municipal public works was henceforth done through partisan-blind formulas based on population, poverty, and unsatisfied basic needs. Given that the PRI enjoyed greater electoral success in underdeveloped municipalities its mayors still received the lion's share of the decentralized federal funding. But the preference for them was not *because* of their partisan affiliation, but simply due to the fact that the PRI governed relatively poor places.

The process of transformation of *Pronasol* into its successor programs has been told only in bits and pieces. Scholars recount the creation of the *Fondo de Desarrollo Social Municipal* (FDSM) in 1996 (which would become the *Fondo de Aportaciones para la Infraestructura Social Municipal* [FISM] in 1998) as a story of decentralization, while the creation of the Conditional Cash Transfer program, *Progresa*, in 1997 is usually couched as one of technocratic innovation.[2] Although each of these programs had their own champions and opponents, the impetus for the revamping of social policy must be understood as a consequence of a political tsunami triggered by two events, one endogenous and the second exogenous: the Zapatista uprising threatening the stability

---

[2] For the most authoritative account of the creation of *Progresa*, as recounted by its main author, see Levy (2006) and Levy and Rodríguez (2005). On the decentralization of social spending, and in particular the creation of the FDSM, see Mogollón (2002), Rodríguez (1997), and the essays by Scott (1998) and Levy (1998) in the volume edited by the Social Development Committee in the Camara de Diputados.

of the political system; and the financial crisis that started in December 1994 which immediately impacted the federal budgetary process and the available strategies for poverty alleviation and clientelism.

Major threats of revolutionary change from below should not be underestimated as a major thrust for elites to engage in preemptive reforms that lead to the creation of effective social programs. Owing to the clever articulation of the Zapatista movement's demands by Subcomandante Marcos and the broad empathy it commanded resonating with citizens fed up with corruption and ineffective government, the Chiapas uprising made it transparent that the persistence of poverty was linked to political corruption, government abuse, and lack of democratic accountability. Most citizens agreed that *Pronasol*'s clientelistic programs did not relieve poverty. The Zapatista rebellion created threats of political instability that, if left unaddressed, could have spilled over into the rest of the country.[3]

Progresa and FISM were born in the heat of true political battles, not dissimilar to those that led to the great shifts of social policy in countries like Britain or Germany in the 1830s and the 1870s. With poverty rising sharply as a result of the economic recession, voter anger and a mounting threat of social rebellion, the new social assistance regime focused on fighting extreme poverty, at a time of serious fiscal restraint. A new social assistance regime emerged, through a compromise between the PRI (its president and the party's subnational politicians) and the opposition, that agreed to tie the hands of the institution of the presidency.

Since the creation of the PRI, the president played a critical role in the clientelistic apparatus. Fiscal resources were highly centralized and the president had huge leeway to decide who got what and when. The system was purposely designed so that when subnational politicians delegated fiscal powers to the president, the president in turn took care to discipline and unite the heterogeneous PRI behind the common cause of hegemonic party survival (Diaz-Cayeros, 2006). With the FISM, resources would now be distributed among subnational governments according to previously specified formulas negotiated within the legislative arena. States and local communities would now decide what projects to fund, not the president and the federal government.

The Zedillo administration was overwhelmed by economic disorder, having to manage the bankruptcy of the banking sector, bail out insolvent state governments, design a program for debtor relief and pursue macroeconomic stability all at the same time. Instead of enjoying a honeymoon in his first year in office (buttressed by the perception that the PRI had won a clean democratic election, albeit on an unlevel playing field in the areas

---

[3] Trejo (2012) suggests that both the 1994 and the 1996 electoral reforms – which paved the road for Mexico's democratization in 2000 – were a direct response to the 1994 Zapatista rebellion and to its transformation into a self-determination movement in 1995. We thank an anonymous reviewer for helping us articulate this point.

of campaign finance and media access), Zedillo inherited renewed guerilla unrest, most notably in Chiapas and Guerrero, and elite-level instability and violence within the PRI, as reflected by the two high-level political assassinations in 1994.[4]

Voters reacted bitterly to the PRI. President Salinas had convinced the public that the austerity and liberalization policies his government pursued would pave the way to sustained economic recovery. Instead, some ten years of economic reform, often painful, culminated in an economic recession of shocking proportions. Voters felt betrayed and began to defect to the opposition. In almost every important local election between 1995 and 1997, the PAN won large city mayoralties and several governorships. The PRD, for its part, found massive voter support in Mexico City and profited from local schisms in the hegemonic party in different parts of the country.

Decentralization in Mexico emerged as a reactive strategy of governance that grew and deepened as events unfolded. At a meeting with governors from both the PAN and the PRI, Zedillo called in 1995 for the establishment of a new federal pact, complaining that "centralization in Mexico today is oppressive and backward, socially insensitive and inefficient."[5] Governors blamed the president for the economic crisis and suffered the dire consequences of fiscal austerity in their state budgets, which depended heavily on federal transfers. Their demands for budgetary and debt relief were loud and ceaseless. Concessions to state governments in those years were substantial. In January, 1996, the general revenue-sharing rate was increased from 18.51 to 20 percent, which together with some minor changes in special taxes and exemptions meant a 10 percent increase in block grant transfers to the states.[6]

Funds for the construction of schools, adult literacy programs, and rural highways were decentralized to the states. But the most substantial decentralization to the states occurred in health, with the management of almost 7,000 clinics and 120,000 health workers transferred to state governments, together with the financial resources to pay for them. Concessions to municipal governments were just as important. In his state-of-the-union address in September 1995, Zedillo announced that two-thirds of the resources previously allocated through *Pronasol* would now be decentralized directly to the municipalities as earmarked or conditional transfers to strengthen Mexican federalism. In unprecedented executive decrees, the federal executive provided explicit formulas for the allocation of funds among the states (Mogollón, 2002), specifying amounts assigned to each state for redistribution to the municipalities and using sophisticated formulas based on poverty gap indicators from the census.

---

[4] The literature on the political crisis is vast. For work published in English see Oppenheimer (1996); Levy and Bruhn (2001); and Camp (2007).

[5] Inauguration of the *Meeting Foro Nacional Hacia un Auténtico Federalismo*. http://zedillo.presidencia.gob.mx/pages/disc/mar95/29mar95.html (consulted January 8, 2007, our translation).

[6] These measures can be seen as a side payment by the president for his party's support in congress of the highly unpopular hike in the VAT rate.

Along with this process of decentralization, a more subtle but profound transformation was taking place with the way in which poverty-alleviation efforts would be pursued. The president delegated authority to make budgetary adjustments to the deputy minister for expenditures, Santiago Levy, in order to achieve fiscal balance. Levy was also the main actor in the negotiation of bailouts for bankrupt state governments. Macroeconomic stability was Levy's overriding imperative, and to that end he resisted pressures from within his party to increase spending. But Levy was also profoundly committed to a vision of creating a poverty-alleviation program based on conditional cash transfers – a vision he spelled out as a scholar researching poverty before he returned to Mexico to join the government.

In an essay written in 1991, Levy (1991) outlined the logic and design of *Progresa*. A very small program in place called the *Programa de Atención de Servicios de Salud para la Población Abierta* (PASSPA) could, with some minor modifications, become the most important program for alleviation of extreme poverty. The proposed centralized program would include: (1) targeting places with the highest poverty indices;[7] (2) providing nutritional supplements; (3) supplying preventive health care and education; and (4) creating temporal sustainability in order to reach a goal of breaking the intergenerational transmission of poverty.

Levy proposed that the program make transfers through a system of vouchers, arguing against generalized price supports. He was quite emphatic that the purpose of the vouchers was not to transfer purchasing power, but rather to condition households to behavioral changes in family nutrition, health, and education. Moreover, Levy noted from the outset that program success would be judged in terms of reduced "infant mortality and morbidity rates, improvements in primary health and [...] hygiene" (1991: 83). In his view, the program should have no other objectives. This outline is virtually identical to the design of *Progresa* that the government adopted six years later, including geographic targeting, complementary interventions in nutrition, health, and education, and program continuation across political cycles. The one element that was abandoned was the use of vouchers, which instead were replaced by direct cash transfers.

The program began in earnest in the summer of 1997, on a small scale. Legislators from all parties denounced it as *asistencialista*, a hand-to-mouth welfare program for poor families that would only create chronic dependency on the cash stipends. But program coverage of families in extreme poverty grew, slowly, and in carefully sequenced stages, from the original 300,000 households to 5 million by 2006. After the PRI lost power in 2000, Vicente Fox chose not only to keep the program but also to expand it into the cities, in keeping with Levy's long-term plan, and change its name to *Oportunidades*. In a country

---

[7] Levy (1991: 82) insisted in his scholarly work that a proper poverty index should take into account the intensity of poverty (i.e., the size of family income gaps that measure absolute distance from the poverty line), rather than the more standard poverty headcounts.

where few programs survive from one presidential term to the next, the continuity of *Progresa/Oportunidades* is responsible for the containment and reduction of extreme poverty during the first decade of the twenty-first century.

As should be already apparent, this dramatic transformation and the phasing out of *Pronasol* would not have occurred had Mexican voters not rebelled against the system. Clientelism requires voters' complicity to survive as a form of electoral exchange. Poor voters willingly became loyal to the PRI because their loyalty served to facilitate access to government transfers and a future stream of benefits. The patron-client relationship was based on reciprocity. The party delivered access to the system of benefits to keep its clients loyal; in exchange, clients reciprocated with their loyalty and support, including turning up for rallies and political campaigns and showing up at the polls.

The perverse nature of clientelism is that voters willingly sustain a system that is corrupt and keeps them poor. The dilemma is one of coordination. Each voter acting alone has powerful reasons to remain loyal. If the voter defects in isolation, she will be punished or cut off from the benefits of the system. And if everyone reasons likewise, the machine can be sustained in equilibrium. To exit the system, the voter needs to know that many others will vote against the machine; otherwise the lone defector will bear the costs of exiting. The equilibrium is perverse because everyone becomes an accomplice of the system even when it is collectively suboptimal. Simultaneously looming behind this process, a real threat of social unrest made politicians more tolerant of technocratic solutions that sought to redress poverty through new policy innovations. *Progresa* was one such experiment. It was a very inexpensive intervention that turned out to be remarkably effective.

Moving away from clientelism and pork barrel politics, Mexico radically slashed the pool of resources at the president's disposal, increasing the available resources to subnational officeholders. Binding rules were established for the distribution of cash transfers targeted to poor families; and decentralized development funds effectively came to reach the poorest local governments to finance much-needed public works. Since *Pronasol* seemed to prove an electoral effectiveness in both the 1991 and the 1994 federal elections, such radical transformation might be somewhat puzzling. However, the combined forces of decentralization and democratic competition induced ambitious politicians – from both the PRI and the other political parties – to shift their support toward programs that provided real benefits to a broad range of citizens.

This second part focuses on the variation in welfare gains across Mexico's municipalities during two decades. The next two chapters take a comprehensive view of poverty relief strategies and their differential impacts upon the lives of the poor. Chapter 5 studies the improvements in access to basic public services (water, sanitation, and electricity); while Chapter 6 analyzes health improvement through the lens of infant mortality. The final chapter provides an understanding of the electoral payoffs of social programs in Mexico.

5

Improving Communities: Transfers for Basic Public Services

> Too often, services fail poor people – in access, in quantity, in quality. But the fact that there are strong examples where services do work means governments and citizens can do better. How? By putting poor people at the center of service provision: by enabling them to monitor and discipline service providers, by amplifying their voice in policymaking, and by strengthening the incentives for providers to serve the poor.
>
> World Bank, World Development Report (2004b)

5.1 INTRODUCTION

This chapter asks about the political conditions and governance structures that facilitate or hinder the translation of social program expenditures into public service delivery that helps the poor. We seek to contribute to a growing literature on public goods provision in developing countries. The story of Francisca told in the introduction to this book illustrates how basic public services can make a critical difference to improve health and prevent premature death. Without access to services like sanitation and health, Francisca's children were very vulnerable: six out of thirteen died of preventable and curable health ailments. This story is hardly unique. Dehydration caused by diarrhea is the second greatest killer of children in developing countries. The World Health Organization (WHO) and the United Nations Fund for Children (UNICEF) calculate that in 2015 there will be 2.4 billion people without basic sanitation, and children will continue to pay the price in disease, malnutrition, and death. Poor sanitation has negative implications for education. Stomach-related illnesses not only prevent children from attending school regularly, but also have a negative impact on their cognitive skills.

By all accounts, life for the poor in Mexico has witnessed significant improvement with the expansion of public services. In 1990 the average municipal-level household coverage of water and sanitation was 65 and

35 percent, respectively; by 2000 coverage had increased to 72 and 50 percent. Such advances notwithstanding, a large proportion of the extreme poor still live without basic sanitation and other public services. In the state of Guerrero, for example, in 2010 one-fourth of the population lived without sewerage and 38 percent had no access to drinking water. The coverage in Chiapas was better, but still one-sixth had no sanitation system and one-fifth were not supplied with potable water. Similar averages could be found in Veracruz, San Luis Potosí, Puebla, and Oaxaca. And even within these states, inequalities are glaring. In rural villages, only a few households enjoy running water and proper sanitation, while in richer towns and cities the overwhelming majority is covered. High rates of infant mortality, as we discuss in the following chapter, are associated with the lack of access to basic services.

What accounts for variations in public service access and delivery? The failure of public service provision in developing countries can be attributed to both supply- and demand-side problems. Corrupt political institutions or unaccountable governments can be blamed for poor provision of services, while badly informed, distrustful, or ethnically divided citizens may generate free-riding and coordination problems as well as insufficient demand for public goods.

In this chapter we focus on supply, asking how the governance of social programs for public good provision and electoral accountability affect the delivery of collective benefits and services. The Mexican constitution grants the municipality responsibility for a wide range of public infrastructure investments, including roads, street pavement, sewers, running water, public markets and lighting, granaries, slaughterhouses, parks, garbage collection and public restrooms. Potable water, sewage systems, and electricity grids make up the bulk of municipal public goods spending. Although municipalities collect some taxes and can spend own revenues on social infrastructure projects, the overwhelming majority of these projects depend upon federal transfers to be funded.

Infrastructure projects can suffer from significant leakage. For example, successful projects sometimes benefit nontargeted populations; unsuccessful projects are often the result of rent-seeking or corruption on the part of politicians and service providers. Our goal is to identify which of the major social infrastructure programs, *Pronasol* and FISM, had fewer leakages, as reflected in their differential effect in expanding the provision of public services. These programs were characterized by radically different modes of governance: *Pronasol* was a centralized program administered from the president's office while FISM is a decentralized program administered by municipal authorities; *Pronasol* was characterized by a high degree of governmental discretion in the targeting of programs and projects, while FISM targets funds to municipalities according to nondiscretionary formulas; *Pronasol* was predominantly a clientelistic program operated from the center to satisfy the PRI's electoral clienteles and extensive patronage networks, while FISM, in sharp contrast, redistributes federal monies to municipalities on the basis of need rather than partisan interest.

5.1 Introduction

The governance of FISM thus works to restrain the manipulation of resource distribution among municipalities, although it does allow local governments considerable discretion to decide resource allocation within their jurisdictions.

This chapter also assesses the extent to which municipal variation in electoral accountability shapes public service delivery. A crucial aspect of accountability stems from voters' capacity to sanction poor government performance (Ferejohn, 1986). Given the constitutional rule in Mexico proscribing reelection at all levels of government, the electoral accountability of municipal governments was necessarily limited.[1] With short time horizons, it could be argued that the temptation has been strong for mayors to behave as "roving bandits" (Olson, 2002), plundering as much as possible while in office.

The ban on reelection defangs the vote, since citizens cannot reward or punish mayors directly for their performance in office. But the vote retains some sanctioning power when applied to the political parties sponsoring mayoral candidates. Political incentives to serve voters largely hinge upon top-down, intraparty mechanisms available to discipline-elected officials. If parties promote local officials and cadres regardless of their records, accountability will be seriously jeopardized. However, electoral accountability without reelection might still be possible, albeit imperfect, if political parties choose to reward with nominations to higher office competent local elected officials with good reputations and performance (Langston, 2011).

Our expectation is that, despite the lack of reelection, higher levels of political competition at the municipal level will increase a municipal government's imperative to improve public service delivery. In monopolistic and hegemonic electoral markets there should be inadequate provision of collective benefits. As Chapters 3 and 4 discussed, voters in monopolistic places were almost condemned to support the PRI, even when it failed to deliver collective benefits. The problem is one of coordination: since each individual voter acting alone cannot defeat the ruling party; individuals are better off consenting to the system, no matter how corrupt or incompetent, so as to continue to have access to the party's spoils system or the mere expectation to receive some future benefits. Voters in hegemonic localities had more leverage than voters in monopolistic places, but as we demonstrated in Chapters 3 and 4, the PRI preferred to target particularistic transfers to these localities so as to prevent its loyal base from eroding.

Incentives are likely to be different where there is electoral competition and partisan alternation in power is realistically possible, or where it has already occurred. In these settings, parties must pay closer attention to voters' interests to be able to win future elections. To evaluate these propositions with empirical data, we measure local "electoral democracy" in several ways. Following Przeworski et al. (2000), municipalities are classified as democratic where partisan alternation in power in office has taken place. We also create an index that

---

[1] This ban on reelection will be lifted starting in 2015.

measures a variety of factors normally associated with electoral democracy, including levels of electoral competitiveness and margin of victory. In addition, we analyze the effect of the cumulative number of years since a municipality first experienced partisan alternation.

Correcting for potential endogeneity between spending, electoral democracy, and coverage of public goods (as well as potential sources of unobserved heterogeneity),[2] our findings show that despite massive investments, the discretionary and centralized funds from *Pronasol* had negligible effects in improving the poor's access to basic public services. In contrast, changes in the provision of potable water, electricity, and sewerage in municipal jurisdictions responded strongly to the decentralized and formula-based appropriations through FISM. Further, our results demonstrate that electoral democracy has a strong impact on improvements in public goods, propping a fairly optimistic view of the value of local electoral competition for the poor's welfare in Mexico. The results are robust to various specifications of the statistical model. We estimate these effects of social programs and local democracy while controlling for the confounding impacts of municipal heterogeneity as captured by shifts in social participation, demography, and economic development.

In contrasting the effects of antipoverty programs and of local democracy on public service delivery, this chapter systematically evaluates the effectiveness of different governance modes for reaching the poor. Together with the next chapter, the discussion provides a clear measure of the leakages entailed in delivering collective benefits primarily through a party's patronage networks relative to less politicized modes of resource distribution. In a nutshell, this chapter and the next provide measures of the scant welfare effects of discretionary antipoverty programs. Political linkages nurtured through discretionary social policy constitute a major barrier to accountability in governance, hindering effective poverty reduction.

The rest of this chapter is organized as follows. The next section provides an overview of the main theoretical hypotheses advanced in the comparative literature to explain variations in the provision of local public goods and services. We draw from that literature to justify the control variables we use in the estimation. The third section discusses the empirical strategy used to assess the policy effectiveness of funding for local public goods provision. We create two types of instruments for the identification of expenditure effects: one using geographic variables, and the other taking advantage of the mismatch between federal and state formulas in the allocation of social infrastructure funds. We follow with a discussion of our empirical results.

---

[2] As we discuss in the next section, unmeasured municipal characteristics might jointly determine the coverage of public goods, the spending allocated to it, and its democratic character. We employ an identification strategy that focuses on the changes in public goods provision over time, rather than the absolute level of provision in the cross-section, while employing an instrumental variables approach to address endogeneity concerns.

5.2 HETEROGENEITY, STATE CAPACITY, AND DEMOCRATIC ACCOUNTABILITY

Well-being hinges not just on family income, but also on access to basic public goods and services. Although public goods can sometimes be privately provided, in general the provision of facilities such as potable water, sewage systems, electricity, schools, and health clinics devolves upon government. What explains differences in the provision of local public goods?

The literature offers four primary explanations for the differential provision of public goods. First, more ethnically homogenous communities seem more capable of providing public goods. Greater social heterogeneity, as measured, for example, through an index of ethnolinguistic fractionalization (ELF), makes it harder for communities to provide public goods (Alesina et al., 1999). This shortcoming is attributed to the idea that collective action when ethnic groups distrust outsiders and ethnic fragmentation breeds conflict among groups.[3]

Studies linking ethnic diversity to public goods provision generally adopt a statistical approach. The association between polarization, as measured by ELF indexes, and failures to provide local public goods, as measured primarily by public expenditure patterns, seems to be a robust finding. However, there is considerable disagreement in the literature regarding the specific mechanisms through which heterogeneity influences public goods provision. It is possible that there is substitution among public goods, in the sense that some places might get less of certain types of goods, but more of others (Banerjee and Somanathan, 2001). Possibly, ethnically heterogeneous societies have a different taste profile for public goods than homogeneous ones, so that the result is driven by preferences, rather than polarization and conflict (Banerjee and Somanathan, 2007; Banerjee, 2004). The literature fails to specify how ethnic differences are reflected in bureaucratic structures and the political system (Posner, 2005), arenas where the provision of public goods is decided.[4]

Nonetheless, this literature suggests that a key determinant of success in local public goods provision is the capacity of communities to work together toward a common goal. In the Mexican context, religious divisions have emerged very strongly during the past decades, becoming an important source of community

---

[3] Studies finding evidence of the impact of social heterogeneity in public good provision across nations and within countries include Alesina and La Ferrara (2000); Khwaja (2007); Miguel (2004); Miguel and Gugerty (2005); Dayton-Johnson (2000); and Baqir (2000).

[4] Political scientists have engaged this literature quite extensively in their own work on ethnic conflict and civil war (Weinstein, 2006; Fearon and Laitin, 2003). The most promising research agenda seems to be the move away from cross-sectional variation to a focus in local experimental settings, in which scholars have tried to understand the conditions under which communities are more able to create networks of trust. Habyarimana et al. (2007), in particular, performed experiments in Kampala, Uganda, testing the willingness of coethnics and members of different ethnic groups to cooperate. Also, in an experimental set up, Wantchekon (2004) tested the appeal of programmatic promises of public good delivery by presidential candidates according to ethnic differences in Benin.

tensions, particularly in the South, and linguistic differences remain prominent, particularly in areas with a strong presence of indigenous communities.

Second, states that in some measurable way are more "capable" might be better able to provide public goods (Kohli, 2001). Failures in the provision of public goods reflect underlying problems arising from weak states that are incapable of taxing, running a bureaucracy or fulfilling basic public functions. Although there are variations in the administrative capacities of bureaucracies and service providers, state capacity tends to be difficult to measure. Very often states are defined as incapable precisely because they do not provide public goods and services. However, a well-documented example of the case of Ceará in Brazil has shown that it is possible to create an autonomous bureaucracy that can provide public goods effectively even within weak states (Tendler, 1997).[5] It is usually very hard to find a variable to measure state capacity that is not confounded with the general level of wealth or development. Nevertheless, it is important to acknowledge that public service provision might be better or worse due to differences in bureaucratic performance. In the Mexican context, there is wide variation in the administrative apparatus of municipal governments. Around half of the municipalities can be thought of as lacking state capacity due to their small size, precarious public finances, and high poverty levels (Cabrero, 1998).

Third, while some cross-country studies show that democracy has a positive effect on the provision of public goods such as education and health (Stasavage, 2005; Besley and Kudamatsu, 2006; Baum and Lake, 2003), others find either no effect in developing countries (Boix, 2003) or no significant effect of regime types at all (Ross, 2006). In a fascinating study on public service provision in an authoritarian regime, Tsai (2007) finds that even when formal mechanisms of electoral accountability are not present, the existence of village solidarity groups in some villages in China made local officials more responsive to their communities, and also more likely to have better local public goods provision than villages without them. The uneven process of local democratization in Mexico provides us an opportunity to test regime differences from a subnational perspective.

Fourth, a growing set of studies focus on moral hazard and electoral control, trying to identify the conditions under which politicians' interests align with voters. The general conclusion emerging from the literature is that electoral competition is not sufficient for good governance. We discuss this last strand of literature in greater detail, given its relevance for our empirical results. Some papers study how improving information among voters works at reducing moral hazard and elite capture, which in turn improves the provision of public services (Khemani and Keefer, 2014). Policymakers have increasingly

---

[5] State capacity can be proxied through fiscal variables, particularly the capacity of local governments to collect revenues and spend on public goods. Zhurakvskaya (2000) has found, for example, that public good provision in Russian cities did not respond to local tax collection efforts, because the center offset those efforts by withholding revenue sharing.

5.2 Heterogeneity, State Capacity, and Democratic Accountability

paid more attention to corruption as an explanation for the difficulties governments face in providing public goods and services.[6] In a particularly poignant example, Reinikka and Svensson (2004) measured an astronomical leakage of 87 percent in a program in Uganda meant to provide grants to schools for nonwage expenditures. That leakage was successfully reduced through greater citizen involvement and information regarding the allocation of funds to local schools.[7] Olken (2006) similarly found that the leakage in a poverty-relief program delivering rice in Indonesia was large enough to offset the welfare gains from having the program in place at all. In a fascinating study, Ferraz and Finan (2008) show that providing information to voters about corruption makes them more likely to sanction bad politicians.[8]

Other studies focus on participatory democracy and citizen engagement in collective decision making. In an important contribution to this literature, Olken (2010) shows that direct participation in political decision making can substantially increase satisfaction and legitimacy.[9] The link between electoral competition and public service delivery has also received some attention. Chhibber and Nooruddin (2004) found that Indian states where electoral competition is stiff (the incumbent faces a strong contest from a single challenger) are more likely to increase expenditure on public goods. They also find that public goods provision in multiparty competition decreases, because in fragmented electorates politicians do not need to build large coalitions.[10]

---

[6] Bardhan and Mookherjee (2006) have shown, in a formal model, that centralized systems of public service delivery are more subject to corruption. However, they also note that local elites might capture subnational governments making them less efficient than centralization. Besley and Coate (2003) have provided a model in which the advantages of decentralization depend on legislative behavior and how jurisdictional spillovers and conflicts, arising from the variance in preferences over public good provision across districts, are mediated by the political system. Despite these theoretical advances, we are only beginning to understand the links between democratic accountability, local public goods provision, and decentralization.

[7] More broadly, in an empirical evaluation of Sen's (1981) influential hypothesis that democracy prevents famines, Besley and Burgess (2002) show that Indian states with greater freedom of the press are more likely to deliver disaster relief. Besley and Prat (2001) reach similar findings for a cross-section of countries.

[8] They exploit a unique natural experiment provided by Brazil's anticorruption program: in 2003 the Brazilian government began to randomly audit the municipal expenditure of federally transferred funds. To promote transparency and accountability, the resulting audit reports were disseminated to the mass media. Exploiting this randomized audit, they found that in municipalities where radio stations were present and higher levels of corruption were revealed, reelection rates were significantly lowered.

[9] The conclusions are drawn from an experiment in which forty-nine Indonesian villages were randomly assigned to choose development projects through direct plebiscites or representative-based meetings. The study shows that direct democracy resulted in higher satisfaction among villagers, increased knowledge about the project, greater perceived benefits, and higher reported willingness to contribute. One of the most intriguing results of the experiment is that changing the political mechanism of allocation – direct versus representative democracy – had much smaller effects on the actual projects selected.

[10] The study focuses on spending rather than on actual provision of public goods, but the results are opposed to our findings in Chapter 4.

In the case of Mexico, Hiskey (2003) argues that in more competitive electoral environments, measured through the effective number of parties, public service provision is sensitive to public spending. In contrast, Cleary (2004) does not find an effect of electoral configuration on public service provision, although he does show that variables related to political participation, such as literacy and turnout, improve public service delivery.[11] Neither of these studies is too conclusive, however, because they both fail to address a problem of endogeneity; namely, that while changes in public good coverage can be the product of electoral competitiveness, competitiveness, in turn, is likely shaped by public goods.[12]

Other studies focus on the effects of particular political institutions on public service delivery. Elective public offices reserved for women leaders in India make local governments more representative by increasing the distribution of public goods preferred by women (Chattopadhyay and Duflo, 2001).[13] In a similar vein, Pande (2000) has shown that better representation of the scheduled caste in the Indian states improved the provision of education and land reform, which are policies that the poor would surely favor.[14] In poor indigenous communities in Mexico, traditional participatory institutions, referred to as *usos y costumbres*, distribute services in a more egalitarian manner than local representative institutions, where political parties tend to distribute services along clientelistic lines (Diaz-Cayeros et al., 2014).

To a large extent these studies get leverage from analyzing the distribution of funds across levels of government. The literature on decentralization is often premised on the notion that local governments are better at providing public services than centralized bureaucracies. In a study of Bolivian municipalities, for example, Faguet (2004) shows that decentralization made public expenditure decisions more effective for the provision of public goods. While decentralized public goods provision is often successful, the initial optimism regarding the virtues of decentralization has been tempered by a greater awareness that a crucial factor that determines whether a local government is capable of providing public goods is the accountability of local politicians to citizens (World Bank, 2004a; Bardhan, 2005).

To sum up, the general thrust of many of these empirical contributions has been to suggest the need to explore failures of electoral accountability and

---

[11] See Platteau (2006) for a discussion of participatory models of local-level development.
[12] In Chapter 7 we will show evidence suggesting that voters respond to public goods expenditures, which means that they are more likely to turn against incumbents when public goods and services fail, and to support governments that deliver better services.
[13] Kearny and Lott (1999) find that across countries greater female representation leads to larger government.
[14] Foster and Rosenzweig (2004) have shown that in India democracy means the empowerment of landless workers, which has led to land reform and higher public good provision, although not necessarily higher productivity. Bardhan and Mukherjee (2006), however, find no trade-off between land reform and increases in income.

ways to enhance good governance. Our approach in this chapter and the following builds on this work. We explore how clientelism distorts the delivery of collective benefits, including basic services and health. There is consensus in the scholarly literature that clientelism corrupts democracy and electoral accountability (Stokes, 2005; Kitschelt and Wilkinson, 2007; Kitschelt et al., 2011). Yet to our knowledge the negative effects of clientelism on government delivery of public goods and voters' welfare have not been systematically measured.

5.3 MODELING PUBLIC GOODS PROVISION

In the Mexican context, access to safe drinking water, electricity, and sewerage, among other local public goods, depends upon provision by municipal governments since the mid-1990s. While education and health facilities are also crucial inputs that impact well-being, their provision in Mexico has been decided from the center. Even after the decentralization of education in 1993 and health facilities a few years later, most of the financing for those two public goods remains federal (Courchene and Diaz-Cayeros, 2000), and the decisions regarding the location and support of schools and health clinics are primarily made by state and federal, not municipal, governments. In the empirical test that follows, we limit the analysis to municipal services, not including education and health provision.

Public spending in the past must account for most of the existing provision of local public goods, while current spending should impact that level only marginally, by investing in the maintenance and expansion of existing public assets. If we do not have data available measuring previous spending and the stock of past provision efforts, using as a dependent variable the *level* of public goods provision observed at a given point in time may involve a serious omitted variable bias. We may falsely attribute very large effects to current spending, only because of its inertial correlation with past expenditures. To solve this problem, the strategy suggested by Banerjee (2004) is to measure public service provision as a *first difference*. That way we avoid wrongly attributing levels of provision from the past to current spending.[15]

Furthermore, independent variables should also be measured as first differences. That is, changes in public goods provision should be affected by changes in municipal conditions, including shifting expenditure strategies. The advantage of measuring independent variables in this way is that even if some unobserved variables are omitted in the estimation, which may account for some of the cross-sectional variance, their omission does not bias the estimation, provided that these variables do not change over time.

---

[15] We employed this strategy in Diaz-Cayeros and Magaloni (2003), as does Hiskey (2003). An alternative specification is provided by Cleary (2004), who estimates levels of public service provision, but keeps the initial level of provision in the right-hand side. This strategy produces a higher R-squared, without changing the substantive findings.

The dependent variable in the analysis is the change in the coverage of public provision of drinking water, electricity, and sanitation services in Mexican municipalities according to census data.[16] Rather than estimating determinants for each service, we averaged the supply of the three public goods to generate a simple index.[17] The index is expressed as the log-odds ratio of the average coverage for the years 1990 and 2000. We chose not to use the mid-census estimations (*conteos*) due to issues of data reliability.[18] The dependent variable hence takes the form of this first difference:

$$\Delta \text{ Public Good Index} = \log[p_t/(1 - p_t)]_{2000} - \log[p_t/(1 - p_t)]_{1990}$$

Where $p_t = \Sigma r_i/3$ and r_i is the share of municipal households covered by a service i, namely, water, electricity, and sewerage in each census decade. We transformed the raw percentages into log-odds ratios because an OLS estimation using percentages yields predicted values that are implausible, falling outside the [0,1] interval (see Tucker, 2006). The transformation to log-odds ratio is also preferable because it fits more closely a normal distribution, and it is more sensitive to differences in the low and high ends of the variable's range (Cleary, 2004). However, a general and well-known problem with a

---

[16] We do not use the marginality or welfare indexes that have been calculated in Mexico by INEGI and CONAPO, because those factor analyses are not strictly comparable across years. More importantly, these indexes include too many census indicators related to *private welfare*, rather than public goods provision (e.g., individuals earning less than one minimum wage or the housing construction materials). We do not use a Human Development Index (CONAPO, 2000; UNDP, 2005) because it measures individual welfare, rather than public services, and we do not have reliable estimations for the HDI at the municipal level for 1990. Our index is highly correlated with all the conventionally used measures of municipal development in Mexico.

[17] We do not perform factor analysis or use other data reduction methods because we believe it is far more transparent to simply average the three services weighting them equally. It is important to note, however, that it is much more expensive to provide sewers than electricity; and that the demands among citizens are most intense for potable water.

[18] We refrain from making comparisons between the census and the population count of 1995 (as in Diaz-Cayeros and Magaloni [2003]), because careful examination of the data suggests that the *Conteos* overestimate the actual improvement in public service provision. The *Conteo de Población* is in fact based on two surveys: the *Enumeración* that counts all households in the country and the *Encuesta* (n=80,000), which has detailed information on families and social services based on 2,500 questionnaires per state. The *Conteo* in this sense is not a full count of public service delivery at the municipal level. For example, the average improvement in potable water provision between 1990 and 1995 is calculated as 9.4 percent; and the increased coverage in electricity is 10 percent. If these figures are correct, there was virtually no change in the provision of those services between 1995 and 2000. Although there was an economic crisis in 1995, it is likely that the techniques used to estimate public service provision in the *Conteos* at the municipal level are somewhat imprecise. We could have compared the provisions between 1995 and 2005, assuming that the bias is systematic among *Conteos*. Preliminary analysis suggests that our main results remain unchanged, although in that estimation we are unable to incorporate an assessment of *Pronasol* spending, given that the program had ended by 1995.

5.3 Modeling Public Goods Provision

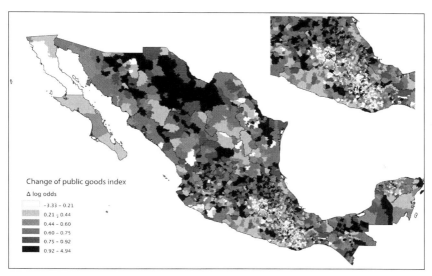

FIGURE 5.1. Change in public good coverage, 1990–2000.

logistic formulation is aggregation. If there is heterogeneity in public service delivery in the localities that comprise the municipality, the model will be correct for the municipal level, but not for lower levels of aggregation (Mookherjee et al., 1998).[19]

The public goods index coverage of the average municipality in Mexico was 58.9 percent in 1990, increasing to almost 69.7 percent by 2000. The average change in provision for that decade was 10.8 percent. Figure 5.1 maps the change in the index across Mexican municipalities. There were large differences in the provision of public services between poor and rich municipalities.[20] For example, in 1990 the first decile of the distribution of municipalities had an average coverage of 30.0 percent, while the top decile's average was almost three times as great, at 85.1 percent.

By 2010, the poorest municipalities had increased coverage to 44.5 percent and the richest municipalities to 91.1 percent. This means that the gap between rich and poor municipalities has somewhat narrowed. Improvements in local public goods progressed more rapidly among the lower half of the distribution. However, in 2000 the median municipality failed to provide these essential public goods to about one-fourth of its inhabitants, while the poorest municipalities still left almost half of their inhabitants without basic services.

---

[19] This Modifiable Unit Areal Problem (MUAP) might be particularly serious if the peripheral areas of a municipality have a much lower provision of public service than its urban center (*cabecera*). This aggregation problem would not be an issue in a linear OLS of direct coverage rates.
[20] The standard deviation of the index was 0.205 and 0.177 in 1990 and 2000, respectively.

Independent Variables

Studies by Cleary (2002 and 2004) and Hiskey (2003) provide important insights into variations in public service delivery in Mexico. However, both studies suffer from a methodological shortcoming in that they fail to address endogeneity concerns, which have been central to the work on impact evaluation in development economics (Rawlings and Schady, 2002). The problems at hand are twofold: first, budget appropriations are probably endogenous to investment outcomes. Funding allocations for social infrastructure projects for water, sanitation, and electricity are not independent from the perceptions policymakers have of where they believe they can get a larger return on their investment. While we seek to understand how much a given service, say potable water, improved as a consequence of public investment, the decisions regarding the allocation of discretionary funds across municipalities are most certainly influenced by engineering assessments of the conditions of the existing social infrastructure around the country and the likely impact policymakers and politicians believe spending in a particular place will have on the delivery of those social services. If this problem is not addressed, the estimations of the effects of policies may be seriously biased.

The same is true for other public services, such as electricity and sanitation. For example, if a politician wants to claim credit for a large improvement in the coverage of electricity in the few years of his short term in office, he might arguably prefer to allocate funds to urban places that already have a relatively well-developed grid, so that a large number of dwellings can improve very quickly. Or politicians might allocate spending in sanitation where it is more urgently needed, for instance, in some regions where the lack of a proper sewage system could produce a cholera outbreak or some other public health crisis. Policymakers in this case might actually be able to allocate resources with the highest priority to the places where no improvement has been observed in the past. These examples suggest that the selection of where to allocate electricity and sewerage projects might be determined precisely by the dependent variable we want to explain. The challenge is to find exogenous variation in expenditure or at least to isolate its exogenous component.

Municipal electoral democracy also exhibits identification challenges. The omitted correlates that account for levels of democracy (including higher electoral competitiveness, the presence of more political parties, and partisan alternation in office) are also likely to be related to changes in public goods provision. Results in the final chapter suggest, in fact, that changes in public goods provision influence electoral behavior. Thus, variables measuring levels of democracy and competition may well be at least partially endogenous, a consequence of the success or failure of earlier governments in delivering services.

To address these concerns, the literature on impact evaluations has become increasingly demanding about the use of instrumental variable approaches in order to obtain solid inferences concerning the impact of public investments.

5.3 Modeling Public Goods Provision

Zhurakvskaya (2000), for example, uses the Soviet legacy of industrial output over agricultural production as an instrument of spending, in order to assess its impact on public goods provision in Russia. Banerjee and Iyer (2005) take advantage of the different political organizations and land tenure arrangements among Indian princely states during the colonial era in order to assess the effect of land distribution on economic performance. Paxson and Schady (2002) use President Fujimori's vote share as an instrument to predict *Foncodes* resource allocations in Peru. In the following section, we explain the strategy employed to instrument the funding of *Pronasol* and FISM as well as the levels of democracy.

Instrumenting Pronasol Transfers

Public good expenditures in *Pronasol* were more concentrated in relatively developed municipalities. Despite widespread poverty in the South of the country, a visual inspection of the map in Figure 2.3 shows that few of those funds were targeted to those areas. *Pronasol* spending is measured as the log of average per capita *Pronasol* public goods expenditure, measured in real terms (1994 pesos).[21] If this spending had an effect on public service provision this variable should be positive.

To instrument *Pronasol*'s expenditures in public goods we employ *alpha*, which is our measure of PRI core support, as explained in Chapter 4. The earlier chapter demonstrated that *alpha* shaped expenditures within *Pronasol* and in this sense satisfies the first requirement for a good instrument – namely, being a strong predictor of our endogenous independent variable. The exclusion restriction – that the instrument be uncorrelated with the dependent variable – is also satisfied. Recall that *alpha* is calculated using data from 1970 until 1988 and is hence unaffected by changes in public goods coverage between 1990 and 2000. The share of core voters in the period 1970–1988 in a given municipality cannot be causally related to changes in public goods coverage, except through the way it shapes expenditures.

We also include an additional instrument for public goods expenditures, the Euclidean distance of each municipality from the railroad network. This geographic variable is exogenous to changes in public goods coverage, yet a remarkably good predictor of *Pronasol* expenditures. Railroads in Mexico were built fundamentally during the late nineteenth and early twentieth centuries. By 1990 no investment in railroad tracks had been made for half a century. Proximity to railroads does not directly influence improvements in public goods, because railroads have become mostly irrelevant for local market activity or passenger transportation (which now pass through the road network). This means that a municipality's proximity to a railroad is orthogonal to improvements in public infrastructure.[22]

---

[21] Estimations for total *Pronasol* expenditure were also run, yielding very similar results.

[22] It is important to note that we do not believe instrumental variable estimations are immune from important methodological criticisms, including that they may fail to address questions of

Although distance to railroads is uncorrelated to improvements in public goods provision, it is a good predictor of *Pronasol*'s expenditures on public goods. This is because the public goods projects that *Pronasol* financed were disproportionately assigned to urban and semiurban localities, which happen to be closer to railroad tracks.[23] Railroads were originally built to connect the main cities and mining towns with ports on the coast and the US-Mexico border. Municipalities that were closer to the railroads were better integrated along trading routes and they developed into more urbanized places. These types of localities happened to also benefit from higher levels of public infrastructure expenditures within *Pronasol*.

Simulated Instrumental FISM Transfers

The second program we evaluate is FISM. The allocation of these funds was in principle determined by a federal formula, but the actual implementation of this program gave room for states to choose how they would apply the formula. FISM allocations raise a problem of identification because unobserved variables may have caused some states to distribute funds among their municipalities according to desired impacts in public goods provision (precisely the variable we are trying to estimate). Fortunately, we can exploit some details regarding the implementation of the federal formula that generate exogenous variation in the funds municipalities receive, captured by the use of a simulated instrumental variable.

The federal formula for the allocation of FDSM created in 1997 was based on calculating gaps in public service provision and poverty, similar to a Foster-Greer-Thorbecke poverty index (Mogollón, 2012; Levy, 1998). These gaps provided estimates of so-called deprivation densities (*Masas Carenciales Estatales*), which determined the amount of funds states would receive.

---

heterogeneity and it is possible that even an "external" variable, such as geography, is nonetheless endogenous (see Deaton, 2010). However, Imbens (2010) suggests that with IV we may be reliably estimating the effects on "compliers" or local average treatment effects. We show that our instruments survive overidentification tests. And the quantile estimations at the end of this section provide some sense of the range over which our findings may be more solid. But in the end it is the substantive links between the actual processes driving the allocation of expenditure funds and political processes rather than purely econometric arguments that should be used to judge whether our instruments are plausible.

[23] Around 17 percent of the total *Pronasol* funds were allocated to drinking water and sewage projects and 13 percent to electricity. A separate breakdown of sewage and drinking water expenditure was not available due to the way *Pronasol* reported its programs. Elsewhere (Diaz-Cayeros and Magaloni, 2003) we tried to estimate the effect of each of the *Pronasol* expenditures separately: water and sewerage, electricity, municipal funds, and the remainder of the funds. The instrumental variable approach does not perform well with individual programs. Our instruments are not able to explain the breakdown of allocations by program, even when they work quite well for overall spending. The developmental impact of the program did not just depend on the expenditure of specific projects in isolation, but on the overall package of investment in a given municipality. Hence we believe the analysis with overall public goods funds is warranted.

5.3 Modeling Public Goods Provision

However, for the distribution from states to municipalities, governors could either use exactly the same federal formula, or choose a much simpler allocation formula based on similar variables (known as "formula 2"), and incorporating precisely the variables we use in our public goods coverage index (percentage of households with water, electricity, and access to sewerage) as well as the share of residents below the poverty line.[24] Nineteen states used the simpler formula, while twelve used the federal formula. Since the federal formula was calculated as a gap rather than just a headcount, it was better targeted to the poor.[25] Once the specific formula was chosen, governors had no discretion in the allocation of these funds to the municipalities. In addition to this choice of formula, during the first years of the FDSM/FISM, one-third of the funds were distributed to states in equal shares, regardless of their population size. State governments, in turn, were bound to distribute the total pool of state resources to their municipalities by their chosen formula.[26]

Our simulated instrumental variable approach captures how much allocations deviated from the counterfactual allocation that would have prevailed had states strictly followed the federal formula, giving greater weight to poverty gaps in fund allocation, instead of the "simpler" formula that most states actually used, which was heavily driven by population and prior public service coverage.[27] Specifically, we regress INEGI indicators of the percentage of households without electricity and sewerage, the illiteracy rate, the poverty headcount of population earning less than one minimum wage and the inverse of the population in 1995,[28] on the per capita FDSM/FISM funds between 1996 and 2000 (in real terms).[29]

---

[24] The federal formula gives almost half of the weight to poverty (0.4616), followed by the characteristics in the dwellings (0.2386, which are not included in "formula 2," related to overcrowding and construction materials), then illiteracy (0.125), electricity (0.114), and sewerage last (0.0608). The simplified formula gives equal weight to all four factors included in the estimation.

[25] The states that use the more targeted formula are Aguascalientes, Coahuila, Chiapas, Guanajuato, Hidalgo, México, Michoacán, Nayarit, Puebla, San Luis Potosí, Sonora, and Tamaulipas.

[26] The formulas have not changed since then; only the census indicators used to calculate them have been updated. The lump sum for each state was reduced to .5 percent of the funds, and eliminated altogether after 2001.

[27] This strategy is similar to Kosec's (2010) simulated instrumental variables estimation, in which she parses out endogenous changes in municipal fiscal effort by recalculating the potential allocation of funds to Brazilian municipalities in a preprimary program using a federal algorithm that simulates the budget allocation, instead of using the actual funds distributed to the municipalities.

[28] The inverse of the population is included due to a transitional rule that gave states for several years a fixed lump sum share of FISM, regardless of size. That coefficient measures the value of being a municipality, since it is the amount of funds each municipality gets in FISM regardless of its size or deprivation indicators.

[29] We have no breakdown of social spending data for 1995 at the municipal level, although there is anecdotal evidence suggesting a very large drop in federal allocations, as a consequence of the

TABLE 5.1. *Decentralized Allocations of Infrastructure Funds*

	(1)	(2)	(3)	(4)
	FDSM 1996	FDSM 1997	FISM 1998	FISM 2000
Pronasol	0.236	0.122	0.024	0.019
(log)	(0.018)**	(0.014)**	(0.011)*	(0.011)
No Electricity	0.414	0.448	0.840	0.833
	(0.067)**	(0.048)**	(0.041)**	(0.042)**
No Sewerage	0.298	0.491	0.867	0.866
	(0.061)**	(0.048)**	(0.045)**	(0.044)**
Wage Poverty	0.469	0.264	0.388	0.402
	(0.077)**	(0.061)**	(0.051)**	(0.052)**
Illiteracy	0.309	0.384	0.728	0.757
	(0.121)*	(0.081)**	(0.065)**	(0.066)**
Population	−0.362	−0.38	−0.013	−0.016
(log)	(0.011)**	(0.010)**	(0.008)	(0.008)*
Constant	5.654	6.685	3.773	4.451
	(0.189)**	(0.155)**	(0.130)**	(0.130)**
State Fixed Effects	YES	YES	YES	YES
Observations	2208	2208	2208	2208
R-squared	0.78	0.79	0.81	0.86

Note: Robust standard errors in parentheses.
* Significant at 5% level; ** significant at 1% level.

The results run separately for each year are reported in Table 5.1. Our simulated instrumental variable is the residual of this estimation, measuring how much FISM allocations per municipality depart from an implicit formula.[30] The simulated instrument can be interpreted as credibly capturing the exogenous variation in appropriations generated by federal law, excluding the endogenous variation due to states' own choices.

Just like the *Pronasol* expenditure variable, we expect FISM to have a positive sign, suggesting that when more money is spent, the percentage of households with access to basic public services will increase.

peso crisis. That year *Pronasol* was abandoned by the incoming Zedillo administration, to be substituted by a new fund for social infrastructure. A third of former *Pronasol* monies included in budgetary item 26 was decentralized in 1996; and the decentralized share became 2/3 in 1997. The FDSM, renamed FISM in 1999, thus became the most important federal transfer to municipalities.

[30] This estimation is similar to Mogollón's (2002) reverse engineering of the FISM formulas. In order to measure expenditure in a similar logarithmic metric to that of *Pronasol*, we made a monotonic transformation of the form: lresidual=log(1582+residual), where 1,582 is the minimum expenditure that ensures all values remain positive.

5.3 Modeling Public Goods Provision

Democracy

To estimate the impact of electoral accountability on public service delivery, we rely on several alternative metrics of democratization. Our first measure focuses exclusively on the impact of partisan alternation in office (a dummy variable where 1 indicates that the PRI lost power in a given municipality in the period between 1990 and 2000, and 0 otherwise). The second measures electoral competitiveness, a dummy variable that takes the value of 1 for municipalities that are marginally won or lost by 10 percent or less of the vote, and 0 otherwise. Our third measure looks at the number of years since a municipality first experienced partisan alternation in office. This can be thought of as a measure of democratic consolidation. Finally, we use an index of "local democratic practice" that reflects the variance in political competition and political change across Mexican municipalities (see Chapter 2). The index ranges from 1 to 7, where 7 reflects highly competitive municipalities in both federal and local elections that have also experienced partisan alternation in office.[31] This index is akin to measures of democracy that attempt to capture graduation in democratic quality, such as the Freedom House or Polity indexes, rather than a sharp categorical distinction between regimes.

Since levels of democracy, alternation in political power and small margins of victory are likely to be endogenous, we also require an identification strategy. We instrument democracy relying on the *alpha* parameter, which measures PRI core support. There is compelling evidence that democracy was more likely to take root in Mexico where the PRI was less entrenched. But we believe areas of core support for the PRI were the consequence of deep-rooted historical processes (including organizational linkages forged between peasant and worker confederations in the aftermath of the Mexican Revolution), which are unlikely to be associated with the change in the provision of public goods in the 1990s, for reasons other than the influence core supporters had on the assignment of public expenditures.

We rely on two additional geographic instruments. First we use the (Euclidean) distance to railroad tracks mentioned earlier. Investments in railroads took place almost exclusively before the foundation of the PRI in 1929. A municipality's proximity to a railroad determined its early chances of development, indicating whether a town was integrated into the main trading routes or stagnated in isolation. Municipalities that were connected to the railroads were thus better able to accumulate capital, tap information and cultural flows, and grow into larger towns. A municipality's location with respect to railroads

---

[31] Hiskey (2003) and Cleary (2004) test their hypotheses in an interactive way, showing that the effect of spending is mediated by the type of electoral competition. Our main concern is not this interactive effect, so we prefer to keep the simpler formulation of a direct control for the possible effect of democratic accountability on public goods provision. For a similar strategy pursuing an interactive effect of democracy on public good provision see Baum and Lake (2003).

hence shaped its long-term economic and institutional development, including its urbanization and propensity to democratize.

In addition, we instrument democracy with the East-West gradient (longitude) of a municipality's centroid. The geography of settlements in Mexico is not determined by the ease or difficulty with which their location facilitates public goods provision. A well-known North-South gradient of development persists in Mexico, wherein the areas of densely settled indigenous communities of Central and Southern Mexico are poorer than the rich towns and cities emerging from mining and cattle-raising activities in the North. But latitude is not a very plausible instrument for the effect of democracy on the changes in public good provision, because it is correlated with virtually every modernization indicator. A less acknowledged geographic feature in Mexico is that a longitude gradient of settlement patterns, in which the pre-Hispanic civilizations of the Toltec, the Maya, and particularly the Olmec, emerged from the southern Gulf of Mexico toward the central highlands, rather than towards the North or the West. Eastern settlements have a longer tradition of being subject to hierarchical social orders, while the West is characterized by more recent settlement in frontier spaces originally populated by nomadic groups.[32] As it turns out the longitude gradient is correlated with democratization, but is not a predictor of public good provision.

Sociodemographic and Fiscal Controls

As controls we use a set of independent variables that are consonant with the debates in the literature. First, we control for changes in literacy. This variable can be thought of as a control for political awareness and citizen demands for public services (Banerjee, 2002). It might also reflect overall levels of development. Cleary (2004) argues that although literacy is correlated with development, it can measure some of the participatory elements of democracy. We include the change in illiteracy, measured as the difference in the percent of population over 15 that could not read and write between the 2000 and 1990 censuses, as an indicator of lack of local empowerment.

For measures of social polarization, religious competition is the most salient cleavage that drives conflict in Southern Mexico (Trejo, 2009 and 2012). The connection between religion and conflict is related to religious organizations' active construction of social networks for pastoral purposes, spurred by the pressures of religious competition. Trejo shows that as a reaction to evangelical inroads in its dioceses, the Catholic Church in Chiapas became more attentive to the needs and demands of poor indigenous communities. This does

---

[32] As Spaniards conquered the Indian civilizations, "extractive" institutions (Acemoglu et al., 2002), including the *Encomienda* and the *Repartimiento*, were set in place, starting in the East and moving toward the center of the country. The inheritance of these institutions persists, making it harder for democracy to take hold in Eastern and Central municipalities compared to the ones in the West and the Northwest. The Yucatan peninsula to the East under these institutions may have in fact suffered from a clear "reversal of fortune."

5.3 Modeling Public Goods Provision

not mean that religious affiliation became a source of violence or contention, but rather that conflicts between citizens and state structures might be more intense in places with more active religious competition. A gap within indigenous groups is less prevalent, since localities tend to be more homogeneous in the ethnic dimension than in the religious one. We have thus calculated a measure of religious fractionalization, which is an index of how divided religious beliefs are in a municipality. We calculate the index defined as $F = 1 - \sum p_i^2$, where p is the share of each of the religious affiliations reported in the 1990 census (Protestantism, Catholicism, Judaism, other religions, and agnostic).[33]

A second indicator of social cleavages we use is the share of "bilingual" and "indigenous population," according to the 1990 census. The indigenous population variable is more inclusive, counting both bilingual and monolingual speakers of indigenous languages. While there is a very high correlation between being poor and Indian identity, the indigenous character of a community might not reflect divisiveness, but in fact improve the provision of public goods. This might be particularly true in places where social organization makes collective endeavors less subject to shirking and opportunism. For example, the most tightly knit communities in Oaxaca use the *Tequio* as a tax-like mechanism for the provision of public goods and services (Diaz-Cayeros et al., 2014).[34] Those municipalities often also use a system of rotation rather than party competition to choose their authorities. These traditional systems, called *usos y costumbres* have turned out to be a very effective form of governance.[35] Hence we do not expect a specific direction in the effect of this control variable.

We include a control for demographic change that might exert pressure on the existing physical infrastructure, measuring the rate of population change between 1990 and 2000 ("Population"). We expect the demographic variable to have a negative sign. We also include a measure of the changes in poverty rates. The measure is a "poverty headcount," defined as the share of individuals earning less than twice the minimum wage according to the 2000 and 1990 censuses. This variable should control for the distribution of poverty in the municipality.

---

[33] Perhaps reflecting the salience of this issue, the 2000 census includes a new category, breaking down Protestantism as Evangelical and non-Evangelical. The fractionalization index of 2000 increases compared to 1990, even without the finer categorization. However, it is likely that the largest increases in religious fractionalization occurred in the 1970s and 1980s.

[34] The *Tequio* is a form of community cooperation for the provision of local public goods. It involves compulsion, in the sense that members of the community must devote some of their labor for a collective enterprise, but it is voluntary to the extent that it accords with the traditional values of most members in the community.

[35] It is possible to use census data to construct an index of ethnic fractionalization going beyond the division between Indigenous and non-Indigenous, incorporating Indigenous subcultures. The ethnicity hypothesis, however, is somewhat peripheral to our project. Moreover, outside a few truly diverse municipalities in Chiapas and Oaxaca, high levels of ethnic fragmentation among Indigenous peoples are relatively rare.

Finally, public expenditure through federal programs is complemented by municipal funds. Public works spending by municipalities constitutes the part of their budget they invest, as distinct from expenditures for debt service and general administration (mostly comprising the municipal payrolls). On average, municipalities during this period spent about half of their budgets on public works. These budgets were much smaller than the total *Pronasol* funds, and relatively similar to FDSM/FISM funds.[36] We include municipally allocated public works spending (Local Public Works Budget or *lworks*), measured as the logged average per capita allocation from 1989 to 2000.

Hence, the reduced form of our estimations has the following specification:

$$\Delta \text{ Public Good Index}_{1990-2000} = \alpha_1 \text{ Pronasol (IV)}_{1989-1994} +$$
$$\alpha_2 \text{ FISM (Simulated IV)}_{1996-2000} +$$
$$\beta_1 \text{ Local democracy (IV)}_{2000} +$$
$$\gamma_1 \Delta \text{ Religious Fractionalization}_{1990-2000} +$$
$$\gamma_2 \Delta \text{ Indigenous Population}_{1990-2000} +$$
$$\gamma_3 \Delta \text{ Bilingual Population}_{1990-2000} +$$
$$\gamma_4 \Delta \text{ Population}_{1990-2000} +$$
$$\gamma_5 \Delta \text{ Poverty Headcount}_{1990-2000} +$$
$$\gamma_6 \Delta \text{ Illiteracy}_{1990-2000} +$$
$$\gamma_7 \text{ Local Public Works Budget}_{1989-2000} + \varepsilon$$

5.4 RESULTS

We now proceed to discuss the main findings. The results of the instrumental variable regressions are presented in Table 5.2. The first column is a naive regression without instrumenting for the endogenous explanatory variables, namely, *Pronasol* and partisan alternation in municipal office. Both variables show positive and statistically significant effects. Our simulated instrumental variable for FISM and local public works budget also impacts the provision of public goods in the same manner. The last columns, instead, provide instruments for *Pronasol* and alternation of political power in office, estimating one variable at a time or simultaneously. The results of the last model can be summarized as follows: FISM retains its strong positive effects on improvements in public goods coverage, whereas *Pronasol*'s impact becomes statistically insignificant. In other words, discretionary pork-barreling fails to deliver welfare enhancing infrastructure to the community at large, while nondiscretionary projects accomplish that feat.

The second finding is that local democratization is a strong predictor of gains in public goods provision. In order to assess the robustness of this finding, Table 5.3 presents the same basic model using our alternative specifications of local electoral democracy. Once again, *Pronasol* and the variables measuring electoral democracy are instrumented simultaneously. The table

---

[36] Public works expenditures by municipalities amounted to 27 percent of *Pronasol* funds.

5.4 Results

TABLE 5.2. *Improvements in Public Goods Coverage, 1990–2000*

	1	2	3	4	5	6
Pronasol	0.05	−0.19	−0.093	0.08	0.105	0.131
	(2.69)***	(1.84)*	(1.25)	(3.44)***	(4.03)***	(1.52)
Alternation	0.064	0.011	0.031	0.49	0.87	0.662
	(3.01)***	(−0.36)	(−1.21)	(2.68)***	(3.74)***	(4.17)***
FISM	0.432	0.481	0.46	0.409	0.387	0.387
	(1.95)**	(1.82)*	(1.87)*	(1.94)*	(1.95)*	(2.00)**
Observations	2399	2375	2375	2375	2388	2369
Endogenous Variable	None	Pronasol	Pronasol	Alt. Power	Alt. Power	Pronasol Alt. Power
Instruments	None	Alpha	Railroads Alpha	Alpha	Railroads Longitude	Railroads Alpha Longitude

Note: All models include a constant term and control variables in first differences: population growth, illiteracy, bilingualism, indigenous population, poverty, and religious fractionalization index changes. All models use robust standard errors. All expenditure variables are logged. Instruments pass the Sargan and Basmann tests of overidentification.

* Significant at the 10% level; ** significant at 5% level; *** significant at the 1% level.
t statistics in parentheses.

TABLE 5.3. *Effects of Alternative Measures of Electoral Democracy*

	1	2	3
Pronasol	0.094	−0.029	0.207
	(1.08)	(0.41)	(1.82)*
Dem. Index	0.111		
	(2.72)***		
Margin < 10%		0.237	
		(1.27)	
Alternation			0.109
			(3.40)***
FISM	0.451	0.469	0.516
	(2.09)**	(1.97)**	(2.01)**
Observations	2332	2332	2369
Endogenous Variable	Pronasol Dem. Index	Pronasol Margin	*Pronasol* Alt. power years
Instruments	railroads alpha longitude	railroads alpha longitude	railroads Alpha longitude

Note: All models include a constant term and control variables in first differences: population growth, illiteracy, bilingualism, indigenous population, poverty, and religious fractionalization index changes. All models use robust standard errors. All expenditure variables are logged. Instruments pass the Sargan and Basmann tests of overidentification.

* Significant at the 10% level; ** significant at 5% level; *** significant at the 1% level.
t statistics in parentheses.

shows that both the index of a minimalist definition of democracy as well as the number of years accumulated since the first turnover in partisan control of local government exhibit positive and statistically significant effects on public goods coverage.

Pronasol has no significant effects on the first two models, while FISM shows robust positive effects in all models. Overall, our results thus suggest that the decentralized and formula-based program, FISM, is robust in its impact upon municipal-level public service delivery. Local electoral democracy, by various definitions, also consistently drives our dependent variable. By contrast, the centralized/discretionary program, *Pronasol*, is clearly not robust in its meager effects.

The possibility that general results for these variables, including *Pronasol*, may hide distinct distributive effects within the total sample of municipalities, leads us to disaggregate the models. The challenges of providing basic public goods in highly marginalized municipalities are likely to be quite different from those facing more developed municipalities. The well-known thesis of the advantages of backwardness implies that poverty-stricken municipalities may exhibit faster improvements in public good coverage than rich municipalities.[37] Convergence might ensue because latecomers enjoy some advantages adopting technologies that may have become cheaper through time or expanding services that are already being provided elsewhere.[38] Furthermore, the administrative and political process through which poor municipalities improve public goods coverage is usually quite different from what obtains in richer municipalities. To explore the presence of this heterogeneity in our data, we perform quantile regressions.

This technique allows us to parse the range in the distribution of the dependent variable over which independent variables exert their influence. OLS remains the most efficient unbiased estimator when the conditional distribution is normal. But when there is strong heteroskedasticity and suspected nonlinear effects, the versatility of the quantile regression is that of allowing an estimation of effects not just at the mean, but at various quantiles of the full distribution of municipalities (q20, q40, q60, and q80). Instead of minimizing the sum of squared terms as in OLS, the technique finds the Least Absolute Deviations with respect to any cutoff point. The quantile regression is also more resistant to outliers. Deaton explains the advantage of quantile regressions:

Quantile regressions are not just useful for discovering heteroskedasticity. By calculating regressions for different quantiles, it is possible to explore the shape of the conditional distribution, something that is often of interest in its own right. (Deaton, 1997: 82)

---

[37] The opposite effect is also theoretically possible: where there is relatively good provision of public goods it might not be so expensive to extend the coverage, while in places with almost no public services the fixed costs might be very high.
[38] The speed of convergence for public service delivery in Mexico is relatively fast. We have estimated that the half-life of unconditional convergence (i.e., the time it takes for half of the initial gap between municipalities to be eliminated) is around eleven years for water and nine years for electricity.

5.4 Results

TABLE 5.4. *Alternation and Improvements in Public Goods Coverage, 1990–2000*

	q.2	q.4	q.6	q.8
^Alternation	−0.176	−0.027	0.036	0.331
	(0.93)	(0.23)	(0.36)	(1.95)*
^Pronasol	−0.26	−0.098	0.102	0.415
	(1.81)	(1.13)	(1.5)	(4.24)***
FISM	1.136	1.046	0.686	0.461
	(5.36)***	(5.23)***	(2.28)**	−1.5
Observations	2369	2369	2369	2369

Note: All models include a constant term and control variables in first differences: population growth, illiteracy, bilingualism, indigenous population, poverty, and religious fractionalization index changes. All models use robust standard errors. All expenditure variables are logged. Instruments pass the Sargan and Basmann tests of overidentification.
* Significant at 10%; ** significant at 5%; *** significant at 1%.
t statistics in parentheses.

Although quantile regression provides a more complete picture than OLS regression, one should be careful in its interpretation. As noted by Angrist and Pischke (2009), one can learn about the characteristics of the distribution, but not necessarily about individuals. Although we may find that a certain treatment (say, democracy) may have a positive effect in the provision of public goods for the lowest quintile of the distribution, that does not mean that the poorest municipalities are necessarily better provided when they have democracy. The estimation only tells us that a regime with democracy yields improvements at that lower tail of the distribution. Quantile regression will allow us to estimate differential effects for our covariates in municipalities that exhibit large improvement (normally the poorest) and in municipalities that exhibit smaller improvements (which tend to be richer).

Tables 5.4 and 5.5 study the differential effect of the two antipoverty programs and two measures of democracy on public goods provision. To be consistent, our endogenous variables are instrumented as before.[39] The results of these models provide interesting insights into the distributive effects of the independent variables: FISM shows positive and strong effects on improvements in local public goods provision in all but the highest quantile. FISM's impact increases for lower quantiles, suggesting that federal transfers for social infrastructure are better able to spur improvements in public goods provision at the lower end of the distribution. Strikingly, the opposite is true for *Pronasol*. The quantile regressions show that the discretionary poverty-relief program produced major improvements in public goods coverage only at the top end of the municipal universe. At the lowest end, it may well have contributed to a deterioration of public service delivery.

[39] This instrumentation means that our IV quantile regression is analogous to the QTE estimator discussed in Angrist and Pischke, 200.

TABLE 5.5. *Democracy Index and Improvements in Public Goods Coverage, 1990–2000*

	q.2	q.4	q.6	q.8
^Pronasol	−0.026	0.082	0.102	0.255
	(0.24)	(0.75)	(2.44)**	(3.31)***
^Dem. Index	0.118	0.105	0.259	0.823
	(2.67)***	(1.69)*	(2.84)***	(5.58)***
FISM	1.235	1.007	0.661	0.472
	(5.67)***	(5.08)***	(2.78)***	(1.43)
Observations	2369	2369	2369	2369

Note: We instrument for democracy and *Pronasol* with alpha, longitude, and distance to railroads. All models include a constant term and control variables in first differences: population growth, illiteracy, bilingualism, indigenous population, poverty, and religious fractionalization index changes. All models use robust standard errors. All expenditure variables are logged. Instruments pass the Sargan and Basmann tests of overidentification.

* Significant at 10%; ** significant at 5%; *** significant at 1%.

FISM performs much better than the decentralized decisions of mayors with respect to their own budgets. This could be the consequence of a "crowding-out" phenomenon, in which mayors see little reason to devote sizeable parts of their budget to public works when they know they have the earmarked FISM funds available. While FISM greatly improved targeting, its decentralized control by mayors might still have an urban bias. Such bias would limit its effectiveness in the improvement of public good provision.

With respect to the democratization, the results of the models show that partisan turnover in power had a strong positive impact on the highest quintiles, but nil effect in all the other quintiles. Apparently, its impact at the high end accounts for the result for the general models in Table 5.2. Perhaps a more fine-grained specification of local democracy can clarify the mechanisms behind this distributive impact. Thus we run the model for the index of democracy in Table 5.5. The results confirm in this specification very strong effects of democracy on improvements in the highest quantile, and also show smaller but positive and statistically significant impacts on the whole range of quantiles.

In sum, we find that the highly centralized and discretionary *Pronasol* program was at best a mixed blessing with respect to welfare enhancing infrastructure in Mexican municipalities. *Pronasol* appears to have widened the gap in public services between rich and poor territories. In dramatic contrast, the decentralized formula-based program, FISM, always has strong positive effects on public goods provision while its impact was skewed in favor of the most marginalized municipalities. The emergence of electoral democracy at the municipal level is also a significant factor accounting for improvements in public services in that decade. However, its distributive profile across

5.4 Results

all municipalities is much less redistributive than FISM. Democratization, in other words, does not entail the rapid catch-up in public goods promise that well-targeted government expenditures can accomplish. Nonetheless, in Mexico in the 1990s, democracy decidedly improved welfare at the local level. We turn now to the question of whether the effects observed in public goods provision, as well as direct transfers given to individuals, impacted well-being, based on an analysis of infant mortality. Did antipoverty programs in Mexico save lives?

6

Saving Lives: Social Programs and Infant Mortality Rates

> Whether the citizen lives or dies is not a concern of the state. What matters to the state and its records is whether the citizen is alive or dead.
>
> J.M. Coetzee

6.1 INTRODUCTION

More than 15 years after the Zapatista rebellion, infant mortality rates among indigenous people in Chiapas today are unacceptably high. According to the Health Ministry, in 2007 there was less than one doctor per 1,000 inhabitants in Chiapas, the lowest rate in the country, and nearly 25 percent of the population, mostly indigenous, had no access to any health service. Most of the indigenous population in that state live in a mountainous region, with only one hospital that serves more than 300,000 people spread across 17 municipalities. In the same zone there are only 6 community clinics offering basic services, and around 166 health units – primitive health centers with no doctors, medicines, or, often, even nurses. The infant mortality in the area is more than 40 per 1,000 live births, almost triple the national average of 16.7 for 2005.

Even when the rural poor can get to a clinic, doctors and nurses are often absent and basic medication is unavailable. Located within Guerrero's municipality of Metlatónoc, Mini Numa is the first community ever to sue the authorities in federal court for denying it basic health services and to win an *amparo* injunction to force the government to redress the situation. The court's ruling was unprecedented in Mexico as it affirmed that basic health is a fundamental right and that the state has an obligation to deliver it. The heroic judicial battle of the Nahua community in Mini Numa began after six preventable deaths occurred in 2007, which resulted from clinics being either too far away or nonoperational. People living in the small village had to walk two hours to get services; and upon arrival, they often found the clinic closed. The community

6.1 Introduction

asked the governor of Guerrero to build a health clinic, but the request was denied. The inhabitants of Mini Numa then built a health clinic themselves, only to have the authorities refuse to staff it. In 2008 the judge of one of the region's district courts ruled in favor of the community and, three months later, a doctor was finally sent to the community to begin providing basic health services. The judge's ruling, however, has met with only partial compliance and the state government has yet to build a new, court-prescribed hospital in Metlatónoc.

Mini Numa's battle is an illustration of the tragic consequences of extreme poverty. Poverty is a multifaceted condition going beyond low-income levels. It can encompass precarious living standards, deficient health, malnutrition, and lack of access to public services. The children of the extreme poor often die of curable diseases, such as diarrhea, respiratory infections, and other contagious diseases that barely affect the children of the nonpoor. In this chapter we discuss the impact of Mexico's antipoverty programs, centering on how they affect the life and death chances of the most vulnerable population, namely infants. As in the previous chapter, our goal is to compare two counterposed types of antipoverty policy – the clientelistic *Pronasol* and the entitlement-based *Progresa/Oportunidades* – with respect to their efficacy in preventing infant deaths in Mexico's poor communities. We also seek to assess whether democracy and electoral accountability play a role in reducing infant mortality.

Despite the dismal statistics still present among indigenous people in Mexico, infant mortality rates have been declining for the past three decades after the country embraced UNICEF's GOBI initiative (Growth monitoring, Oral rehydration, Breastfeeding and Immunization), and the child survival revolution. Although mortality remains unacceptably high, there has been substantial improvement between 1990 and 2000, particularly in the poorest states. Our goal in this chapter is to assess the extent to which the various antipoverty programs contributed to this decline.

Our work contributes to a vibrant debate within the political science literature on the effects of political regimes on infant mortality rates (IMR). Existing comparative literature has focused on how democracy reduces mortality (Przeworski et al., 2000; Navia and Zweifel, 2003; Zweifel and Navia, 2000; Ross, 2006; Gerring et al., 2005; Lake and Baum, 2001; Baum and Lake, 2003). We depart from this literature in that we study the effects of the design of public policies in the reduction of IMR. Our work shows how improved provision of public goods, such as drinking water, sewerage, and electricity impact IMR; we also look at the impacts of conditional cash transfers (CCTs) versus discretionary transfers to individuals based on patron-client networks.

Social infrastructure programs such as FISM or *Pronasol*'s public goods programs might have an indirect effect on infant mortality through their impact on sanitation and the construction of health clinics and roads. Clientelistic programs such as *Pronasol*'s *crédito a la palabra* (a subsidized credit program) might have an indirect effect on infant mortality by increasing household's income. CCTs, for their part, might have both direct and indirect effects on infant health. Household's increase in cash availability facilitates access to health services. But CCTs also might have a direct effect related to how the program conditions the cash transfer on regular health visits and women health education programs.

The chapter proceeds as follows. The next section briefly discusses the existing comparative literature on infant mortality and how we depart from the conventional approach by assessing policy interventions rather than focusing exclusively on regime type. The third section reviews the national trends for IMR, discussing data quality issues that emerge from shifting from national to local measurements of infant mortality. The section calls for a better understanding of the processes of data collection and reporting in the use of off-the-shelf datasets, which anchor most cross-national research strategies. In particular, the section discusses problems of underreporting and excessive reliance on forecasting models in available IMR datasets in Mexico. The fourth and fifth sections estimate statistical models of changes in municipal IMRs and explore the distributive effects of various poverty-relief interventions and local democratization.

6.2 COMPARATIVE STUDIES OF INFANT MORTALITY

There is an important debate within political science regarding the effect of political regimes on infant mortality. In their path-breaking study of democracy and development, Przeworski et al. (2000) found that democratic regimes generate a host of impacts on demographic behavior, fertility rates, the spacing of children, and their chances of survival. Controlling for regime-selection effects, democracies lead to lower population growth, higher life expectancies, fewer child deaths, and thus enhanced well-being. A crucial element in these findings is that the mechanism for improvement in human development is not simply a higher level of health spending by democracies. What democracies seem to do better than autocracies is to empower women to make free choices about their own fertility and to enjoy higher relative wages.

Lake and Baum (2001) explore the effect of regime type on public health outcomes and public goods provision, finding that democracies are more likely to reduce IMR. Navia and Zweifel (2003) find similar effects, controlling for regime-selection bias. In their most recent work, they show that, beyond a direct positive effect of democracy in reducing IMR by around 5 percent, policy interventions purportedly aimed at reducing IMR, such as immunization campaigns, generate positive effects only in democracies. They posit that these findings are consistent with the likelihood that democracy provides the public services that citizens actually want.[1] All of these studies are based on cross-national comparisons using readily available official statistics.

---

[1] Gerring et al. (2005) argue that, within democracies, there are some institutional characteristics (which they call centripetalism) that lead to greater improvements in human well-being. In

6.2 Comparative Studies of Infant Mortality

Kudamatsu (2012) shows that democracy in Africa decreased IMR by an astonishing 18 deaths per 1,000. His analysis differs from previous work in that he uses individual-level data from the Demographic and Health Surveys (DHS), which permit an identification of the effect of democracy by comparing children born to the same mother under different political environments. The mechanisms underlying the findings are related to the improvement of health interventions leading to more medical attention at birth, breastfeeding, and, in general, better health services.

Using historical data from the United States, Miller (2008) found an effect of female enfranchisement upon the survival of children (an improvement ranging between 8 and 15 percent). This analysis is based on a careful reconstruction of IMR across the United States, taking advantage of the differential timing of enfranchisement. In this account, the mechanism that explains the outcome is a shift in legislative behavior once women were given the right to vote, which is followed by rapid increases in local public health spending. This is one of the few studies providing an explicit link between IMR and political arrangements mediated by budgetary priorities and legislative behavior.

Ross (2006) has cast doubt on cross-national analyses of IMR, calling for a greater awareness of the problems of validity in available datasets. In particular, he shows that if missing data in autocracies with relatively good development performance are taken into account, the main findings in the literature tend to disappear. The econometric estimations he proposes include country fixed effects, to control for likely omitted variable biases incurred in the prevailing work. Democracy seems to have no effect in reducing infant deaths.[2]

The only analysis exploring these issues in Mexico is the work by Tania Barham (2011) evaluating the impact of *Progresa* on IMR. In her carefully designed study, she calculates that *Progresa* diminished infant deaths in rural areas, as reported in vital registration statistics, by around 11 percent (i.e., too fewer deaths per 1,000 live births). This effect is found in municipalities where the program was implemented by random assignment at an early date, as compared to a control group of municipalities chosen for inclusion, but left untreated. The statistical approach she uses takes advantage of the experimental setting of these temporal waves in the introduction of *Progresa*, in order to isolate the effect of treatment on otherwise nearly identical rural communities. Hence Barham (2011) finds a clear link between one poverty-relief program and the decline of child mortality. But what about the earlier programs administered under the umbrella of *Pronasol* from 1989 to 1994? Or the far-reaching

---

particular, their statistical analysis suggests that centralized versus decentralized political systems, proportional representation versus SMD electoral rules, and parliamentarism versus presidentialism are associated with greater reductions in IMR.

[2] However Gerring et al. (2005) retort that democracy's most important effect on IMR is cumulative, rather than immediate: the effect of democratic transitions in a given country is rather small, while the accumulated years of democracy empower citizens and preserve lives.

decentralized strategy for municipal provision of basic public services since 1996? How have these strategies contributed to the reduction in IMR, compared to *Progresa/Oportunidades*?

There is general agreement among the public health community that public policy interventions have contributed to the reduction of IMR. IMR trends in Mexico are historically preceded by important policy initiatives, including the widespread distribution of oral rehydration salts since 1984, efforts to extend universal vaccinations since the 1990s and the improvement of water quality with the chlorination program in 1992 (Sepúlveda et al., 2006). But studies have failed to specify the channels and mechanisms through which policies affect outcomes. The link is plausibly posited but untested. Statistical analyses of the determinants of IMR based on health surveys, to which the public health community has been very attentive, have failed to determine how important the influence of specific policy interventions are vis-à-vis socioeconomic and physiological factors, because individual-level databases rarely include many policy related and social variables – let alone political ones.

Our working hypothesis is that the antipoverty programs we have analyzed, all of them, should have indirect and/or direct effects on infant mortality. First, social infrastructure projects from *Pronasol* and FISM affect IMR indirectly by improving access to drinking water, sanitation, electricity, roads, and health clinics. The previous chapter modeled how these programs shaped improvements in public goods provision and showed that formula-based public goods transfers within FISM were more effective at targeting the poor than the discretionary pork-barreling projects within *Pronasol*. Here we focus on understanding how improvements in public goods provision during the 1990s shaped reductions in IMRs at the municipal level. Second, we model the direct and indirect effects of *Progresa* transfers and *Pronasol*'s clientelistic allocations on IMR. Our expectation is that private good transfers within each of these programs shape IMR by increasing a family's disposable income. After some time, the CCT program's more direct impact on targeted health monitoring should translate into a much larger effect in infant death.

6.3 ISSUES IN MEASURING IMR

Infant deaths provide an undeniable indicator of well-being linked to development policy. Notwithstanding the deprivation of poor regions like Oaxaca, Guerrero, Hidalgo, and Chiapas, overall IMRs in Mexico have declined substantially in the past twenty-five years. These reductions coincided with important innovations in public health and the implementation of different poverty-relief strategies. Although statistical sources vary in their estimates, it is fair to say that IMR in Mexico fell from around 50 deaths per 1,000 in 1980, to levels slightly above those found in developed countries (19 per 1,000 in 2005). The same trend is observed in the children under five years of age (Sepúlveda et al., 2006).

6.3 Issues in Measuring IMR

Still, failures in government policy and the overall social environment in which poor children live are key determinants of mortality. An early study on poverty in Mexico concluded that 43 percent of deaths in 1974 were preventable (Coplamar, 1982), in the sense that timely health interventions could have saved their lives. Despite great strides in public health in the intervening years, the percentage of preventable deaths has barely changed. Twenty years after the landmark Coplamar study, the Health Ministry estimated preventable deaths still at around 38 percent during 2000–2004 (*Secretaría de Salud*, 2006). For the specific case of infants, the Health Ministry calculates the percentage of preventable deaths in recent years at around 80 percent. Most infant mortality is related to common infectious diseases, which are preventable with simple medical interventions if appropriate and opportune care is available.

The reduction in infant mortality in Mexico is part of a worldwide phenomenon, and a clear continuation of downward trends observed throughout the century (Roberts, 1973; Bobadilla and Langer, 1990). Mexico is usually considered a success story because it is one of only seven developing countries on track to meeting Millennium Development Goal Number 4: to reduce the underfive mortality rate by two-thirds by 2015 (Bryce et al., 2006).[3] Notwithstanding the national trend of declining mortality during the past decades, there is significant regional variation within Mexico, with some regions experiencing sharper reductions in IMR than others.

To study the regional variation of IMR in Mexico, we first need to tackle an important problem related to the availability of data at the municipal level, which is our unit of analysis. The tragedy of child deaths often goes unnoticed – and therefore uncounted – by both government officials and the public at large. The main thrust of the Ross (2006) critique is that many countries without democracy have better outcomes in IMR, but are frequently not included in international health data due to inadequate reporting. Statistical analysis based on publicly available datasets often entail case-wise deletion of missing values, which can lead to dubious conclusions. Moreover, with the exception of Kudamatsu's (2012) use of individual-level survey data, the cross-sectional literature has often not been very conscious of the measurement issues that plague demographic studies of infant mortality. Specifically, the most widely used IMR datasets from the World Health Organization (WHO), the United Nations Children's Fund (UNICEF), and the World Bank involve a mix of official country data based on vital registration statistics, census information, and survey data.

The problem with using IMR data without understanding their provenance is that estimates can differ according to the methods used to generate them. In particular, IMR statistics are plagued with two problems that determine their quality, namely, the way in which they deal with underreporting and the technical choices made in forecasting models. Researchers need to be mindful of the advantages

---

[3] Mexico is expected to reach 15 deaths per 1,000 by 2015 (comparable to US rates in the 1970s).

and disadvantages of the different methods employed to measure IMR and to be explicit about their reasons for choosing one data source over another.

Arguably the most comprehensive effort to deal with the issues of data quality and comparability in IMR across countries has been done by UNICEF.[4] Infant Mortality Rates are calculated by UNICEF as the best fit model combining direct survey responses, indirect census estimations and official vital registration statistics. Direct estimations of IMR in Mexico are made using the reconstruction of birth cohorts reported in health surveys, such as the internationally sponsored Demographic and Health Survey (DHS) from 1987 and the *Encuesta Nacional de Dinámica Demográfica* (ENADID) from 1997. An alternative source of IMR data for Mexico comes from official vital statistics collected by the civil registry, as reported by the national statistical office (INEGI).

Both UNICEF and direct estimations from surveys show much higher IMRs than vital registration data. The gap between sources is in the range of around 20 deaths per 1,000. This means that, given the general decline of IMR over the years in Mexico, underreported deaths in vital statistics are an increasingly relevant problem in counting actual infant deaths, defying the downward secular trend. Increases in infant mortality calculated through vital statistics might represent efforts by public officials to improve the registration of children. But they might also signal periods in which the reduction of infant deaths in fact stagnated (say in the early 1970s and late 1980s).

There is hence an obvious challenge in using vital statistics data as an indicator of IMR, particularly since the poorest localities are the least likely to register births and deaths. In addition, according to INEGI, around 40 percent of births in Mexico are registered after a child is more than one year old. In short, calculating infant deaths from vital registries is not very reliable. One of the limitations of the Barham (2011) study on the effects of *Progresa* on IMR is precisely that it employs vital statistics.[5]

INEGI calculates an alternative disaggregated IMR through demographic models from the relatively reliable census data, estimating deaths and births by mother cohort. Their method does not interpolate or extrapolate and calibrates yearly estimates through independent models of fertility patterns.[6] As

---

[4] The methodology developed by Hill et al. (1999) to fit the best curves to the available information has become the standard for official estimations of international IMR made by the Inter Agency Group for Mortality Estimation, which includes the World Bank, UNICEF, WHO, and the UN Population Division (UNPD). Those estimates are calculated for the purpose of benchmarking progress toward the Millennium Development Goals.

[5] To use vital statistics we need to assume that the quality of the official records remains constant over time or vary in the same manner in all places under study. This might be reasonable in a short time frame, but is clearly not a tenable position for longer periods.

[6] It is based on demographic indirect estimation models, in which the difference in the age structure between censuses is used to infer the missing individuals in the various age cohorts.

6.4 The Determinants of IMR Decline

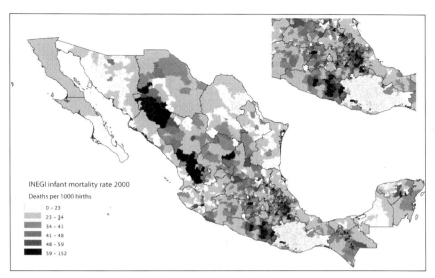

FIGURE 6.1. Geography of infant mortality rate in 2000.

shown in Figure 6.1, municipal IMRs calculated by INEGI have an average value of 47.5 per 1,000 in 1990 and 34.6 in 2000.[7] The level of those indicators and the decline over the decade are consistent with the calculations of IMR obtained from health surveys, such as ENADID. If we accept the INEGI estimations, municipal vital registration data suffer from underreporting. In the average municipality only 40 percent of the infant death ratios are registered; and in the bottom quartile of the municipalities only one quarter of the ratios between deaths and births are ever registered.[8]

6.4 THE DETERMINANTS OF IMR DECLINE

In order to explore the determinants of the performance of municipalities in children's health, and in particular, the role of antipoverty policies in the reduction of infant mortality, we estimate a statistical model in first differences. The

---

[7] The change in IMR across Mexican municipalities over the ten-year census interval does not exhibit a simple North-South divide, since there is substantial variation across municipalities within any given state. This suggests that state-level analyses are probably not particularly reliable for understanding the determinants of IMR. For a statistical analysis at the state level using survey data see Lozano et al. (2006).

[8] Underreporting is correlated negatively with the level of development, but the correlation is not so strong that one can use the level of development as a proxy for the correction factor that should be used to adjust vital registration data.

dependent variable is the change in every municipality's IMR between 1990 and 2000. The differentials use indirect estimations based on the reconstruction of births and deaths according to census data, as calculated by INEGI. The model includes improvements in basic public goods, variables measuring antipoverty policies, and municipal changes in political regime. Controls for demographic and health interventions include changes in the level of female illiteracy (as a proxy for maternal capabilities), changes in the rate of infant delivery under doctor supervision, shifts in the quality of birth registrations, population growth and changes in the poverty headcount.

$$\Delta \text{IMR}_{1990-2000} = \alpha_1 \text{ Pronasol Spending }_{1989-1994} +$$
$$\alpha_2 \text{ Progresa Coverage }_{1997-2000} +$$
$$\beta_1 \text{ Democracy (Instrumented) }_{1990-2000} +$$
$$\gamma_1 \Delta \text{ Public Goods}_{1990-2000} +$$
$$\gamma_2 \Delta \text{ Doctor Deliveries }_{19990-2000} +$$
$$\gamma_3 \Delta \text{ Delay in Registration }_{1990-2000} +$$
$$\gamma_4 \Delta \text{ Population}_{1990-2000} +$$
$$\gamma_5 \Delta \text{ Poverty}_{1990-2000} + \varepsilon$$

It should be noted that municipalities with strong declines in mortality are found throughout the country. Places with most improved infant well-being cluster near the Huasteca region, the mountainous zone of Puebla and the state of Chiapas. Coastal municipalities and most northern ones have witnessed much smaller improvements over the decade. A Moran test for spatial autocorrelation, however, found no systematic spatial patterns in the declines of IMR across neighboring municipalities, so no spatial correction is made in the estimations.

The independent variables of interest are three antipoverty policies. The first is the household coverage of *Progresa* by the end of 2000. Since *Progresa* transferred cash and nutritional supplements while requiring medical checkups for children, IMR should decline as a consequence of greater coverage, which would be indicated by a negative sign. Mothers benefiting from *Progresa* take their children in for regular physical exams and vaccinations, and also receive information on breastfeeding, oral rehydration therapy, and basic hygiene. Given that *Progresa* was allocated according to a system of targeting at locality and household levels, it is important to control for the poverty profile of municipalities so that the substantive indicator reflects the effect of the intensity of *Progresa* participation, given a certain poverty level.

We also include the prevalence of clientelism in each municipality, as measured by the per capita private goods provision targeted to individuals and groups through *Pronasol*. This variable might affect IMRs thorough an income effect among benefited households. Given that these transfers were not conditional on health interventions, but rather on political behavior, the relative

6.4 The Determinants of IMR Decline

effect should be much smaller than the one observed for conditional cash transfers.

The third policy variable is the change in the index of public goods provision of water, sewerage, and electricity used in Chapter 5, as an indicator of the improvements in local public goods. This variable reflects infrastructural investments under *Pronasol* and the decentralized funds of FISM after 1996. As demonstrated in the previous chapter, local public goods provision improved only slightly through *Pronasol* expenditure, whereas decentralized funds in FISM were much more effective in expanding public service delivery. We expect this variable to show a negative sign, since greater coverage of public goods should be associated with lower IMR.[9]

To measure democratic practices at the municipal level, we follow an approach similar to the previous chapter, where we used alternative specifications for electoral democracy. The analysis poses a problem of econometric identification, which we address following the approach used in Chapter 5.

We include two indicators of state capacity from vital statistics. The first is the change in the share of babies delivered by doctors in each municipality.[10] The second is the change in the average delay of registering children after they are born. The lower the state capacity, the more we expect families to delay registering their children. These state capacity indicators should show a positive sign.

As a measure of poverty, we include changes in the percentage of the population living below two minimum wages (using one minimum wages makes no difference in the results). Widespread poverty limits the choices and capabilities of mothers and families, so we expect a positive sign in this level variable, indicating a greater difficulty in reducing IMR where poverty is more prevalent.

---

[9] We also ran regressions disaggregating the components of the index – changes in water, sanitation, and electricity. We also tested for the inclusion of a variable measuring the per capita expenditures in regional hospitals from IMSS-Solidaridad. These were *Pronasol* expenditures that were devoted to the construction of hospitals, such as the one built in Guadalupe Tepeyac that was never staffed. Results were robust to those variables.

[10] We have information on the availability of nurses in the public health system, the location of the 11,551 hospitals and clinics previously run by the Health Ministry, now decentralized to the states, and the population with no access to the social security system (IMSS and ISSSTE). We also collected data on doctors and the number of beds and doctor's offices. Unfortunately, we have this information only at the end of the period of study, which precludes their use in first differences. We were unable to obtain municipal-level information of the expansion of IMSS-*Solidaridad* (called IMSS-*Coplamar* in the 1980s, and now IMSS-*Oportunidades*), which used the infrastructure and funds of the social security institute to cover population in some of the poorest areas of the country. Specific public health interventions, such as the introduction of rehydration therapy or the water chlorination program of 1992, might have contributed to reducing children deaths at low costs during those years. We could not locate a data source for any of these interventions. Of all these variables, only nurses and access to social security were correlated with IMR declines, but this is probably only a reflection of their underlying correlation with poverty profiles.

TABLE 6.1. *Determinants of Changes in IMR in Mexico, 1990–2000*

	1 Change in IMR (1990–2000)	2 Change in IMR (1990–2000)	3 Change in IMR (1990–2000)	4 Change in IMR (1990–2000)
Change public Goods index	−2.521 (2.64)***	−2.49 (2.57)**	−2.531 (2.42)**	−2.559 (2.72)***
Alternation	−0.317 (0.56)	−0.062 (0.09)	−19.301 (1.92)*	−6.362 (1.82)*
Clientelism	0.494 (2.20)*	1.359 (1.03)	−0.585 (0.94)	−1.125 (0.81)
CCT	−58.779 (6.55)***	−64.782 (4.82)***	−101.024 (4.15)***	−62.378 (4.47)***
Observations	1817	1817	1814	1814
R-squared	0.18	0.17	0.16	0.12
Endogenous Variable	None	Clientelism	Alternation	Clientelism Alternation
Instruments	None	Alpha Erosion	Railroads Longitude	Railroads Longitude Alpha Erosion

Note: All models include a constant term and control variables in first differences: population growth, illiteracy, poverty, and doctor delivery and delay in registration changes. All models use robust standard errors. Instruments pass the Sargan and Basmann tests of overidentification.
* Significant at 10%; ** significant at 5%; *** significant at 1%.
t statistics in parentheses.

Table 6.1 shows the results of our IV-regressions. The first column reports the results of a simple regression that does not instrument for clientelism and electoral democracy. Model 2 instruments for clientelism, model 3 for electoral democracy, and model 4 for both variables simultaneously.

The main findings can be summarized as follows: the conditional cash transfer program of *Progresa* always exhibits a strong and statistically significant effect. Clientelism increases IMR in the first model; but once instrumented it fails to have discernible effects on changes in infant mortality. Improvements in local public goods (water, sanitation, and electricity) have consistent negative effects, indicating that their expansion in the 1990s helped to reduce IMRs. Democracy, as reflected in municipal alternation, shows a similar effect to that found in the previous chapter. There seems to be some effect of greater accountability in health outcomes brought about by electoral contestation.[11]

[11] Our variable of lack of state capacity measured as delay in registration has strong positive effects, suggesting that IMR is higher where the state has little reach. Surprisingly, health infrastructure as reflected in doctors delivering babies has no effect on reducing IMR. The sociodemographic variables all have predictable effects on IMR. Illiteracy strongly impacts IMR, while parental

6.4 The Determinants of IMR Decline

TABLE 6.2. *Effect of Democracy on Changes in IMR in Mexico, 1990–2000*

	1	2	3
Dem. Index	−0.673		
	(0.97)		
Margin		0.537	
		(0.16)	
Years Alternation			−0.598
			(1.77)*
Pronasol private	−0.451	0.567	−0.833
	(0.32)	(0.42)	(0.65)
Change in public goods index	−2.503	−2.496	−2.552
	(2.62)***	(2.56)***	(2.76)***
CCT	−63.086	−55.831	−57.908
	(4.21)***	(3.60)***	(4.35)***
Observations	1786	1786	1814
R-squared	0.17	0.18	0.14
Endogenous	Dem. Index	Margin	Years Alternation
Variable	Clientelism	Clientelism	Clientelism
Instruments	Railroads	Railroads	Railroads
	Longitude	Longitude	Longitude
	Alpha	Alpha	Alpha
	Erosion	Erosion	Erosion

Note: All models include a constant term and control variables in first differences: population growth, illiteracy, poverty, and doctor delivery and delay in registration changes. All models use robust standard errors. Instruments pass the Sargan and Basmann tests of overidentification.
* Significant at 10%; ** significant at 5%; *** significant at 1%.
t statistics in parentheses.

Table 6.2 estimates similar models using various specifications for electoral democracy. As in the last column of Table 6.1, the models in Table 6.2 instruments for clientelism and electoral democracy simultaneously. A clear pattern emerges from the data suggesting that only alternation of political power at the municipal level makes a difference in health outcomes for the poor, rather than overall levels of electoral competitiveness. The cumulative years since a municipality first experienced political alternation in power and the alternation dummy variable in the 1990s (reported in Table 6.1) have negative and statistically significant effects on IMR. Yet, the index of democracy and close margins of victory do not seem to impact health. In any event both expansion in public goods coverage and the spread of Progresa always reduce infant mortality rates.

> education seems to consistently bring improved health outcomes. Demographic dynamics at the municipal level make it harder to improve children's health. Reductions in poverty also have strong negative effects on IMR.

TABLE 6.3. *Quantile Regression of Infant Mortality Change, 1990–2000*

	q.2 Change in IMR (1990–2000)	q.4 Change in IMR (1990–2000)	q.6 Change in IMR (1990–2000)	q.8 Change in IMR (1990–2000)
chpubgoods	−1.632	−2.627	−2.572	−1.934
	(2.96)***	(2.68)***	(2.10)**	−1.45
^Alternation	−0.219	−5.038	−6.103	−6.967
	(0.08)	(2.62)***	(2.03)**	(2.73)***
^ clientelism	−4.297	−1.978	0.481	1.411
	(2.17)**	(0.9)	(0.19)	(0.68)
oportoo	−50.147	−63.604	−61.956	−66.076
	(3.58)***	(3.88)***	(3.58)***	(3.25)***
Observations	1814	1814	1814	1814

Note: Alternation and clientelism are instrumented with alpha, erosion, distance to railroads, and longitude. All models include a constant term and control variables in first differences: Pronasol hospitals and clinics, population growth, illiteracy, indigenous, poverty, doctor delivery, and delay in registration changes. All models use robust standard errors. Instruments pass the Sargan and Basmann tests of overidentification.
* Significant at 10%; ** significant at 5%; *** significant at 1%.
t statistics in parentheses.

6.5 QUANTILE REGRESSIONS

The challenge of improving infant health in highly marginalized zones is likely to be different from reducing deaths in wealthier places. Because of convergence, highly marginalized municipalities tend to exhibit faster improvements in health than rich ones. To explore this heterogeneity in our data, we perform quantile regressions to estimate differential effects for our covariates in municipalities that exhibit large improvements (normally the poorest) and in municipalities that exhibit smaller changes. Because of the way the data is coded, municipalities that exhibit the largest reductions in IMR are in the lowest quantiles.

Table 6.3 dissects the differential effects of our main variables of interest on infant mortality. Our two endogenous variables are instrumented in the same manner as before. The results of the quantile regressions are striking. *Progresa* shows a consistently strong negative effect on IMR for all quantiles. Similarly, expansion in public goods coverage reduces IMR across the board. Clientelism lowers IMR only in the bottom quantile (q.2), suggesting that under some conditions destitute poor benefited from this form of political linkage. It should be emphasized that any effect of clientelism pales in comparison to *Progresa* and to actual improvements in public goods.

6.6 FINAL REMARKS

When transferring funds to individuals based on their political loyalty becomes the overriding consideration in the design of social policies, the developmental

6.6 Final Remarks

goal of using social programs to help the poor is distorted. That does not necessarily mean that social policies are irrational or always wasteful. Public administrators tend to think that better management of personnel, better planning and oversight, and improved mechanisms for controlling corruption are the best way to make sure that public policies can help the poor. Our analysis suggests, instead, that democracy and the empowerment of women are more promising solutions than seeking to reform governance by administrative design.

Results in this chapter demonstrate that the creation of better-designed social policies targeted to poor women has had a decisive impact on development by saving the lives of children. New social programs such as FISM and *Progresa* that came as a result of stronger checks and balances increased electoral competition, and decentralization improved the provision of municipal public goods and allowed poor families greater access to health services.

Our results also demonstrate that there were some clear effects of local democracy on the reduction of IMR. Municipalities that experienced an alternation of power between political parties are better at preserving infants' lives than municipalities that remained under the exclusive hegemonic control of the PRI.

Democracy does not necessarily lead to increases in funding for social programs or a greater budgetary priority for social expenditures, nor does it induce a normative consensus in society to address the plight of the poor. But the introduction of checks and balances brought about by democracy generated the possibility for a compromise among politicians, which led to a better architecture of social policies. The social policies chosen in Mexico combined elements of decentralized decision making for the municipalities, with centralized control by the federal government over the conditional cash transfer program. As the federal government allocated fewer funds to the goal of fighting poverty, compared to the largesse witnessed under *Pronasol*, it also shifted away from the expensive clientelistic strategies of vote buying in favor of a greater orientation toward public goods provision and the empowerment of the most vulnerable citizens through *Progresa*.

There are some painful lessons for Mexico and its clientelistic past: thousands of children likely would have remained alive had the transformation of programs occurred a few years earlier. As mentioned in the introduction, Subcomandante Marcos was right in pointing out that children died from curable diseases and no one took notice. *Pronasol*'s claims about "putting an end to poverty" are assessed against a clearly defined metric: Was the program able to save the lives of the most vulnerable? Our results suggest that its effects were at best marginal; some poverty alleviation took place, but it was marginal compared to what better-designed poverty-relief policies achieved.

7

Electoral Payoffs of Antipoverty Programs

> They [the PRI] are giving away the construction materials because of the governor's campaign. That doesn't matter, we need it, and when the candidate comes we will put up banners to show our support and [our gratitude]. He promised the material and here it is," says Petra. "In contrast, those from the PAN give very little, just 15 bags of cement; with that one can't do anything. And those from the PRD, poor devils, they give nothing.
> Quoted in Masiosare supplement of *La Jornada*, February 12, 2006

7.1 INTRODUCTION

The PRI governor of Yucatán handed out thousands of portable washing machines to poor women prior to the 2000 presidential elections. He personally distributed 1,003 machines at a rally in Umán's central plaza. PRI supporters were called to City Hall to turn over their voter identification cards to a local PRI leader and sign up to receive the washing machines at the upcoming rally. The governor's convoy arrived early in the morning, and Governor Cervera Pacheco himself headed the rally, to chants of "Long Live the PRI!" (*New York Times*, June 18, 2000). Similar reports of overt vote buying came from all over the country. As in previous elections, the PRI handed out groceries and construction supplies and threatened to cut off subsidized milk rations to nursing mothers if they failed to show up for rallies in support of the PRI's candidates. Party cadres gave poor housewives bags of rice, beans, and other foodstuffs purchased by a federal government charity headed by the First Lady. As they handed out these goods, party cadres registered the names of the people and made copies of their electoral identification cards. These were the typical vote-buying tactics in campaigns that the PRI's electoral machine employed and continues to employ at election time.

More serious than campaign handouts, however, were the efforts to coordinate officials who administered government social programs to use them

7.1 Introduction

on behalf of the PRI's campaigns. "The federal government's social programs are PRI programs, and we're going to use them to win the presidency," said Manuel Bartlett, a party heavyweight and former interior minister who at the time was working in the PRI's presidential campaign (*New York Times*, June 18, 2000). In the weeks before election day, it was not uncommon in Mexico to come across long queues of people waiting outside public buildings to receive a variety of benefits from social programs – for example, peasants waiting to receive their *Procampo* checks or mothers expecting subsidized food.

Nevertheless, the recently instituted social assistance program, *Progresa*, would prove more difficult to manipulate than *Pronasol* because party officials could no longer control the operation of the program. PRI brokers and some of the program's village organizers made every effort to frighten beneficiaries by telling them they would be cut off from *Progresa* if they did not pledge support for the PRI's candidate. In an attempt to lessen beneficiaries' fears, Carlos Jarque, the secretary of social development, distributed a letter reminding them that the program did not obligate them to vote for any candidate. Back in 2000 that letter might not have been sufficient to reassure *Progresa* recipients that they were entitled to their benefits regardless of their vote choice. In those elections, poor voters whose lives had been improved by *Progresa* went to the polls burdened with anxiety. On the one hand, they feared that party officials would cut their benefits if they failed to signal their allegiance to the PRI. On the other, they feared that if the PRI lost the elections, the incoming administration would punish them for supporting the PRI and the program would be terminated.

After the PRI lost power in 2000, it gradually became clear to *Progresa/Oportunidades* beneficiaries that the CCT program was more insulated from political manipulation than preceding social programs. "One can be PANísta, PRIísta or PRDísta and still receive benefits from *Oportunidades*," a Oaxacan mother of five told us in an interview in 2009. It is clear from our interviews in Oaxacan villages that the poor perceive important differences between the CCT and other social programs, and that they consider it an entitlement rather than a political handout that comes and goes with the election cycle.

This chapter attempts to evaluate voters' responses to different strategies of vote buying. There are not many studies that answer elementary questions about the electoral yields of government programs in a systematic manner. Most empirical studies of distributive politics have focused on the logic of electoral investment – who gets what, where, and when (Ferejohn, 1974; Schady, 2000; Dahlberg and Johansson, 2002; Calvo and Murillo, 2004; Stokes, 2005; Brusco et al., 2004; Magaloni, 2006; Magaloni et al., 2007 are some examples), bypassing the issue of how voters actually respond to vote-buying efforts.

Our study employs both aggregate municipal-level electoral returns and individual-level survey evidence to assess the electoral consequences of two decades of antipoverty programs in Mexico. Recent scholarship has begun to explore the electoral payoffs of government transfers and programs (Magaloni,

2006; Magaloni et al., 2007; De la O, 2015; Hseih et al., 2011; Zucco, 2013). All these studies show that voters respond positively to government transfers, a finding that should surprise no one. Our approach moves beyond this research by comparing the electoral payoffs of various types of government programs. How many more votes does clientelism buy relative to entitlements? How many more votes do private transfers buy relative to public goods? These empirical questions are highly relevant for theorizing about distributive politics. Only by understanding the electoral consequences of different vote-buying strategies will we be able to comprehend why politicians choose distributive policies and their beneficiaries as they do.

7.2 THE PAYOFFS FOR ELECTORAL INVESTMENTS

Recall from earlier chapters that we categorized Mexican social programs according to the type of benefits delivered – private or collective – and to their discretionary or nondiscretionary design. Discretionary private goods are what we have called *clientelism*. About a third of *Pronasol* expenditures from 1989 to 1994 fall into this category. Discretionary transfers of public goods geographically targeted, commonly classified as pork or pork-barreling, made up the larger remainder of *Pronasol* funds. Nondiscretionary distribution of private goods or entitlements is the third combination, which covers *Progresa/Oportunidades*, starting in 1997. The last combination is the nondiscretionary distribution of public goods, represented by the FISM program enacted in 1995.

Our theory of *conditional party loyalty* holds that a party machine targets particularistic transfers to reward the loyalty of its core supporters. The machine targets these benefits to loyal voters that are identified *ex ante*, according to their known political affinities and ongoing interactions with party agents. If it does not do so, its core voters may become detached and evolve into swing voters. Although the relationship is voluntary, an implicit (and often enough, quite explicit) threat of punishment sustains it. Voters stay loyal to the party because they receive their benefits and because they know these can be denied to them for political reasons.

Hence, our expectation is that clientelism should exhibit the highest electoral return. Discretionary transfers more easily targeted to the machine's core voters are less subject to the problem of voter opportunism. But the logic of this political linkage implies a form of arm-twisting. Core voters respond to these transfers because they need to signal loyalty to the party in order to obtain similar benefits in the future. The perverse nature of this relationship is that voters can be bought off with an array of material inducements that prove not to be welfare-enhancing in the long run.

Discretionary public goods or pork-barreling projects are riskier investments since they are targeted to places with typically smaller cores where project

7.2 The Payoffs for Electoral Investments

beneficiaries include many nonsupporters. These transfers thus entail a sizeable problem of potential voter opportunism and, for that reason, we expect pork to return lower electoral yields on average than clientelism.

With respect to the electoral payoffs of nondiscretionary private and public goods, our vote-buying theory does not generate *a priori* expectations. Nonetheless, it makes intuitive sense to expect that voters will reward parties that transfer benefits to them which entail notable income and consumption gains. Thus, we expect beneficiaries of *Progresa/Oportunidades* to reward incumbents for improvements in their welfare regardless of the partisan identity of their benefactor. As for formula-based social infrastructure transfers, their electoral return should be no lower than that for discretionary pork-barrel projects, but not particularly higher since, in a federal system like Mexico's, credit-claiming is more likely to generate rival partisan claims in municipalities under divided vertical government.

Our study of the electoral consequences of all these programs employs both individual-level survey evidence and aggregate electoral results for estimating their actual vote yields. We employ exit polls for the 2000 and 2006 presidential elections.[1] For our purposes, exit polls of election-day voters are better than postelectoral surveys, which in Mexico are characterized by substantial overreporting in favor of the winning candidate as well as implausible turnout rates. Preelectoral surveys, for their part, tend to have smaller samples with variable levels of undecided voters. They often do not capture last-moment shifts in sentiment and they cannot isolate actual voters through likely voter models.

We supplement our survey research with the systematic analysis of aggregate vote swings in the 1994, 2000, and 2006 presidential elections. Aggregate electoral data are necessary to calculate the electoral returns for many public goods, whose benefits are diffuse and poorly captured by conventional surveys. Surveys are well suited to the study of recipients of private goods in *Progresa/Oportunidades* but not those of the public goods distributed through *Pronasol* and FISM.[2]

A second reason why it is difficult to study distributive politics through survey research is that it is practically impossible to rank-order beneficiaries

---

[1] We could not locate any exit poll that identified *Pronasol* beneficiaries for the 1994 presidential elections. We did analyze a *Los Angeles Times* postelectoral poll for the 1991 midterm elections and a Gallup preelectoral poll for 1993 (results are available upon request).

[2] The President's Office during the *Pronasol* years designed surveys asking respondents whether they knew that projects were being provided in their community, whether they or their friends had actually witnessed the projects being built and whether they had directly benefited from them. Unfortunately, the overriding concern in the design of those surveys was to measure the image of the president and the effectiveness of the government's publicity campaigns. Those long questionnaires were not carried out at times of electoral activity, but during what were called Solidarity Weeks. Worse, the surveys filtered respondents, *completing* the interview only for those that reported knowledge of the program. These surveys are deposited at the Roper Center (MXOTAP1992-SOL10992 and MXOTAP1993-SOL10993).

according to the benefits they report having received. We are interested in measuring the yields for electoral investments in a bottom-line pesos-per-voter calculation. This task is simply easier to accomplish with aggregate electoral data than with election surveys limited by short questionnaires and interview times.

Finally, survey research is often inadequate for the study of clientelistic practices because many individuals avoid reporting the benefits received when these are understood to be illegal or corrupt. Specifically, in the comparison of programs we seek to make, survey respondents might be more willing to report benefits received from *Progresa/Oportunidades* than from *Pronasol*, creating a problem of underreporting for the latter program.[3] Although techniques such as list experiments can deal with these flaws, Mexican pollsters in the 1990s did not collect their data with such problems in mind.

7.3 THE POLITICAL CONTEXT OF PRESIDENTIAL ELECTIONS AFTER 1988

The three elections we analyze in this chapter were all dramatic events. The 1994 election, while cleaner than the 1988 contest, was marked by considerable political violence before and after election day. The 2000 election was the watershed of the Mexican transition to democracy with the upheld defeat of the PRI by Vicente Fox. The controversial 2006 election was the closest race in the country's history, pitting the two parties that had contested PRI hegemony since 1988 against each other.

The 1994 presidential election took place in a year of significant political turmoil, punctuated by the Zapatista uprising in the Southern state of Chiapas which erupted on the first day of 1994 and by the assassination of the PRI's presidential candidate on the campaign trail in March. Although the substitute candidate, the technocrat Ernesto Zedillo, went on to score a comfortable triumph, without serious postelectoral conflicts, the long-standing *Pax Priista* had been shattered.

Initially, analysts thought that these events would jeopardize the peaceful transfer of power, sustained for over sixty years, since the last major political assassination and the creation of the PRI. For the purposes of this book, the Zapatista uprising is particularly noteworthy, since it emerged despite the political success of *Pronasol*, touted throughout the Salinas term as the

---

[3] In a survey designed to assess public opinion regarding *Pronasol* in 1992 (MXOTAP1992-SOL10992), 47 percent said *Pronasol* projects were carried out in their own neighborhood. According to a *Los Angeles Times* poll carried out by Belden-Rusonello in 1991, 32 percent of respondents claimed to have benefited from *Pronasol* (MXLAT1991-258). A Gallup-IMPO poll that same year (MXUSIA1993-I93057) reported that only 19.4 percent of respondents claimed to have received benefits from the program. In short, it is very unlikely that one can reconstruct the distributive impact of *Pronasol* through survey data.

7.3 The Political Context of Presidential Elections after 1988

definitive strategy for eradicating poverty in the country. The Zapatistas made it clear that poverty relief had yet to reach ample sectors of the destitute poor, especially among its indigenous peoples.

The 1994 presidential election was also special in that it took place after six years of structural transformation of the national economy. Mexico had joined the North American Free Trade Agreement in 1993 and was more fully integrated into international capital markets. By most accounts, macroeconomic stabilization had been successful and domestic consumption was rising, although economic growth remained anemic. Thus, the election as a referendum on economic performance, one of the PRI's central strategies for the campaign, was by no means a foregone conclusion. The second strategic line was the constant reminder of welfare gains delivered through *Pronasol*. Despite the Chiapas uprising, the Colosio assassination, and prevailing discontent with the national economy, the PRI was reelected with just under 50 percent of the vote and a whopping margin over its two major rivals. In the next section, we analyze the contribution of *Pronasol* to the PRI's electoral success in 1994.

Ernesto Zedillo initiated his presidency with the Tequila Crisis, which sent Mexico into a deep, albeit short, recession. Poverty reached alarming and unprecedented levels in the first two years of his presidency. According to the estimates shown in the first chapter, over 80 percent of rural citizens and over 60 percent of urban dwellers could not meet "basic capacities" (i.e., fulfill minimal nutrition requirements and provide health and education for their families). In reaction to the economic recession, the PRI lost a string of local elections in the aftermath of the crisis and then its majority in the Chamber of Deputies in the 1997 midterm elections. Legislative politics were utterly transformed. For the first time in its history, the PRI was obliged to compromise with the opposition in order to pass ordinary legislation. The establishment in 1997 of *Progresa*, as we discussed in earlier chapters, represented a turning point in the design of social policy. With *Progresa*, Mexico witnessed the advent of social entitlements for its poorest citizens. During the Zedillo administration, social infrastructure funds were also decentralized and the distribution of these funds increasingly fixed through poverty-based formulas. By the 2000 presidential elections, the PRI had renounced or been forced to renounce its discretion in the administration of antipoverty programs.

The 2000 presidential election marks the great divide in Mexico's electoral history, when the PRI lost control of the presidency. PAN candidate Vicente Fox won with 43 percent of the vote, six points above the PRI's candidate. Despite strong growth rates prior to the elections and high presidential approval rates, the PRI could not win the election because voters were fed up. They had lost confidence in the PRI and perceived that, if returned to power, the party would escort the country into yet another postelectoral recession (Magaloni and Poiré, 2004; Magaloni, 2006). Importantly, the elections were administered by the autonomous Federal Electoral Institute (IFE), which made electoral fraud at the ballot box and in the vote count practically impossible for the PRI. While the average voter was euphoric upon unseating the PRI, a more cautious mood prevailed among the poor, especially those benefiting from government programs such as *Procampo* and *Progresa*. The main question for them was whether the incoming PAN administration would retain these programs or scuttle them.

After numerous international policy evaluations supporting the effectiveness of *Progresa* in reducing extreme poverty, the Fox administration decided to continue with the program, but rebaptized it with a new name, *Oportunidades*. The expansion of the rural program and its extension to cities under Fox made for impressive coverage of poor households throughout the country. At the end of 1999, *Progresa* had reached approximately 2.6 million families in extreme poverty, about 40 percent of all rural households. By the end of 2005, coverage under *Oportunidades* had doubled to almost 5 million families, two-thirds in the countryside and the remainder comprising urban and semiurban households. By 2006 more than half of all families living under the poverty line in Mexico were recipients of these transfers.

Aside from *Oportunidades*, the Fox administration introduced a new social insurance program to remedy the truncated nature of health care delivery in the country. According to the 2000 census, some 58 percent of the population was not covered by the social security system (including the IMSS *Solidaridad* hospitals and clinics built with *Pronasol* funds). *Seguro Popular* was an ambitious program created to extend health coverage to this uninsured population. The program began in five states in 2001 and by the end of 2005 had been implemented in all thirty-one states plus the Federal District, affiliating almost three million families. In contrast to *Oportunidades*, centrally administered by the federal government, *Seguro Popular* was partially decentralized and potentially more subject to political manipulation in its selection and subsidization procedures. Coverage and spending varied widely among states and some doubts remain concerning the criteria for affiliation. Despite these shortcomings, Scott (2006) calculates the incidence of benefit distribution and concludes that affiliation in the new insurance program is more propoor than any other healthcare service except for *Oportunidades* and IMSS-*Oportunidades*.[4] Thus, the innovations in welfare policy engineered by the Fox government clearly entailed an important extension of tangible and needed benefits to the poor.

At the close of the Fox administration, the 2006 presidential election was the most contested election in Mexico's postrevolutionary history. The front runners were Felipe Calderón, from the PAN, and Andres Manuel López Obrador, from the PRD. The margin of victory, after a recount of around 10 percent of total votes, was slightly more than half a percentage point. Many interpret

---

[4] Scott further argues that the piggy-backing of *Seguro Popular* onto the poverty relief program, allowing for automatic affiliation of families already registered in *Oportunidades*, could only improve its targeting efficiency in favor of the poor.

7.3 The Political Context of Presidential Elections after 1988

the tight contest as the outcome of a pitched ideological battle that divided right from left, rich from poor, and North from South. From this perspective, the 2006 election was a prospective exercise, with a clear choice between right-wing continuity and left-wing populism. Yet the PAN's triumph would not have materialized without the support of ample sectors of the poor, urban and rural, that voted for the right-wing party retrospectively as a result of *Oportunidades*.[5]

The PRD did not recognize its defeat, claiming that the election had been rigged. López Obrador based his accusations of electoral fraud on several arguments. The first was that the computer program used to tally precinct-level vote totals had been rigged and inconsistencies in the vote count were apparent. He demanded a complete recount, although election law stipulated that ballot boxes uncontested by party representatives at the precinct level did not qualify for a recount. His second argument was that, throughout the campaign, the PAN had manipulated social transfers to the poor in order to buy their electoral support, severely undercutting the fairness of the election.[6]

The claim that fraud was orchestrated in electronic form is hard to document and is a task that goes beyond the scope of this chapter.[7] But the accusation that the PAN used its access to patronage, pork, and clientelism to generate electoral support, particularly from the poor, is worth addressing. It is conceivable that the PAN used its power over federal resources, following the old practices of the PRI, to coerce or bribe poor voters. In particular, Alianza Cívica, one of the most important and prestigious NGOs engaged in electoral observation, had warned for months that the PAN was using federal social programs as vote-buying currency (Alianza Cívica, 2006). This perception was seconded by Fundar, an NGO for citizen oversight in budgetary matters (Fundar, 2006). The accusations could not be taken lightly, given the reputation and credibility of the sources.

President Fox and the Social Development Ministry (*Sedesol*) had anticipated these types of accusations, and as a result adopted a strategy of *blindaje electoral*, i.e., safeguards to shield federal programs from electoral manipulation (*Sedesol*, 2005). These safeguards retained the original prohibition from 1997 against the expansion of the CCT program in any federal election year. Further, *Sedesol* came to an agreement with the United Nations Development Program (UNDP) to make a thorough study of the operation of all its social programs during the election year, including surveys of beneficiaries and

---

[5] The *Seguro Popular* also played a decisive role, as we show elsewhere (Diaz-Cayeros et al., 2006).
[6] Lack of fairness was also claimed with respect to the torrents of negative, disparaging, and fear-mongering advertising that presumably swung the election in the PAN's favor.
[7] Given irregularities in the vote count acknowledged by all, the debate remains centered on whether there was legal cause for a full recount or the irregularities could be attributed to random human error at the precinct level. See the opposing views of J. A. Crespo and Javier Aparicio in the special edition of *Política y Gobierno*, "Elecciones en México", 2 (2009).

nonbeneficiaries, in order to gauge the occurrence of vote buying and coercion (PNUD, 2007).[8]

Our position on this contentious issue is that *Oportunidades* made the PAN's victory in 2006 possible, but that voters responded to the program freely. Vote buying and credit claiming are complementary facets of democratic politics. However, their scopes can overlap, ranging from voters responding freely to programmatic appeals and the benefits received through social programs to voters supporting a party out of fear of losing their benefits for political reasons. The institutional design of a given program is decisive, but popular perceptions may not turn on knowledge of their operation.

Oportunidades made an explicit effort to publicize the principle that program benefits were not contingent upon political behavior. The program posted a notice on all materials assuring beneficiaries that their participation in the program was not tied to partisan sympathies nor could their benefits be withdrawn for political motives. Beneficiaries were also constantly reminded that their benefits would continue so long as they complied with program requirements of school attendance and periodic visits to the health clinic. However, in a country with such a long tradition of clientelism, we cannot know whether beneficiaries actually believed these statements. Our intuition is that it takes some learning on the part of poor voters in Mexico to feel secure about their entitlements. The fact that Vicente Fox did not reverse *Progresa* after the PRI's defeat in 2000 surely helped to assure them that welfare benefits were no longer vulnerable to election cycles nor to the political whims of the leadership.

7.4 INSTRUMENTAL VARIABLES IN THE STUDY OF VOTE SWINGS

To model the electoral payoffs of antipoverty programs, this section studies vote swings between presidential elections (1988–1994 and 1994–2000 for the PRI, and 2000–2006 for the PAN). Using interelectoral vote swings as dependent variables helps to address the potentially serious problems arising from omitted variable bias. To the extent that an independent variable remains constant between elections, its omission should not bias the results. Following Tucker (2006), we calculate all electoral data in log-odds ratios, in order to keep estimates between the range of 0 and 1 and to ensure normality in their distributions.

A methodological problem we face in the study of electoral payoffs of antipoverty programs is endogeneity (as well as reverse causation). When incumbents assign discretionary resources, they surely do so in anticipation of voters' responses. This implies that explanatory variables are likely to be correlated

---

[8] One of the authors was commissioned to carry out part of the evaluation.

with the error terms of simple OLS regressions, producing biased and inconsistent estimates.

To model vote swings for 1988–1994 as the *product* of *Pronasol's* investments per capita in private and public goods, we take an instrumental variables approach. Potential candidates for instruments, as in the previous chapters, are related to physical and human geography. In particular, we use rugged terrain, the landlocked status of a municipality and the average distance from railroad tracks. These variables plausibly influenced investment decisions. The uneven nature of terrain, for example, is a natural factor taken into account when funding public infrastructure projects. It is harder and sometimes excessively costly to build and pave roads, dig ditches and water wells, construct health clinics and schools, and the like, where the terrain is rough and mountainous.

However, to be valid, instruments must work their effect only through expenditure, and thus be exogenous and uncorrelated with vote swings. We can be confident that by using geographic variables a problem of reverse causation is not present, because, for example, rugged terrain does not vary according to how voters behave; and railways in Mexico have not expanded at all since the 1940s. But to be truly convincing as instruments, we must believe that changes in party success are not dependent on these instrumental variables. Taking ruggedness as an example of the issue at hand, the PRI was historically entrenched in places where it was most difficult for opposition parties to successfully present candidates. In the 1960s, for example, the PAN mostly presented candidates in large cities of the Central highlands. But by the 1990s swings for or against the PRI were not particularly related to remote areas: when a PRI splinter occurred it was not uncommon to see massive swings in mountainous regions. To be sure there was gradual erosion of PRI support in the north of the country as democratization proceeded, but coastal municipalities had no particular political configuration making them more or less likely to swing in favor of one party or another. Hence landlocked municipalities had no specific pattern of vote swings as compared to the coast or the border. Furthermore, by the 1990s the places with historical proximity to railroad tracks had no particular advantage in modernization or specific political alignments, because by then the crucial developmental role was being played by highways. These geographic variables are hence good predictors of *Pronasol* investments but are uncorrelated with vote swings. Our diagnostic tests suggest that neither changes in vote shares nor in turnout are correlated with the residuals of a regression using these variables.[9]

Thus our models employ geographical instruments as correlates of entrenched poverty to predict logged per capita private and public good allocations in *Pronasol* (*private PC^* and *public PC^*). Our expectation is that the

---

[9] We are able to reject an F test of regression residuals being correlated with the instruments (see Deaton, 1997). Strictly speaking these overidentification tests are not decisive because they require that at least one of the instruments must be valid.

TABLE 7.1. *Effects of Programs on Vote Swings (Instrumental Variables Estimations)*

PRI Vote Swing 1988–1994		PRI Vote Swing 1994–2000		PAN Vote Swing 2000–2006	
Private PC^	0.052 (0.008)**	Progresa^	1.886 (0.389)**	Oportunidades^	0.607 (0.108)**
Public PC^	0.034 (0.011)*	FISM^	0.070 (0.037)*	FISM^	0.069 (0.028)**
PRI 88	−0.890 (0.024)**	PRI 94	−0.605 (0.028)**	PAN 00	−0.237 (0.015)**
Alpha	0.043 (0.014)**	Alpha	0.076 (0.031)*		
Decline	−0.022 (0.034)				
Constant	−0.755 (0.034)**	Constant	−1.158 (0.252)**	Constant	1.756 (0.381)**
N = 2338		N = 2346		N = 2344	
F(35,2302) 141.22		F(34,2311) 65.12		F(33,2310) 65.12	
Pr>F 0.000		Pr>F 0.000		Pr>F 0.000	
R2 0.619		R2 0.564		R2 0.336	

Note: Regressions are run with robust standard errors and state fixed effects.
* Significant at the 95 percent level; ** significant at the 99 percent level.

electoral yield for private goods should be significantly higher than that for public goods. The regression controls for the PRI's vote share in 1988 (*PRI 88*) and the *alpha* and *erosion* parameters discussed in Chapter 4. Higher vote swings in favor of the PRI (or smaller swings against it) should characterize places with large cores (*alpha*) and slow *erosion*. We also expect smaller vote swings in places where the PRI performed exceedingly well in 1988. The regressions use state-fixed effects to control for other local patterns of politics stemming from, for example, the partisan identity of incumbent governors, party chapters' mobilizational capacity, the concurrency of gubernatorial races, and the different types of local party system configurations. Results are reported in the first column of Table 7.1.[10]

All the coefficients perform as expected and all but one reach reasonable levels of statistical significance. *Pronasol* was a decisive factor in accounting for municipal vote swings in favor of the PRI in the 1994 presidential elections, even after controlling for state-fixed effects and the divergent electoral histories of municipalities since 1970, as measured by *alpha* and *erosion*.

[10] We examined swing data in all presidential elections for spatial autocorrelation in GeoDA, failing to find any significant concern. Therefore, we do not include a spatial lag in these estimations.

7.4 Instrumental Variables in the Study of Vote Swings

These results reveal a powerful impact of clientelistic transfers vis-à-vis public goods. The vote-buying effect of private goods almost doubles that of collective ones. In terms of votes-per-peso it was significantly more effective for the PRI to distribute particularistic transfers to individuals and small groups of producers than to invest in social infrastructure projects or public goods provision for communities at large. Nonetheless, public goods provision also generated some voting support for the PRI.

Our results thus cast doubt on the existing analyses of *Pronasol*. Although myriad observers have accredited this program as a key factor in the PRI's electoral recovery in the 1990s, most empirical analyses have concluded that *Pronasol*'s electoral effectiveness was disappointing. Bruhn (1996: 162) finds no evidence that *Pronasol* expenditures helped the PRI and undermined the left. Hiskey (1999: 128) concludes that the "political impact of *Pronasol* funds is noteworthy for its insignificance." Although Molinar and Weldon claim to find positive effects for this program, their results are counterintuitive because vote gains are generated only in states where gubernatorial elections were held in 1991. "In states where elections for governor were not scheduled in 1991, the PRI did somewhat *worse* in the federal elections for every extra peso spent on *Pronasol* " (Molinar and Weldon, 1994: 137).

The columns in Table 7.1 present analogous results for the election that stamped the transition to democracy, but centered on the nondiscretionary social transfers introduced by the Zedillo administration. The 1994–2000 vote swings are a function of the instrumented municipal-level coverage of *Progresa* in 2000 (*Progresa^*) and the instrumented per capita expenditures in FISM (*FISM^*). The table also presents the analysis of 2000–2006 vote swings, this time for the PAN as the incumbent party, as a function of the instrumented change between 2000 and 2006 in the coverage of *Oportunidades* (*Oportunidades^*) and in the predicted per capita expenditures through FISM (*FISM^*). These regressions also use state-fixed effects to control for the idiosyncrasies of state-level politics.

Although we recognize that transfers within these programs were determined by objective formulas not easily manipulated, it is plausible that the expansion of *Progresa* and *Oportunidades* were politically determined. That is, the formulas constrained the politicians and policymakers to target the poor but they were not constrained in terms of phasing-in program expansion across states and municipalities.[11] This leeway to skew implementation compels us to instrument change in coverage in *Progresa* and *Oportunidades* to eliminate potential problems of endogeneity – that is, the possibility that higher increments in coverage were in part driven by expectations of electoral results. For the case of FISM, as discussed in the previous chapter, the fact that funding

---

[11] It is important to note that an important randomization trial was executed in the early phase of the program in 1997 and completed in 1999. Parallel and subsequent expansions after 1997 did not involve random assignment.

was determined by formulas does not rule out the possibility that the choice of the specific elements included in the formula and the distribution resulting from them were the product of political calculations by the incumbent party. Geographic instruments, as in the 1988–1994 model, are good predictors of allocations of *Progresa/Oportunidades* and FISM but are uncorrelated with the dependent variables.[12]

Regression results perform as expected. Both *Progresa* and *Oportunidades* generated strong positive effects on the incumbent parties' vote swings in the 2000 and 2006 elections. *Progresa* proved to be particularly potent in favoring the PRI in 2000, about three times more effective in vote gains than *Oportunidades* for the PAN in 2006. FISM also impacts vote swings in the expected direction. More per capita investment in social infrastructure at the municipal level translates into higher vote swings for the incumbent party in both elections.

To have a sense of the range of effects, Figure 7.1 simulates the vote-buying effects of the various programs, distinguishing between private and public goods. The graph on the top simulates the effects of the discretionary program (the two basic categories of *Pronasol* transfers) and the other graphs those of the formula-based ones (*Progresa/Oportunidades* and FISM).

The findings for *Pronasol* are striking, with far larger payoffs extracted from private goods. Relative to pork-barreling or discretionary public goods allocations, particularistic transfers are vastly superior for buying votes. For example, if the PRI spends 100 pesos per capita in private goods, the simulation predicts a swing of around one point in that party's favor, while the same expense in public goods would not generate a positive vote swing. Moreover, against the 100 pesos per capita in clientelism, expenditures for pork would need to be almost six times as large in order to replicate a similar gain in votes. That does not mean that electoral investment in public goods is useless, since any money for pork may prevent adverse negative swings. However, there is no question that clientelistic transfers were more effective at producing electoral support for the PRI *throughout the whole range of expenditures*. Public goods also produced swings of considerable magnitude for this party at higher levels of expenditure, but never outpacing the yield from private goods.

The graphs for swings of the incumbent in 2000 (the PRI) and 2006 (the PAN) simulate the effects of nondiscretionary transfers for private and public goods. The electoral payoffs of nondiscretionary private goods (or entitlements) behave quite differently from those of particularistic transfers. The electoral swings for entitlements are not always higher than the payoffs from

---

[12] Instruments for the 1994–2000 regression include traits of physical geography (temperature, landlocked status, longitude, and latitude). Instruments for the 2000–2006 model are very similar (rugged terrain, landlocked status, longitude, latitude, and distance from railroad tracks). Also included as control variables are the CONAPO poverty index, population size, the Human Development Index for 2000, and Progresa's municipal coverage in 2000. The instruments passed overidentification tests.

7.4 Instrumental Variables in the Study of Vote Swings

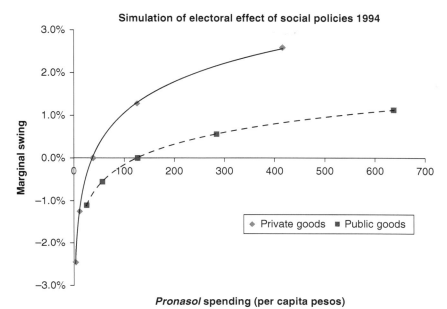

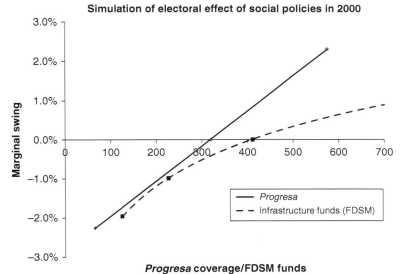

FIGURE 7.1. Simulated electoral returns of social programs.

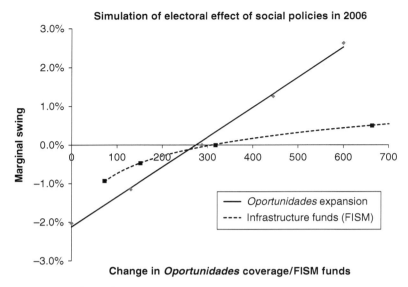

FIGURE 7.1 (cont.)

public goods. In these estimates, positive vote swings for the PAN in 2006 emerge only after better than half the municipality's households receive benefits. Hence, the Fox administration's interest in expanding *Oportunidades*. At very high levels of CCT coverage, vote swings easily outperform those observed from investments in public goods provision. When poverty relief through entitlements reaches a large critical mass within poor communities, the impact on electoral support for the benefactor (PRI and PAN alike) is stunning.[13] In contrast, districts with fewer inhabitants living in abject poverty (medium- and large-sized cities) are less generous, requiring stronger investment in public goods in order to generate additional voting support for the incumbent. Portfolio diversification, as we claimed earlier, is practically inevitable in more competitive contexts.

7.5 INVESTMENT YIELDS FROM CCTS

This section supplements the previous section's findings with survey research. The study of antipoverty programs with individual-level data also presents

---

[13] The exact mechanism involved is disputed. Earlier research on *Progresa/Oportunidades* (De la O, 2006; Cantu, 2006) argued for an "implementation effect" favoring the party in charge of operating the program (the PRI until 2000 and the PAN afterward). This is similar to the proincumbent bias noted by Zucco (2010a and 2010b) among *Bolsa Familia* beneficiaries, which he seems to attribute to the poor's deference to authority. In the next section, we assess individual-level evidence to resolve this question.

7.5 Investment Yields from CCTs

serious challenges of selection bias. Thinking in terms of medical research and experiments can help to conceptualize some of the problems involved in studying these types of policy interventions. To estimate the effects of a drug or medical treatment, ideally one would like to have two individuals that are identical in all respects (age, diet, gender, lifestyle, ethnicity, etc.) except for the "treatment." Medical research solves this issue through experimental design wherein a group of individuals with similar characteristics are randomly selected and divided into two groups, one receiving the "treatment" and the other (the "control" group) not.

As envisioned by its creator, Santiago Levy, *Progresa* was originally designed to allow for experimental evaluations. Communities with similar characteristics were identified at the onset of the program, but only a randomly selected group began to receive benefits immediately, while the others were incorporated 15 months later. In two innovative studies, Green (2005) and De la O (2013) take advantage of the program's randomization or the delay in incorporation to assess the effects of *Progresa* on turnout and voting choices. These studies arrive at opposite conclusions. Green finds that *Progresa* had no effect on voting choices, while De la O obtains a rise in turnout and an increase in the incumbent's vote share.

A problem for our purposes to compare the variety of electoral strategies across elections is that there is no experimental setting available for *Pronasol*, FISM, and *Oportunidades*. If we want to compare the political impact of the various social protection programs, we must rely on observational data. We can, however, use statistical methods to deal with potential selection problems. That is, we contrast treated and untreated individuals by matching comparable persons in terms of the nonrandom set of characteristics that make them potential targets of selection into the program, but with some selected while the others are not. Specifically, we use a nonparametric technique, propensity score matching (PSM), to compare individuals along these lines (Ho et al., 2007; Rosenbaum and Rubin, 1983).[14] The treatment variable in this quasi-experiment is being a *Progresa* or *Oportunidades* recipient. We used a similar strategy in Diaz-Cayeros et al. (2009) to evaluate the electoral impacts of *Oportunidades* and *Seguro Popular* on voting decisions in 2006.

In matching, the most common indicator of interest is the mean impact of the treatment on the treated. This indicator is also known as the average treatment effect on the treated (ATT). In the case at hand, we are interested in the comparison of the mean probability of voting for a given party from the treated group and its matched nontreated group. The method is based on an

---

[14] In this technique, assumptions of linearity are not necessary, because matching is done nonparametrically. With the propensity score the challenge is to find a scale within which the assumption of nonconfoundedness holds (Imbens, 2003). There is no direct test that can assure that this assumption holds. We follow the common practice of checking whether the propensity scores of the treated and control groups have a similar distribution (a balance test by blocks).

assumption of unit homogeneity. This means that the outcome of the nonparticipant can be taken as an indication of what would have happened *holding all other relevant variables constant*. In this sense, the hypotheses tests do not control for covariates, since they are already incorporated into the choice of observations to be compared.

Propensity score matching is relatively simple to perform. The first stage involves a probit (or logit) estimation of every individual's probability of being selected as a *Progresa/Oportunidades* beneficiary. The second stage is a simple test of means, where treated observations *sharing similar propensity scores* are compared to untreated ones.

To ascertain the electoral payoffs of *Progresa* and *Oportunidades*, we employ two exit polls performed by the newspaper *Reforma*.[15] *Reforma's* research department is credited with conducting some of the best electoral survey work in Mexico. Their questionnaires are rather comprehensive, including self-reporting of enrolment in *Progresa* and *Oportunidades*. The 2000 exit poll sampled 3,380 voters in 119 municipalities (including *delegaciones* or boroughs in Mexico City); the 2006 poll included 5,807 voters spread among 122 municipalities throughout the country.

The 2000 exit poll shows a relatively even distribution of votes for the PRI's candidate, Francisco Labastida, in rural and urban localities. By contrast, the 2006 poll shows that support for Felipe Calderón varied considerably according to whether voters lived in rural or urban areas. The urban-rural gap in Calderón's support is clear from both the survey and the official vote tally. According to official tallies, in rural areas his vote share was 29.7 percent, while in urban areas he reached 38.3 percent of the vote.

The descriptive statistics of the surveys (Table 7.2) show that *Progresa* recipients voted more frequently for the incumbent party's candidate, Francisco Labastida – there is a 24 percent point gap in his favor between recipients and nonrecipients. Vicente Fox from the PAN seems to be particularly affected by *Progresa*, producing a 21 percent gap against him. Similarly, the 2006 poll shows that the PAN's candidate received more support among beneficiaries of *Oportunidades* – 37 percent of beneficiaries voted for Calderón versus 32 percent of nonbeneficiaries, a gap of 5 points. If one were to view only the average vote shares for the three main presidential candidates in the 2006 elections among nonbeneficiaries of either program, a fierce tie between Calderón and López Obrador emerges, with Roberto Madrazo from the PRI in a distant third place overall. Among beneficiaries of the programs, however, Calderón outpaces López Obrador by double digits. Any one of these spreads is enough to have tilted the national election in Calderón's favor.

But the crucial inference that one wants to make is whether voters in 2000 supported the PRI because they received benefits from *Progresa*, or because some of the correlates of Labastida's vote are also related to the selection criteria of

---

[15] We thank Alejandro Moreno for making these polls available to us.

7.5 Investment Yields from CCTs

TABLE 7.2. *Percentage Voting for Major Candidates and Program Beneficiaries*

	2000 Elections *Progresa*		2006 Elections *Oportunidades*	
	Beneficiary (%)	Nonbeneficiary (%)	Beneficiary (%)	Nonbeneficiary (%)
Vote for PAN	25.4	46.9	37.2	32.3
Vote for PRD	16.4	17.0	25.9	31.7
Vote for PRI	57.7	33.5	23.1	17.9

beneficiaries into the social program. The same question arises with respect to the effects of *Oportunidades* on the support for the PAN in 2006.

Table 7.3 shows first-stage probit estimations of our PSM for *Progresa* and *Oportunidades*. In estimating the propensity scores, we use individual data from the survey merged with municipal-level data. The merger is important in our case because we know that selection into *Progresa/Oportunidades* was shaped both by income measured at the individual level in household surveys *and* by locality-level development indicators.[16] The merger follows electoral precinct identification at the polling points sampled for the exit poll.

The combination of variables used to calculate the propensity score was inductive: we included variables with predictive power, while satisfying a balancing property among blocks of observations.[17] We did not include variables that measure vote choice or are closely related to it in a voting model, such as party ID or presidential approval, since those are the outcomes we are interested in studying. We use a rather exhaustive specification for predicting beneficiaries: we follow the practice of trying to include variables that are statistically significant predictors of selection into the program and that meet the balancing property. Thus, these models are similar to each other but not identical.[18]

---

[16] We also employ a municipal-level variable for coverage of the program because this shapes an individual's probability to be chosen, as program managers decided to increase the coverage in rural sites where the program was already in place (the so-called densification process).

[17] The balancing property checks whether the propensity score within each partial range produces random treated and nontreated groups for the independent variables. Formally, it does not constitute a test of nonconfoundedness, but can allow one to reject a propensity score that most likely does not satisfy it.

[18] Propensity score matching produces a dataset in which observations falling under a common support (i.e., observations with similar probabilities of being treated, but with some in the treatment group and others not) should satisfy what is known as the "balancing property." If a matched dataset is balanced, there should be minimal differences in the distributions of the covariates that are used to calculate propensity scores between the treated and control groups (Ho et al., 2007). In the estimations, we have checked for balancing by testing whether the means of the covariates are the same across various blocks of observations (Becker and Ichino, 2002). In all estimations the balancing property was satisfied. The estimations were run using the PSCORE routine for STATA developed by Becker and Ichino (2002). We use a nearest neighbor match with bootstrapped standard errors.

TABLE 7.3. *First-stage Probits for Propensity Score Estimation*

Model 1: Propensity Score, *Progresa* Beneficiary (2000)		Model 2: Propensity Score, *Oportunidades* Beneficiary (2006)	
Individual socioeconomic indicators			
Age	−0.023 (0.016)	Age	−0.046 (0.011)**
Education	−0.123 (0.035)**	Education	−0.183 (0.025)**
Income	−0.090 (0.026)**	Income	−0.041 (0.011)**
Woman	0.146 (0.075)*	Woman	0.115 (0.050)*
Peasant farmer	0.099 (0.119)	Peasant farmer	0.158 (0.087)
Family size	0.072 (0.039)		
Aggregate socioeconomic indicators			
Rural precinct	0.519 (0.098)**	Rural precinct	0.577 (0.056)**
Usos y costumbres	0.213 (0.143)	Indians (municipal share)	0.298 (0.189)
No water supply (%)	0.850 (0.372)*	No water supply (%)	0.166 (0.215)
No electricity (%)	−4.062 (0.721)**	No electricity (%)	−0.487 (0.477)
No sewerage (%)	0.708 (0.329)*	No sewerage (%)	−0.847 (0.243)**
		HDI (2000)	0.701 (0.847)
Geographical correlates			
Northing	0.001 (0.000)**	Rainfall	0.0003 (0.000)**
Easting	0.0002 (0.000)	Easting	0.0001 (0.000)
Population density	0.0000 (0.000)**	Temperature	0.0001 (0.000)
Distance to roads	0.028 (0.007)**	Distance to roads	0.010 (0.005)*
Distance to rails	0.007 (0.002)**		
Distance to city	0.002 (0.001)		
Landlocked	−0.301 (0.117)**		
Policy-related variables			
Progresa coverage, 2000	4.743 (2.556)*	*Seguro Popular* insured	1.236 (0.058)**
Private goods % of funds in *Pronasol*, 1989–1994	−0.347 (0.331)	Change in *Oportunidades* coverage, 2000–2006	1.403 (0.272)**
Constant	−1.857 (0.351)**	Constant	−1.430 (0.716)*
Observations	2379	Observations	5019
LR (20)	328.88	LR (17)	1205.68
Prob>LR	0.0000	Prob>LR	0.0000
Pseudo R^2	0.168	Pseudo R^2	0.246

Note: Robust standard errors in parentheses.
* Significant at the 95% level; ** significant at the 99% level.

7.5 Investment Yields from CCTs

TABLE 7.4. *Effects of* Progresa *and* Oportunidades *on Vote Choice in 2000 and 2006*

	Vote in 2000 Effect of *Progresa*			Vote in 2006 Effect of *Oportunidades*		
	National	Rural	Urban	National	Rural	Urban
Vote for PRI candidate	0.167 (0.058)**	0.286 (0.071)**	0.087 (0.050)[a]	−0.049 (0.027)[a]	0.020 (0.064)	−0.071 (0.039)[a]
Vote for PAN candidate	−0.088 (0.043)*	−0.195 (0.072)**	−0.041 (0.050)	0.113 (0.032)**	0.113 (0.058)*	0.126 (0.039)**
Vote for PRD candidate	−0.060 (0.046)	−0.084 (0.064)	−0.023 (0.039)	−0.065 (0.037)[a]	−0.144 (0.045)**	−0.039 (0.037)
Approval	0.228 (0.082)**	0.383 (0.126)**	0.108 (0.110)	0.370 (0.060)**	0.500 (0.116)**	0.309 (0.060)**
Pocketbook	0.309 (0.098)**	0.655 (0.106)**	0.207 (0.134)	0.412 (0.051)**	0.366 (0.089)**	0.422 (0.080)**
PID PRI	0.132 (0.051)**	0.248 (0.079)**	0.098 (0.064)	−0.061 (0.030)*	−0.046 (0.057)	−0.045 (0.035)
PID PAN	−0.056 (0.034)[a]	−0.130 (0.056)*	−0.031 (0.047)	0.114 (0.030)**	0.124 (0.059)*	0.142 (0.034)**
PID PRD	−0.038 (0.033)	−0.062 (0.056)	−0.054 (0.037)	−0.004 (0.028)	−0.046 (0.046)	−0.019 (0.031)

Note: Nearest Neighbor Matching Method with bootstrapped standard errors in parentheses.
* Significant at the 95 percent level; ** significant at the 99 percent level; [a] significant at the 90 percent level.

In table 7.4 we present differences-of-means tests between treated and untreated respondents, which is the program's impact indicator or the ATT. In our case it corresponds to the comparison of the mean probability of voting for a given candidate between a treated group and its matched nontreated group. For our purposes, it is not necessary to include all relevant controls normally employed in vote choice models in order to infer the political effects of a given policy intervention.

The first thing to highlight is that both programs produced significant vote returns for the incumbent parties that implemented them. In 2000, beneficiaries of *Progresa* were 17 percent more likely to support the PRI's candidate. This probability jumps to 29 percent for rural beneficiaries, the program's original target population, with respect to nonbeneficiaries within the rural subsample. In the cities, any impact of *Progresa* was negligible across the range of political variables. The results also demonstrate that the CCT program hurt the PAN, but not so much the PRD. Thus, our results contrast with Cornelius (2004), who finds positive but rather marginal effects of *Progresa* in favor of the PRI (around 7 percent, just a bit more than in De la O, 2013). Cornelius's study, however, is agnostic about selection bias problems.

In the case of *Oportunidades*, beneficiaries were 11 percent more likely to vote for the PAN's candidate than nonbeneficiaries with very similar propensity scores – that is, individuals with the same sociodemographic and community-level characteristics. Program beneficiaries were, at the same time, 7 percent less likely to vote for the PRD's candidate and 5 percent less likely to support the PRI's candidate. Thus, our results validate López Obrador's concerns about *Oportunidades* as a strategy to steal votes from the left. But they do not support the claim that program beneficiaries were manipulated or coerced into voting for the PAN. Rather, *Oportunidades* worked to create an electoral constituency for the right-wing party among poor voters, who otherwise probably would have voted for the PAN's rivals. These results are opposed to Poiré and Estrada (2007), who report no favorable effect for the PAN nor any negative impact on support for other parties. These authors also ignore problems of selection bias.

Importantly, *Oportunidades* beneficiaries registered similar gains for the PAN in both subsamples. Given the dual expansion of the CCT program in those years, this result is consistent with expectations about beneficiaries' response to new welfare benefits, regardless of partisan predispositions. The first wave of expansion occurred in rural municipalities between 2001 and 2004. The second one began in 2002, in a rapid extension of the program to urban contexts with modified selection procedures (including self-selection by potential beneficiaries with agency review of their applications). Both phases involved similar numbers of new beneficiaries.

Rural gains for the PAN, however, came almost exclusively at the expense of the left, while its urban gains were mostly charged against the PRI. It bears emphasizing that the effects of *Oportunidades* are smaller by half among rural beneficiaries than was the case for *Progresa*. Rural expansion of the program increased recipients about 60 percent over those incorporated by 2000, in the range of PAN gains in the countryside by 2006. With respect to the cities, the urban electorate is over twice as large as the rural one. While the urban premium for *Oportunidades* is smaller than the rural one for 2000, in absolute terms the PAN's urban support in 2006 grows precisely as a result of its gains among the urban poor.

The last rows of Table 7.4 report the effects of the program on presidential approval, pocketbook evaluations, and partisan identification. These attitudes and assessments are, of course, strongly associated with vote choice, in most studies of electoral behavior. Consistently, the effect of the program on treated versus untreated voters is to increase presidential approval, reflect stronger pocketbook evaluations, and reveal more partisan identification in favor of the incumbent party. These results are in line with the effects on vote choice and, indeed, undergird them.

7.5 Investment Yields from CCTs

We highlight three implications from these results. First, it is clear that *Progresa* and *Oportunidades* produced high electoral payoffs for incumbent benefactors. While at first sight *Progresa* apparently reaped more votes for the PRI than did *Oportunidades* for the PAN, the payoffs from the latter may have been decisive in the PAN's victory in 2006. The program enabled the PAN's victory by generating support among the poor for this party's candidate *at the expense* of his rivals (see also Magaloni et al., 2009). A similar dynamic in vote buying among rural beneficiaries of *Progresa* in 2000 proved insufficient for maintaining the incumbent party in power.

Second, these results suggest that *partisan loyalties are conditional*, as argued in Chapter 3. If one compares two individuals nearly identical in sociodemographic and municipal-level traits, one treated and the other not, their partisan identities are likely to be different as a result of these benefits. Welfare benefits appear to create or re-create partisan identification. In the Mexican case, *Progresa* reinforced the rural poor's loyalties to the old ruling party, while *Oportunidades* helped the PAN generate new partisan sympathies in the same voter group and its urban counterpart. It is worth noting that the program works to decrease partisan identification with the PRI, but does not affect identification with the PRD. Notwithstanding the electoral success of the program in its two phases of implementation, predispositions among the poor in favor of the left perhaps remain latent and capable of being mobilized in future elections.

Third, a crucial way in which *Progresa* and *Oportunidades* shaped voting decisions is by spurring higher voter satisfaction with government performance (approval) and with their own material well-being (pocketbook evaluations). The impact of *Progresa* and *Oportunidades* on voters' self-reported material improvements is impressive. For example, a rural *Progresa* beneficiary was 60 percent more likely to report that her material well-being had improved than a rural nonbeneficiary. Similarly, both programs cause a significant increase in presidential approval. In rural localities, recipients of *Oportunidades* were 50 percent more likely to approve of Vicente Fox as president than nonrecipients.

These patterns of preference beg the question of credit-claiming for *Oportunidades*, since it is an outgrowth of *Progresa*, introduced by a rival political party in 1997 and credibly claimed by the PRI as its own. Of course, the inherited program was almost entirely rural in its community coverage in 2000 and more narrowly distributed. The relative impact of this program's expansion can be plausibly inferred by contrasting the columns of the table reporting rural subsamples. First, *Oportunidades* in 2006 does not affect rural beneficiaries' support for the PRI nor their level of identification with that party. This suggests that the PRI suffered no adverse effects from rural expansion of the CCT program and that it was able to retain much of the rural support generated by *Progresa* until 2000. But secondly, if rural voters had credited the PRI for *Oportunidades*, they should not have returned higher yields for the PAN. These gains, combined with the high rates of presidential approval in the same subsample, would argue in favor of the opposite interpretation – namely, that beneficiaries in the countryside accurately credited the PAN for program maintenance and expansion.

7.6 THE EFFICACY OF VOTE-BUYING STRATEGIES

We began this chapter by asking about voters' responses to different instruments of electoral investment. We classified these according to whether they deliver private or public goods and according to the level of government discretion in policy implementation. Our results provide a clear measure of the electoral benefits of clientelism relative to other vote-buying instruments, and unveil one powerful reason why politicians in the developing world have a strong preference for this form of political linkage. Clientelism produces high electoral yields at low cost and low risk. Politicians mobilize electoral support with selective inducements, and voters respond positively to these favors. Not only do they value the benefits as such; by staying loyal to the machine, they assure access to a future stream of benefits.

A second reason why clientelism exhibits high electoral returns, we have suggested, is because party machines can screen voters *ex ante* and target benefits to those who are most likely to vote for them – namely, loyal voters. In targeting their core voters, machines minimize the risk of voter opportunism. Our results also demonstrate that discretionary private goods have far higher electoral returns per peso spent than public goods projects. One possibility is that voters prefer excludable benefits over public goods that everyone can enjoy, as in Wantchekon (2004). However, it seems implausible that voters not value public infrastructure projects that improve their welfare, often more than particularistic favors.

Another possibility explaining the lower electoral return of public goods projects, as suggested by our theoretical approach, is that they entail higher risk of voter opportunism. The PRI targeted public goods projects, as our results in Chapter 4 demonstrated, disproportionately to small-core districts in an attempt to buy off swing voters and even opposition backers. The electoral returns of these investments are hence lower because it costs more to buy nonloyal voters and because the machine cannot twist their arms to assure good behavior at the ballot box.

Despite having uncovered remarkable electoral efficiency for clientelism, we should note that our results leave room for optimism. Poor voters handsomely rewarded incumbents that were credited with establishing or expanding CCT programs. The delivery of welfare-enhancing benefits through entitlements and sustained policy innovation matters for a governing party's electoral prospects. The influence on voting decisions exerted by such programs, singly and in combined form, is logically tied to a retrospective calculation that overshadows prospective ones. What is ironic in 2006 is the partisan identity of the two sides

7.6 *The Efficacy of Vote-Buying Strategies* 181

of vote buying, with the right delivering policy benefits unassociated with its historical reputation against the left credibly promising changes in distributive policies in the future. In the end, the average beneficiary reasoned in line with the saying, "Better a bird in the hand than two in the bush." The Spanish version exaggerates the discount rate of the future: *Más vale un pájaro en mano que cien* (100) *volando*. Effective vote buying, in line with folk wisdom, is usually based on tangible exchanges from the past rather than welcome promises to the future. Vote buying of this sort is fully consistent with democracy and, as the two previous chapters have demonstrated, it is welfare-enhancing where clientelism is not.

We end our discussion in this chapter by reflecting on the limits of electoral accountability. Our results in this book reveal a paradox of pseudo-democratic and democratic politics. Clientelistic parties and patronage politics persist despite the fact that these fail to enhance the poor's welfare, as Chapters 5 and 6 compellingly demonstrated. These practices persist because they exhibit high electoral returns.

This chapter has demonstrated that voters reward clientelism over other "vote-buying strategies," including the provision of public goods and the distribution of welfare-enhancing targeted benefits through entitlement programs. Understanding why voters respond in this apparently irrational manner is critical for advancing knowledge on the workings of democracy and electoral accountability in developing societies.

Following Magaloni (2006) our approach stresses a collective action dilemma. Each individual core voter acting alone has powerful reasons to remain loyal to the machine, even if this is corrupt, because she wants to continue to receive benefits and spoils today and into the future. The clientelistic linkage implies a credible threat of punishment to those who defect to the opposition (Magaloni, 2006). The PRI's clientelistic practices, as the narratives at the beginning of the chapter suggest, demanded a clear choice from a loyal voter: either stick with the machine or be denied benefits. Only voters loyal to the machine are given access to its spoils. The credible threat of future punishment for disloyalty plays a central role in keeping voters loyal and to a large extent accounts for the high electoral yield of clientelism, despite the fact that this form of political linkage is not welfare enhancing.

The problem is one of voter coordination. If all core voters could coordinate to vote against the machine, they might arrive to a Pareto optimal equilibrium where politicians supply welfare-enhancing benefits and public goods. But if each individual voter defects in isolation, she will solely bear the cost of opposing the machine. Often only middle-class voters are able to bear the costs of exiting the machine and make "ideological investments." The poor are more likely to remain trapped in clientelistic linkages.

8

Conclusion: The Politics of Entitled Social Protection

> Mexico is the country of inequality. Nowhere does there exist such a fearful difference in the distribution of fortune, civilization, cultivation of the soil and population. [...] This immense inequality of fortune does not only exist among the caste of whites, it is even discoverable among the Indians.
>
> Alexander von Humboldt (1811)

8.1 A POLITICAL TRANSFORMATION

With these words Prussian geographer and explorer, Alexander von Humboldt, described Mexico at the beginning of the nineteenth century. The paragraph could have been written to refer to most other Latin American countries today. Income inequality is one of the most distinctive traits of the region. This book has recounted how a Latin American developing country combated poverty in myriad ways and what it took for competing political parties to relinquish discretion in the allocation of public transfers, limiting the capacity of incumbent governments to distort antipoverty programs for partisan or electoral purposes. The book traces a major political transformation in Mexico's emerging democracy, which led elected officials and bureaucrats to serve the poor. We have demonstrated how clientelism distorts incentives to alleviate poverty. We have also explained how a society can transit from this type of suboptimal equilibrium in distributive politics to one in which governments deliver public goods and politicians become more accountable. From both a historical and a comparative perspective around the world, these kinds of transformations are relatively rare.

In Mexico millions of families were lifted out of extreme poverty through the establishment of a new system of social protection.[1] Despite lags in the remote areas of the country, the poor unquestionably benefit from properly

---

[1] This progress is real. In 1996, according to official statistics, 37 percent of Mexicans were extremely poor, in the sense that they could not meet basic nutritional needs. This percentage

8.1 A Political Transformation

targeted transfers, and enjoy better sanitation and access to local public services than before.[2] This book argues that what underlies this progress is a monumental political transformation.

The transition to democracy empowered Mexico's poor citizens. When winning votes in democratic elections became decisive for the fate of politicians, the policymaking arena changed. Contrary to what many observers at the outset feared, the transition to democracy did not reinforce clientelistic ties, but resulted instead in the design of effective social policies. The ability of political parties to manipulate social transfers was curbed, and more competent and autonomous bureaucrats were pushed to better target social assistance to the poor.[3]

The Mexican state deployed its considerable capacity and resources, including teachers, doctors, nurses, and social advocates, within a centrally controlled bureaucratic agency to extend a Conditional Cash Transfer program to virtually every village and irregular urban settlement in Mexico. At the same time, investment funds for social infrastructure successfully combined federal revenue-sharing (targeted transfers skewed in favor of the poorest municipalities) with effective decentralization (with local elected officials in charge of project selection). Removed from the national partisan considerations that drove the allocation of such funds in the typical dynamic of pork-barrel politics inherited from the past, investment in public works has translated into the delivery of water, sewerage, electricity, and other basic services in a more efficient and inclusive manner. And changes in social policy have had impacts beyond the income effects of cash transfers. Thousands of children who would otherwise have died have been saved by timely interventions.

Throughout the developing world most social programs are still characterized by clientelism and political manipulation. Can the experience of Mexico shed light on how to improve the design of social protection and poverty relief reforms elsewhere? In this conclusion we recapitulate our theoretical contributions, summarizing the main empirical findings of our study, and push for an agenda of future research that embraces conditional cash transfers as a legitimate strategy of social protection, rather than a defective intervention falling short of the social-democratic ideal of a contributory universalistic welfare state. In outlining this agenda, we provide a comparative institutional perspective

---

dropped to under 19 percent by 2012 (CONEVAL, www.coneval.gob.mx/Medicion/Paginas/Evolucion-de-las-dimensiones-de-la-pobreza-1990–2010-.aspx accessed August 20, 2013).

[2] See also CONEVAL (2013) for trends in access to health care, whereby the population without access has been reduced from 60 to 20 percent. Note, however, the dismal performance of basic education and low-quality health services, particularly in very poor indigenous communities.

[3] We do not deny that as the transition to democracy proceeded, social programs subject to political manipulation have multiplied, given the interest of many state governments in creating programs based on clientelistic exchange. But federal social policy, affecting all thirty-two states, has clearly shifted in the direction of less discretion and more propoor targeting.

on poverty alleviation through cash transfers. We suggest that this entitled social protection is here to stay, and is not better nor worse than other institutional solutions for poverty relief, such as the welfare state, church-based charity, or private philanthropy. In the final section we speculate about the future of social policy in Mexico.

8.2 DEMOCRATIZATION, STATE CAPACITY, AND THE DEMISE OF CLIENTELISM

At least since the classic work by Scott (1972b), social scientists and many policymakers understand that clientelism is a false solution to the quandaries of the poor. But for politicians clientelism is an extremely attractive strategy for assuring political support. Although the scholarly literature provides good accounts of the conditions under which clientelism thrives, there is lesser consensus about the factors that lead to the demise of this form of intermediation between politicians and voters.[4]

Clientelism depends on both supply and demand conditions that allow political machines to broker votes and entice citizens to pledge them. Kitschelt and Wilkinson (2004) note the profound association between modernization and the erosion of clientelism, summarizing the channels through which economic development undermines both demand and supply factors. On the demand side, they suggest that with modernization social networks become territorially larger, which create voter loyalties to larger groups; lower discount rates make voters more patient in awaiting the benefits of programmatic promises; and the cognitive sophistication of poor voters enhances their capacity to see the causal process linking public policies with personal benefits.

On the supply side, Kitschelt and Wilkinson (2004) note that the monitoring problem of local brokers becomes more challenging as social networks expand and citizens are spatially more mobile; there will be greater constraints on parties obtaining the resources to pay increasingly expensive votes as citizens become richer; the greater heterogeneity of voters may create greater trade-offs for politicians and deter them from continuing with particularistic appeals; and media exposure may hinder the capacity of parties to engage in corruption, fraud, and favoritism.[5]

---

[4] See, among others, Baland and Robinson (2007); Calvo and Murillo (2004); Keefer and Vlaicu (2008); Kitschelt and Wilkinson (2007); Medina and Stokes (2006); Nichter (2008); Stokes (2005); Stokes et al. (2013); Wantchekon (2004); Weitz-Shapiro (2014), and the review by Hicken (2011).

[5] Kitschelt and Wilkinson (2007) also provide some thoughts regarding the links between the prevalence of clientelism and ethnic heterogeneity, but the literature seems not to have advanced enough yet (on either the theoretical or empirical fronts) to provide a clear hypothesis regarding the causality between modernization, ethnic composition, and clientelism. See, however, the foundational work by Wantchekon (2004) showing a promising research avenue on these issues based on field experiments.

8.2 Democratization, State Capacity, and the Demise of Clientelism

The experience in Latin America suggests, however, that the demise of clientelism can take a very long time, even under conditions of economic development.[6] Furthermore, the historical experience with clientelism in European democracies should warn against a simple modernization story being taken as the explanation for the difference between countries that embraced the programmatic design of social transfers, and those that have not, even under long consolidated democratic regimes.

In the European context, the historical emergence of clientelism is often understood as an institutional process intrinsically linked to the emergence of political parties and democracy. As initially formulated by Martin Shefter (1994) and explored more fully in the essays collected in Piattoni (2001), demand conditions for clientelism depend fundamentally on cultural norms and voter attributes that may be relatively unchanging, making some countries more susceptible to this form of political intermediation. But most of the variation in clientelism across Europe, following the institutionalist account, lies on the supply side.

According to Shefter (1994), when the enfranchisement of voters occurred historically after a charter of bureaucratic autonomy for public servants had been established, clientelism and patronage ceased to be an option and parties decided to mobilize voters more readily on the basis of programmatic appeals. As noted by Piattoni (2001), this institutional approach seems to be accurate for continental Europe, but is harder to reconcile with cases that successfully reformed highly clientelistic systems, like the United States and Britain.

Stokes et al. (2013) suggest a mechanism for the reform of clientelism that seeks to reconcile a modernization account with the institutionalist one just described. In their view, the thrust to abandon clientelism emerges from within political parties, responding to shifts in the electorate. In their account party leaders are at odds with their copartisan brokers because of problems of agency loss. Public resources intended for clients are appropriated by intermediaries who are interested in capturing rents and not only in winning elections. The agency problem emerges because brokers have local knowledge and monitoring capacity that leaders lack. In their model party leaders are concerned about excessive leakage of scarce financial resources within their organizations. Reforms in machine politics are driven by this motivation, not an effort to curb corruption per se.

---

[6] In the "Democratic Accountability and Linkages Project," Herbert Kitschelt and his associates find through expert survey judgments compelling empirical evidence of an association between clientelism and underdevelopment (Kitschelt, 2011, figure 4). A similar association is reported in Stokes et al. (2013: 155) using Latinobarometro and Afrobarometer survey data. Note, however, that in the subnational data of actual clientelist transfers reported here (as well as in Magaloni et al., 2004), the relationship between clientelism and development may well be nonlinear. In the Mexican case, at least, very poor municipalities received fewer clientelistic transfers than those at intermediate levels of development.

Using this theoretical framework, Stokes et al. (2013) seek to explain the demise of clientelism in Britain and the United States, precisely the cases that are more difficult to explain in the Shefter model (Hicken, 2011). The largest weight of their explanation, however, is not institutional. Primacy is given to the effects of industrialization and economic growth on voters. As the electorate became richer, they argue, it was harder for parties to monitor their behavior; and as costs of communication were reduced, parties could appeal more directly to voters. Given the conflict posited with party brokers and confronted with these modernizing trends, "leaders were only too happy to slough off their machines" (Stokes et al., 2013: 201).

This is not the place to adjudicate between explanations for the demise of clientelism in the United States and Britain. But our evidence, drawing from the case of Mexico, suggests that changes in bureaucratic autonomy had powerful effects on clientelism, independent from modernization processes. In our discussion of social policy reform in Mexico, we noted that a more professional administration of federal agencies tasked with social policy was made possible by a process similar to that described by Barbara Geddes (1994) in Brazil, where politicians found it to their advantage to allow bureaucracies to decide resource allocation without partisan considerations. Similar stories are told regarding the reform of the postal service in the United States, from a system of patronage structured around party careerism, to what Carpenter (2001) has characterized as reputational autonomy built on the basis of a "coalition of esteem" among the publics at large.

The main thrust of social policy in Mexico changed, as clear and transparent formulas, instead of political discretion, determined the allocation of decentralized social funds and the selection of beneficiaries of CCT programs.[7] Although we recognize that serendipity played a role in this transformation, in the sense that one individual's role (Santiago Levy) in both designing and skillfully gaining support for his new architecture for social policy played a critical role in these changes, there is no question that the autonomous bureaucratic capacity of the Mexican state loomed large as an enabling condition for these changes to take place. The social policy bureaucrats (and the indefatigable promoters on the ground, like Enrique Bentzul) were able to put in place a program that works and to implement credible evaluations of its performance. Political actors initially opposed to the policy changes had to tolerate the new programs. As the programs expanded, beneficiaries became further empowered, shifting the balance of power within the ruling coalition and achieving permanence for *entitled social protection*. PRI politicians in Mexico would probably have preferred to keep their party machines; and politicians from the other parties,

---

[7] It is worth noting that the fiscal federalism and decentralization scholarly literatures provide good explanations of the distributive politics implications of discretion versus rule-based allocations of fiscal transfers. But they give little guidance as to why or how rules for distribution actually emerge.

8.3 The Range of Poverty Alleviation Programs in Mexico

in fact, spent substantial resources trying to build machines of their own in the states. But agencies in charge of social policy, at least at the federal level, became professionalized and relatively free from political influence.

A final comment is in order with respect to the links between clientelism and the process of democratization. The literature has noted the importance of ballot secrecy for the weakening of clientelism. For example, throughout Latin America, an important discussion has involved the use of the Australian ballot as an effective way to prevent electoral corruption.[8] In one of the most interesting contributions, Baland and Robinson (2007 and 2012) studied the effects of Chile's adoption of the secret ballot, including a decrease in the value of political brokers and, perhaps most remarkably, a decrease in land values (owning large expanses of land with captive blocks of voters became less valuable for the oligarchy). Research in Argentina, and elsewhere, however, has suggested that political operatives on the ground can often monitor votes even when they are secret.[9]

For the specific case of Mexico, Larreguy (2012) has exploited, in a truly creative manner, the difference between electoral precincts drawn to respect the boundaries of rural communities with communal *ejidos* and those that do not. He shows that monitoring is more likely when the "fit" between those two territorial units is close than when they are only loosely matched. In his evidence, the PRI successfully obtains more votes in places where it can easily monitor voters in their *ejido* community. He also shows that the provision of public goods (public education facilities) suffers in those same places easily monitored. Hence, politicians choose clientelistic intermediation with those *ejidos'* poor inhabitants. It is clear that even in the presence of the secret ballot and after the decline of PRI hegemony, it is feasible for clientelism to survive, particularly in small, poor, and isolated communities.[10]

8.3 THE RANGE OF POVERTY ALLEVIATION PROGRAMS IN MEXICO

Clientelism has commanded much attention among development specialists, particularly in Latin America, but it has seldom been studied, as in this book, in the context of the range of options for social policy interventions available to politicians.[11] The decentralization of federal programs for the construction of basic social infrastructure in favor of the municipalities in Mexico

---

[8] See Gingerich (2013) and Gingerich and Medina (2013).
[9] See Auyero (2007); Brusco et al. (2004); Stokes (2005); Calvo and Murillo (2013).
[10] Calvo and Murillo (2013) reconstruct partisan networks in Chile and Argentina, showing that organizational capacity plays a critical role in the sensitivity to the proximity of party members, even in urban settings.
[11] For exceptions see the essays in Kitschelt and Wilkinson (2007); Kitschelt and Kselman (2013); Larreguy (2012).

led to the creation of poverty-formula-based transfers that have transformed the way municipalities undertake basic public works projects. The *Fondo de Infraestructura Social Municipal* (FISM) has become a reliable source of federal monies not conditioned by partisan alignments. By decentralizing control over the selection and execution of local public goods projects, the federal government created incentives for mayors to be more attentive to citizen demands and more effective in the use of these resources. It is probable that corruption in public works, or at least some of the leakage in the flow of resources among levels of government, has also been reduced. Resources have flowed away from state capitals and metropolitan areas to more peripheral and underdeveloped municipalities, where a higher social impact of infrastructure funds can be achieved.

In contrast, *Pronasol* left poverty seriously unattended. Political discretion is a key explanatory variable accounting for the distortion of that antipoverty program. Ample discretion remained for government officials to fund and operate projects through the party's clientelistic networks. There was also a great deal of corruption in the implementation of *Pronasol*. Government officials at all levels of government –federal, state, and municipal – diverted resources for personal gain because there was virtually no public scrutiny of resource employment. Given the lack of transparency and accountability in *Pronasol*'s operations, it is not at all surprising that a massive amount of government resources meant to alleviate poverty ended up in the wrong hands. Very few of these investments reached the extreme poor.

To be self-sustaining, clientelistic linkages require voters' complicity. Poor voters willingly support a party machine because it gives them access to a steady stream of benefits and favors. Voters willingly sustain a system that is corrupt and keeps them poor. To exit the system, the voter needs to know that many others like her will vote against the machine, for otherwise she alone would bear the costs of defection. The equilibrium is perverse because everyone is an accomplice of a system that is collectively suboptimal.

This book has argued that the impetus to restrain clientelism in Mexico first came from a voter rebellion against the system. Massive voter defection after the peso crisis of 1995 brought about a reshuffling in the workings of the institutional apparatus, fundamentally transforming presidential-legislative relations, the balance of power between the president and the party, and between the federal and subnational governments. The critical moment was the loss of majority control by the ruling party in the lower chamber of Congress after the 1997 midterm elections.

All these changes, however, fall short of institutionalizing a universalistic system of social protection in the mold of the European welfare state. For many critics on the left, the new programs represent a defeat in the effort to create truly redistributive arrangements of social solidarity through which risks can be shared fully among citizens and the most disadvantaged members

8.4 Poverty Relief in Comparative Historical Perspective

of society protected. CCTs are decried for displacing an agenda of social reform instead of being hailed as a triumph for the democratically empowered poor majority.

8.4 POVERTY RELIEF IN COMPARATIVE HISTORICAL PERSPECTIVE

Beyond the Mexican case or the current debates on clientelism, how should we think about poverty relief strategies in the context of a redefined role for the state in the provision of social protection in the twenty-first century? In order to do so we should understand the transformation of clientelistic poverty relief into social entitlements from a comparative historical perspective. We can gain, in fact, a richer perspective of the experiences of poverty relief strategies by looking at the deep historical origin of entitlements and cash transfers, well before the advent of the welfare state.

Targeted transfers and entitlements should not be judged primarily on the basis of how they compare to an ideal-typical welfare state like the ones developed in the advanced industrial democracies during the twentieth century. Conditional cash transfer programs are not defective systems devised by neoliberal technocrats to avoid caring for the poor. They are a new institutional strategy for poverty relief emerging at the outset of the twenty-first century, in response to democratic challenges faced by policymakers from across the political spectrum. Responsive to citizen demands at a time of fiscal retrenchment, governments have become more efficient and more effective in their resource deployment. Depending on the bureaucratic capacity of the state, those strategies may well succeed in bringing an end to extreme poverty, not just in Mexico but throughout most of Latin America.

Latin American nations failed to develop welfare state systems like those of Sweden or Canada – and it remains highly unlikely they ever will. Behind the lofty ideals of the welfare state proclaimed by many governments in the region since the early twentieth century, what has prevailed in practice throughout the region is a discriminatory and regressive system of state transfers benefiting corporatist interests and the middle classes. The counterfactual against which antipoverty policy reforms should be compared is this truncated welfare state, or the alternative of leaving the poor to be tended by private philanthropy or religious charity.

While the new systems of social protection may be criticized as a step backward in their evolution toward the welfare state, Latin American nations have never been on a clear path toward the creation of European-style solidarity systems of redistribution. The welfare state in Latin America has remained truncated, benefiting only a fraction of the urban working class. Furthermore, the adoption of pension, health, and social security reforms in several countries in Latin America during the past decade suggests that, despite the evidence of overall retrenchment in expenditures (Haggard and Kaufman, 2008), many countries have in fact expanded the coverage of risk-mitigating social security institutions (Mares and Carnes, 2009).

The social protection regime emerging from the neoliberal adjustment at the turn of this century is undeniably far removed from the social democratic ideal. In some regards, as stressed by critics on the left, the new arrangements are a reversion to features characteristic of poor relief strategies during the liberal era of the nineteenth century. Poor relief institutions were in place for several centuries in several European countries before the advent of the modern welfare state, and had been transplanted in a rather tentative, embryonic manner to many Latin American cities, also during the nineteenth century. The political motivations and constraints explaining these forms of social protection are poorly understood, whether before the emergence of the modern welfare state or after the fiscal crisis impelling its retrenchment.[12]

The new institutional responses to poverty in the twenty-first century can be traced from a comparative historical perspective to processes occurring before the advent of the welfare state. A good place to start is with the very prominent debates assessing the effects of the English Poor Laws.[13] In his classic work, Karl Polanyi (1957 [1944]) argues that a critical institutional shift (The Great Transformation) occurred in England with the abolishment of the so-called Speenhamland system of poverty relief to be replaced by the New Poor Laws of 1834. This shift would shape the way in which the state dealt with poverty from then on. The Poor Law Reform of 1834 was motivated by a vigorous debate in Britain and in continental Europe, to a large extent neglected by current scholarship. The debate is important because it demonstrates that targeted systems of poverty relief existed well before the late nineteenth and early twentieth centuries, when poor relief was substituted by welfare state systems of social protection. In the developing world, this replacement did not occur, but poverty relief systems did have precedents in the colonial period and postindependence in the nineteenth century.

A connection between the early strategies of poverty alleviation and the emergence of the welfare state in Europe is now better appreciated (Kahl, 2005;

---

[12] In contrast, the political economy of contributory social insurance programs, within the encompassing term of "the welfare state," is quite well understood. The enormous success of the occupation-based insurance systems of social protection in Europe has generated a rich scholarly literature addressing, for example, the role of labor union density and left-wing parties in the emergence of these systems; the combination of business and labor interests in risk-sharing, giving rise to variations in institutional configurations; and during the era of retrenchment, the role of deindustrialization, risk induced by globalization, or shifts in workers' skills. The literature is vast, but a good place to start is Baldwin (1990); Esping-Andersen (1990); Huber and Stephens (2001); Iversen (2005); Mares (2004); Pontusson (2005).

[13] An exception is the path-breaking work by Lindert (1998 and 2004). A less comparative, but relevant literature was generated in the United States, studying the path to a very different model of social protection that never evolved in the template of continental Europe or Scandinavia (see Skocpol, 1992; Gordon, 2000; Piven and Cloward, 1993).

8.4 Poverty Relief in Comparative Historical Perspective

Van Kersbergen and Manow, 2009). Specifically, the budding scholarship has highlighted the importance of Catholic versus Protestant traditions of charity (and the peculiar Calvinist version). Going back to the pre-welfare-state era allows us to understand the full range of strategies for poverty relief that were available and attempted by governments at various moments, and how they were distinct from the polar extremes of clientelistic practices and welfare-state redistributive compensation.

Tracing the origins of entitlement and cash transfer systems of poverty relief to nineteenth-century liberalism also highlights the role of church-based charitable organizations, mutualist societies, and other philanthropic forms of associational life that, for many decades if not centuries, were the mainstay of poverty assistance in Europe, Latin America, and the United States before the advent of poverty relief. The political conditions under which liberal social reformers wrested control of social policy from the Church and forged new forms of social policy shed some light on the emergence of contemporary systems of social protection as progressive rather than regressive developments.

In his *Memoir on Pauperism* published in 1835, Alexis de Tocqueville noted that there were two alternatives for "welfare" (p. 26): either the Catholic model of charity found on the continent, or what he characterized as the Protestant model of public charity, found in England. Indeed, during much of the premodern and modern eras, European nations dealt with poverty through a relatively uniform model of parish-centered charity organizations. The English Old and New Poor Laws were in fact institutional innovations in response to the model based on the Church.

To understand the political conditions that give rise to poverty relief strategies in the world today, it is useful to highlight the history of the country with the longest tradition of poverty alleviation programs, England. The English Poor Laws were established as a compulsory system of poor relief administered and financed by local governments (parishes) through the Elizabethan Acts of 1597–1598 and 1601. Able-bodied males were supposed to be put to work, children given apprenticeships, and the so-called deserving poor (old or disabled) relieved with "competent sums of money." The system was secular, public, and national in scope, but administered by local government.

The so-called Speenhamland system was introduced in 1795, to a large extent, as a reaction to the challenges posed by the French Revolution, to provide compensation for the poor through local parishes, for the first time ensuring a minimum income to the poor. Eliminating this system in 1834 was a momentous decision that occurred only after a sea change in English politics. As Polanyi notes, "The Parliamentary Reform Bill of 1832 disenfranchised the rotten boroughs and gave power in the Commons once and for all to the commoners. Their first great act of reform was the abolishing of Speenhamland" (p. 101). The Poor Law Reform of 1834 was a critical moment in the evolution of modern capitalism, according to Polanyi, since it created unfettered labor markets, abolished most outhouse poor relief, and replaced it with poorhouses.[14]

The larger part of the debate over the English reform concerned the issue of whether poverty relief created the correct incentives for work.[15] The main conclusion of the Report of the Poor Law Commission in England was that poor relief fostered massive voluntary unemployment. The "mythology" of the Old Poor Law has been debunked by recent scholarship, starting with the influential essay from Blaug (1963), who suggested that the 1834 report's findings regarding the effects of poor relief on incentives to work were unfounded. The evidence regarding the use of relief by able-bodied men was highly suspect.[16] Moreover, recent scholarship suggests that the Old Poor Law and Speenhamland may have, in fact, played a critical role in preventing famine and chronic malnutrition (Kelly and O'Grada, 2010). But as noted by Block and Somers (2003), the dispute over weak work incentives generated by direct income transfers to the poor has loomed large in later debates over entitlements in countries like the United States.

Perhaps a more instructive precedent of the importance of poor relief before the advent of the welfare state, less tainted by the misinformed discussions of the effects of poor relief on the poor, is the case of the Netherlands. According to De Vries and Van der Woude (1997), transfers for income support in Dutch municipalities, primarily for the poor, unemployed, or dependent persons in urban areas and mostly during winter months, may have accounted for as much as 3–4 percent of the national income since the mid-eighteenth century. They may have reached up to 15 percent of the population by the nineteenth century (Lindert, 1998).

The origin of the system of charitable and poor relief institutions in the Netherlands can be traced back to the revolt against Spanish rule and the

---

[14] Himmelfarb (1997) provides a succinct description of the system: The Poor Laws dated back to the sixteenth century when the dissolution of the monasteries obliged the government to make provision for the indigent who had previously been cared for by the church. Toward the end of Elizabeth's reign, the laws were codified, providing alms ('outdoor relief') and almshouses ('indoor relief') for the aged and infirm, apprenticeships for children, and temporary shelter and work for the able-bodied in workhouses or poorhouses. Although the system was nation-wide, the administration was local, each parish being required by law to levy taxes (poor rates) on householders to pay for the relief of those having a 'settlement' (a legal residence) within its bounds. This system, applied at different times and places with varying degrees of rigor or leniency, survived two centuries of revolutions, wars, and momentous social and industrial changes. (pp. 5–6)

[15] Malthus' *Essay on the Principles of Population* (1826[1798]) is usually credited as one of the main intellectual forces behind the critique of the Old Poor Laws. While providing comparative evidence of demographic checks around the world, he also mounted a powerful critique of what he believed was an ineffective, if not altogether pernicious, system of poverty relief.

[16] Block and Somers (2003) provide a good account of the intellectual history of this debate and attempt to explain the survival for over a hundred years of a factually incorrect assessment of the effects of the Poor Laws, paradoxically shared by both left and right, including the likes of Marx and Malthus.

8.4 Poverty Relief in Comparative Historical Perspective

expropriation of Church property by the provinces in 1574. Continuing the Catholic tradition of charity, but under a Calvinist model, parishes and Reformed deacon boards (consistories) from various denominations became responsible for poor relief (De Vries and van der Woude, 1997: 656).

In 1682 a clearly decentralized system emerged in which cities and villages became legally responsible for the support of "their" poor. By the second half of the seventeenth century a coordinated network of religious and public agencies were in place, and remained so until the twentieth century. As this system became financially more burdensome and under a mounting critique of the incentives for work it may have generated, not dissimilar to the one voiced by many in the English setting, efforts were made to transform the outdoor relief efforts into workhouses. But those municipal poorhouses were never particularly successful, so that the basic outline of the poverty transfers system of the Netherlands survived well into the beginning of the twentieth century.[17] The modern welfare state of the country was built on this foundation.

From a historical vantage point, what were the alternatives to the poor relief systems of income transfers? In the case of the Catholic countries, the system of compensation to the poor remained primarily under the control of the Church.[18] The state did not succeed in wresting control of these compensatory resources away from religious corporations. Thus, instead of public funds playing a complementary role as in England and Holland, systems of almsgiving were based primarily on voluntary philanthropy and Church endowments. No system was deemed superior to the other at the time, and, in fact, a moral argument was made justifying the voluntary charity system as superior on the grounds that it created mutual obligations between persons (Tocqueville, 1835 [1997]).[19]

---

[17] De Vries and van der Woude (1997) note that the exceptional character of Dutch social policy is not to be found in the size of the payments but in the size of the population deemed eligible for support (pp. 660–661). This is consonant with the findings of Lindert (1998) in which only Belgium reached a coverage similar to that found in the Netherlands during the nineteenth century. What explained the differences in generosity and coverage of poverty relief programs in the era predating the welfare state? Lindert (1998) has lucidly argued that at least in the case of England, with the abolition of Speemhamland, it is possible to think about this "retrenchment" in poor relief as a response to the democratic enfranchisement of a middle class, which was no longer willing to pay for an arrangement deemed to benefit the extremes in the income distribution. Research on the links between poor relief and regime change in this era is sorely needed.

[18] Outside of Europe, Turkey and probably all of Northern Africa had a different approach to poverty relief, based on what we would think of today as philanthropic organizations or foundations. In Islamic societies the Waqf was established as a trust fund for the purpose of satisfying public needs. This institution predates European trust organizations by half a millennium, since European charities did not create trusts for charity until the thirteenth century (Kuran, 2001). Under Islamic law the Waqf was regulated in its establishment and operation by the state, but its assets were privately provided. The administration, although connected to mosques, was autonomous (in the person of the trustee, the mutawalli). In the eighteenth century, perhaps around 6 percent of the population in Istanbul was fed by Awkaf (Kuran: 850).

[19] Alexis de Tocqueville's *Memoir on Pauperism* (1835) sought to provide a more comparative perspective on the issue of the Poor Laws. He argued, similarly to most of his contemporaries, that

In Italy, for example, as late as the end of the nineteenth century, institutions for pious works (*opere pie*) were very numerous, although poorly endowed. According to a contemporary study (Emminghaus, 1870) of the more than 20,000 institutions operating throughout the Italian peninsula and Sicily, the vast majority of them had insufficient resources to run their own administration, let alone to provide relief to the poor. Venice (and probably other cities, including Florence) was an exception, with around 13 percent of its population receiving some form of support (Emminghaus, 1870). But by leaving poverty relief to voluntary almsgiving and private philanthropy, the Italian state had, for all practical purposes, abandoned the poor.

A particular element of the Italian model of *opere pie* was brought to Spain by the Bourbon kings in the 1760s with the establishment of *Montepios*, official agencies providing pensions for survivors of public functionaries, that evolved into lending institutions and, in a residual fashion, providers of beneficence to the poor (Chandler, 1991). In the case of New Spain (now Mexico), the Bourbon innovation was the direct precedent to the establishment of the *Sacro y Real Monte de Piedad y Animas* (now the *Nacional Monte de Piedad*), founded in 1775 as a pawnbroker and still functioning today. The scale of these interventions was not trivial. For example, from 1775 to 1792 the *Monte de Piedad* in New Spain engaged in almost one million transactions (Villamil, 1877).[20]

During the nineteenth century debates regarding "pauperism" wrongly conflated the prevalence of poverty with the count of the population actually receiving transfers. The assumption that pauperism could be equated with poverty led Tocqueville, for example, to claim that Portugal and Spain had lower poverty rates than England. The empirical evidence showed only that a greater share of inhabitants received aid in England than elsewhere. As late as 1875, studies commissioned by the British Parliament to explore poor relief around the world noted, in a discussion about the Russian peasantry, that widespread peasant poverty notwithstanding, "absolute pauperism or want of food is rarely met" (Doyle, 1875: 404).[21] In the same report, Portugal was characterized as follows:

In Portugal pauperism does not exist [...] This evil which accompanies the development of industry in the large centres of operatives, and which casts large populations into

---

poverty relief had the unintended effect of *increasing* poverty rates. He believed that the English system was fraught with the risk of creating a compulsory system with the wrong incentives for able-bodied workers ("creating an idle and lazy class, living at the expense of the industrial and working class" [p. 30]), reducing social mobility (p. 33), but perhaps most crucially from his perspective, removing the "moral tie" between rich and poor that charity entailed (p. 31). He believed that transfers to the poor would eventually "culminate by bringing a violent revolution in the State" (p. 37).

[20] Francois (2006) provides an assessment of Monte de Piedad suggesting that although the institution probably had little impact in terms of poverty relief, it provided middle-class women with access to a financial institution. She argues that this prevented the downward mobility of white women.

[21] A similar assertion was made for the principality of Bucharest: "Pauperism, properly so called, has no existence in these principalities. By the rural law of 1834 every peasant was created a

permanent conditions of brutish ignorance and misery, does not exist in our country, which is more agricultural than industrial. (Doyle, 1875: 469)

In the case of New Spain, Alexander von Humboldt knew better. In his careful statistical analysis of the demographic and social conditions at the end of the eighteenth century, the German scholar calculated that between 15 and 20 percent of the population in Mexico City was completely destitute. He understood well that poverty in the countryside was even worse. "Mexican Indians ... offer a picture of extreme misery" and the "natives live only from hand to mouth" (Humboldt, 1811: 139). He characterized poverty in rural settings as a consequence not just of the culture or the Indian character, a commonplace among European observers at the time, but he linked poverty to the deficiency of colonial administration, the racial divisions of the caste system, and a general situation of disempowerment of Indian communities. He did note that conditions in mining towns were probably better, a pattern in poverty profiles that persists in Mexico even today.

The Catholic model of continental Europe was transferred to the Spanish crown possessions, although with adaptations in both the colonial and post-independence periods. During the colonial period, a combination of hospitals funded by private beneficence, almsgiving through the Church (including the resources channeled to the needy through the tithe), public granaries (*alhondigas*) to deliver food during droughts and famines, and pawnbroker institutions conformed a fragmented system of social protection for the poor.

Perhaps the most notable example of the hospital model in Mexico would be the Hospital de Jesus, the first hospital in the hemisphere founded by Hernan Cortez himself in 1524, sustained until 1932 by the Pignatelli family, the heirs of the *conquistador*, and still operating to this day. Juan de Dios Peza (1881) describes the system of hospitals that took care of the poor in the latter part of the nineteenth century, to which he adds orphanages, the poorhouse, and incipient vaccination campaigns.

Almsgiving (through the moral duty of *caritas*) and beneficence (*bienfaisance*) were the prime mechanisms through which the poor were compensated for their misfortunes during the liberal era of the nineteenth century. In Mexico, the first law establishing and regulating nonreligious benevolent charity organizations was decreed in 1899. This law was subsequently modified and reformed multiple times after the Revolution, but remains in place today.

This piecemeal package of poor relief, anchored by charity and philanthropy, is the origin of the frequent accusation that social programs aimed at the poor are merely *asistencialistas*,[22] connoting minimum assistance that is degrading, creates dependence and possibly alienation, and is inadequate to the

---

landowner [...] Some people are 'badly off', but there is none of the squalid misery which is to be met with in the cities of Western Europe" (Doyle, 1875: 480).

[22] There is no obvious translation of this term, which is well understood throughout Latin America, but may be referred to as "handouts," "welfare," "charity," "paternalism," or "aid dependence"

task of helping the poor to escape from their destitution.[23] Yet this same package is historically grounded in an early modern approach widespread in continental Europe and bequeathed to Latin America through Spanish colonialism.

Tocqueville was concerned with the moral implication of moving away from a model of charity, which in his view connected citizens in mutual obligations in a way a state transfer would never do. In the United States conservatives often argue that entitlement programs, such as Aid to Families with Dependent Childern (AFDC), make recipients dependent on the state and remove the natural incentives for work. AFDC is the most important entitlement program in the United States, emerging from the New Deal.

Arguably, one of the most striking features of the debate surrounding means-tested relief in the United States is how much of the rhetoric resonates with the much earlier debate surrounding the Poor Laws in England. As Skocpol (1992) argues, the broad popular acceptance of common public schooling was not present for the case of social protection for the poor (p. 92).[24] In contrast "local communities did not so readily compete to emulate and outdo one another in their provisions for the poor and the dependent" (p. 93). Although the United States developed Almshouses and "outdoor relief" in the English model, the support of either the federal government or local legislatures for these efforts at compensation were more driven by the distributive politics imperatives of political parties than by efforts to benefit the poor. Indeed, the rise of entitlements has the same origin, as parties sought at both state and national levels to outbid each other in legislating benefits for veterans and their families after the civil war. In their timing, entitlements for soldiers coincided with the rife clientelism of machine politics throughout the North.

In a remarkable turn of public discourse, in the United States citizens have, in fact, internalized a stigma associated with the understanding of "being on welfare" as a derogatory term, very different from a situation of participating

---

(see the online translation tool Linguee). http://www.linguee.com/spanish-english/translation/asistencialismo.html (accessed March 2, 2013).

[23] The critique of social programs as *asistencialistas* is not limited to critics on the left. See, for example, the critique of Mexico's poverty relief programs by Carlos Slim, one of the richest men in the world: "Slim: programas asistencialistas no resuelven pobreza," October 3, 2006. http://www.eluniversal.com.mx/primera/27727.html

[24] Lindert (2004) has shown quite persuasively that the initial head start of the United States in the provision of free primary education was a consequence of the combination of democratic pressures voiced through popular vote; and decentralization, which allowed autonomous local authorities to raise the revenue necessary to meet local popular demands. Comparisons with France and England before 1914, and the rest of Europe during the twentieth century, suggest, however, that the same decentralization may have become a disadvantage for the US education system at a later phase, as some regions lagged behind in as far as education was concerned and the central government did not become a compensatory force for equalization, tolerating among other things the disenfranchisement and dismal provision of education services to blacks in the South.

in the "welfare state" (Gordon, 1994), which at least for "liberals" or "progressives" should have a positive connotation. Although this is not the place to provide a nuanced account of the rise of entitlements in the United States, from a nineteenth-century perspective the critiques are not particularly novel or buttressed by hard evidence.

Skocpol (1992) has helpfully clarified that social policy in the United States developed through regulations and social spending that indeed buffered citizens from market dislocations, family crises, and material want, just like in Europe. But rather than creating "sets of regulations and benefits devised by male bureaucrats and politicians for the good of male wage earners and their dependents" (p. 525), the United States protected mothers and soldiers. This first phase of social protection for the disabled, elderly, widowed, and orphaned was accompanied by female enfranchisement and expansions in health expenditures to protect children and mothers (Miller, 2008). This process never quite developed into a "maternalist welfare state" (Skocpol, 1992: 526) focused on families, but it does signify that the United States was not as much a laggard in social protection as the literature on the European welfare state would lead us to believe.

The American case also suggests a rather important connection between social protection and the threat of conflict and protest which the more or less linear evolution of welfare state development in Europe tends to obscure. In their now classic work, Piven and Cloward (1993) suggest that poverty relief in the United States was determined by cycles of protest and threats of civil unrest, which were counterbalanced by market forces seeking to prop strong incentives to work. In their study of poverty relief, specifically the most important means-tested program in the United States from 1935 to 1996, Aid to Families of Dependent Children (AFDC),[25] the poor seldom had any voice in government, and therefore did not necessarily benefit from many of the social policies enacted. But at times of social turmoil the poor can make their voices heard loud and clear. This resonates strongly with our discussion of the Zapatista uprising as an impetus for the reform of social policy in Mexico.

8.5 ENTITLED SOCIAL PROTECTION: AN EMERGING PARADIGM?

Most scholars have a great admiration for the history of social democracy and its success at creating a comprehensive welfare state system in Europe. They do acknowledge that the influences that led to the development of institutions that generated solidarity, socialization of risks, and redistribution are not the exclusive province of the left, but that one can trace their origin to preemptive reforms like those of Bismark in Germany. And recent scholarship has allowed

---

[25] The program was replaced by the Temporary Assistance for Needy Families, TANF, a joint federal-state cash assistance program.

a better understanding of how there were also other influences, including a religious one noted by Kahl (2005), that are not dissimilar to some of the processes observed in Latin America, where the Catholic Church has had such a prominent role in charity and tending to the poor.[26]

The liberal reforms of the nineteenth century in England do not appear as particularly progressive from the vantage point of the welfare state literature. And the US American historical development, moving away from partisan-controlled bureaucracies to provide clientelistic transfers under the guise of social protection, to be substituted by entitlements are usually seen as small achievements compared to the monumental task of creating full-fledged welfare state institutions. But all these are remarkable stories of social reform.

Our previous discussion, however, should recast the image of one of the three worlds of Welfare Capitalism. The "conservative welfare regimes" from Esping-Andersen (1990) should perhaps be conceived in a new light. The truncated welfare state of Latin America is not retrenching because it was never too complete to begin with. It is rather being complemented by new forms of poverty assistance programs, which have precedent in the fragmented, local, and Catholic inheritance of social protection systems inherited from the past. Conditional Cash Transfers do not simply represent a neoliberal abandonment of the ideal of a comprehensive welfare system for compensation and redistribution. They are part of a less centralized or less unified approach to social protection, which was characteristic of poverty relief systems existing before the twentieth century.

The failure of Latin American welfare states to develop should be understood as only one more element within a complex system of aid to the poor. The fragmented systems of poverty relief in Latin America have always included private philanthropy, public interventions targeted to specific groups or behaviors, and the coexistence of some more or less comprehensive universalistic systems to share risks of disease, unemployment, or old age.

Entitlement transfers are often regarded as inferior because they usually involve less money than the massive mobilization of financial resources associated with the welfare state. Hence the amount of cash deployed by the state, rather than the coverage and targeting or the effects on well-being, became the metric of success. It is an inappropriate standard. Can the demographic and financial conditions that allowed for the two waves of expansion of welfare state be reproduced in the future? Can the political conditions that enabled a coalition of progressive reformers to be entrusted with such an enormous amount of power and resources be repeated? We do not think so. But this does not mean that welfare states are doomed. We are fitfully learning in the current

---

[26] The history of Christian Democracy in France, according to Kalyvas (1996), might also have created piecemeal reforms with local delivery social protection, which are the basis of the more competitive but still universalistic welfare state found there.

8.5 Entitled Social Protection: An Emerging Paradigm?

retrenchment era how to reduce costs while respecting acquired rights and protecting the less fortunate members of society.

Mares and Carnes (2009) suggest that the future of Latin American social protection is not easy to surmise under a simple linear monocausal story where globalization pressures inexorably erode the truncated social protection institutions already in place, nor by a political account where reformist programmatic parties on the left or the right articulate a new vision of how to create social policies for the realities of the twenty-first century. Mares and Carnes (2009) demonstrate "the existence of significant variation across policy areas in the trajectories and distributional implications of social policies in developing countries" (p. 110), quite at odds with the conventional wisdom emerging from a narrow subsample of countries that covers fourteen–eighteen OECD economies (p. 94). In their view, means-tested policy solutions are the significant product (relatively neglected by scholars) of a political equilibrium supported by a coalition of the middle classes and the poor. This equilibrium differs from the much discussed privatization scenario where welfare states unravel and become dismantled under the forces of globalization and fiscal restraint. It also diverges, of course, from universalistic coverage with redistribution and socialization of risks. In what they label the "targeting" regime, there is a high degree of redistribution of resources from rich to poor, but risk is fundamentally individualized, meaning that "individuals face risk alone and not as part of a broader community of risks" (Baldwin, 1990, p. 3). Risks are not socialized because the state exhibits very low extractive capacity, and because citizens are willing to accept only a very short temporal lag between the contribution and the receipt of benefits.

The two cornerstones of the new forms of social protection are, we argue, the establishment of conditional cash transfer programs and the use of decentralized social funds to produce public goods. Those strategies are very different from both old poor relief and welfare state interventions. The differences can be summarized in terms of the financing of transfers, their redistributive effects, the fragmentation of the institutions involved, and the role of women.[27]

Financing. The first major difference between classic welfare state interventions and CCTs (and most of the new social protection interventions) is that the former are financed from contributory payroll taxes for both workers and employers while the later are financed from general taxation. In contrast to the Poor Laws of the nineteenth century and other forms of poverty relief from the modern era, CCTs are centralized in their administration: the responsibility to provide for the poor is in CCT is usually met by national governments rather

---

[27] We do not know enough about the long-term intergenerational effects of these programs and whether they should be conceived as temporary or permanent. A large impact from the point of view of a locality or municipality is the possibility of beneficiaries migrating obtaining higher standards of living elsewhere. The long-term health effects might be powerful. And there might be lifetime income effects generated from the differences in human capital.

than each local parish or municipality. Compensation is hence accomplished at the national level. In this sense, although there is no socialization of risk among occupational classes or industries, in the manner of the welfare state, the new forms of social protection still pool risks across the national population. The financing of public works through decentralized social funds also comes from general revenues. Rather than expecting local governments to privatize public services, or to pay for them with their own revenues, the compensatory logic of these systems is that regional redistribution can be achieved through formulas that provide more resources to the neediest local governments.

Redistribution. The systems of *entitled social protection* will not generate dramatic changes in the distribution of income. But to the extent that they are well-targeted they have an important income effect that reduces poverty instantaneously, and they might even improve at the margin the measures of income distribution. Even though CCT transfers are a very small portion of social expenditures, they constitute a very large part of the income of families in extreme poverty. In combination with targeted expansion of basic public services, these benefits may well suffice to provide the very poor with a gateway to what Deaton has called the "Great Escape" (Deaton, 2013). With CCTs children will no longer die prematurely and we should expect that people will be able to live healthier and longer lives. Decentralized funds for the provision of local public goods can be mildly redistributive, but this will depend fundamentally on the allocation formulas created to distribute them. In the Mexican case they are highly redistributive toward poor places, but this is not an intrinsic characteristic of their design. It is conceivable that such funds could be structured to favor the largest urban metropolitan areas, with very large demands for public good, rather than in favor of poor municipalities.

Institutional fragmentation. The motivation to introduce or expand entitled social protection system does not necessarily come from the imperative of serving a large social class or group, but usually from specific challenges of destitution faced by smaller groups, including the elderly, the unemployed, indigenous peoples, or single mothers. This suggests that from an institutional standpoint, there is no reason to expect a single coherent national system of entitled social protection to emerge in Mexico or elsewhere. The combination of pressures emerging from the democratic process channeling citizen demands and specific capacities of the state in various arenas and realms might determine the coverage and relative coherence of the various policy interventions. The generosity of benefits might be defined through the political process in ways that defy the idea of a minimum support or income line. After all, the definition of the relevant poverty line to establish thresholds for targeting and who deserves to be included in the social benefits will be endogenous to political processes. Perhaps the process of creation of new forms of social protection through the cumulative but fragmented social choices will gradually lead to more comprehensive coverage. Decentralization and federalism might play a role here, in closing off the route to the welfare state, leading to more piecemeal reforms for the creation of specific transfers to specific groups, many of them managed by local or state governments. That was precisely the story of entitlements for soldiers and mothers in the United States in the later part of the nineteenth century. In this sense, an important issue is whether the centralization of entitled social assistance will continue in the future. In the Mexican context, for example, the addition in 2006 of income supplements for the old (70+) in very poor communities has been replicated by many state governments and after 2010 turned into a national entitlement program for persons 65+. There is no definite trend toward centralization or decentralization, but there is no question that the institutional architecture will remain fragmented.

The role of women. The English Poor Laws sought to distinguish the deserving poor by emphasizing that aid would be targeted preferably to women. In the United States the emergence of entitlement involved the imperative of protecting mothers and widows. Mothers have in fact played a crucial role in the expansion of social services benefiting the poor, particularly in the realm of health and provision of services for children.[28] We should expect that the systems of social protection of the future will continue empowering women, rather than providing transfers to male heads of households. In poor communities, women will have the greatest impact in the choices they will make regarding their own fertility, everyday practices of hygiene and provision of a healthy environment, the allocation of scarce proteins within the household, or the priorities given to different children to continue in school. This will probably still be short from a maternalistic welfare state, but it will at least ensure that women are not at a disadvantage regarding their potential role in development.

8.6 THE FUTURE OF SOCIAL PROTECTION IN MEXICO

What future awaits the millions of poor Mexicans who witnessed the transformation of social programs we studied in this book? The question is not just about whether we can expect sustained improvements in well-being for poor families in the coming years, but more fundamentally, about whether Mexican citizens have become empowered by the democratic process to demand high-quality local public goods and social programs delivered as entitlements emerging from an underlying social pact, which seeks to promote a more equitable distribution of capabilities and life chances. Or will the country revert to a system of political representation with weak accountability, in which voters are captured in a web of dependence, passively waiting to receive transfers and benefits from corrupt governments that provide as little services as they can get away with?

A critical element for the permanent transformation of social policies regards the role of women (and men) that come to expect better performance from state institutions. The conditionality of *Oportunidades* means that communities

---

[28] Miller (2008).

throughout the country have learnt to demand that teachers actually attend their classes and that nurses and doctors keep health clinics open during regular business hours. The decentralization of social infrastructure funds to municipalities has empowered mayors to choose projects that resonate more clearly with the preferences of local dwellers, and many communities have learned to create mechanisms for the oversight of municipal expenditures.

Is the transformation of social policies in Mexico breaking the transmission of poverty across generations? We have shown that children were more likely to survive and therefore have greater chances to enjoy a more productive adult age thanks to the programs that the political transformation we have studied brought about. But are the children of *Oportunidades*, who have enjoyed better public services, likely to have better life chances and well-being than their parents? The prospect for improved livelihoods must be at the core of the final verdict of the success of these programs.

Despite improvements in accountability, the linkages between citizens and politicians in municipal governments in Mexico have been very imperfect. In particular, the institutional anomaly of the rule of nonreelection perverted accountability, because local politicians could not be punished or rewarded for their performance in office. The municipal three-year terms were so short that a typical complaint was that the first year a mayor devoted to learn how to do his or her job, the second year actually doing it, and the third year looking for their next appointment. Without reelection there are few incentives for building up programmatic reputations, and many observers have noted that corruption is more likely when there is complete certainty that one cannot continue in the job, even if performing well. The administrations of municipal government also have a dramatic turnaround every three years, even when mayors are elected from the same party.[29]

The governance of municipal institutions is not particularly conducive to much citizen involvement either. Although in principle citizens may engage in planning exercises and voice their views in town council meetings, in practice there is very little voter information regarding public decision making at the local level and very little oversight of municipal public servants. Hence, although mayors have more money they can autonomously use to provide public services and expand coverage of basic infrastructure, they do not have the right incentives to think about the long-term impacts of investments in public goods on the well-being of their citizens. For example, even though expanding the provision of water is one of the main priorities of almost every mayor in poor Mexican municipalities, there are no incentives for their administrations to be very concerned regarding the long-term impact of clean water in public health. The mayor may be interested in generating a contract for a firm to

---

[29] However, approval of municipal reelection promises to realign these incentives. Local administrations will probably have longer time horizons once the prospect of mayors staying in office for more than one term is opened up.

8.6 The Future of Social Protection in Mexico

expand the existing network of pipes around the town, but has little incentives to provide water systems to villages in the periphery or to ensure that existing systems are maintained and the quality of water is strictly enforced through the oversight of chlorination and frequent testing of the water supply.

In fact, our findings regarding the impact of social programs on infant mortality rates (IMR) suggest that there is little that mayor can do to improve health outcomes. They may increase coverage of local public goods, but have no authority on the quality of federal and state health interventions; no budgetary or oversight authority over health clinics; and are explicitly excluded from the functioning of *Oportunidades* (in order to ensure the protection of the program from political manipulation, it is important to note). Our estimations suggest that the single most powerful intervention to save the lives of children was the incorporation of families into the conditional cash transfer program *Progresa/Oportunidades*, followed by the democratic quality of governance as reflected in the alternation in office.

Unfortunately, there is little evidence suggesting a significant change in social mobility in Mexico. The evaluation of the long-term effects of the social programs that have been in place over more than a decade is elusive, in part due to the inherent difficulties of scientific inference in which there are many confounding variables that may explain the changes in well-being, but also because the Mexican economy has underperformed, both compared to its historical record before the debt crisis, and in comparison to peer countries in Latin America.

Our hope for a better future comes from the innovation of social programs that strengthen democratic accountability through the empowerment of poor citizens, who are now able to demand the quality of public services and entitlements they deserve. Inequality and poverty will remain a reality in every country. But extreme destitution will be overcome when deprivation from basic human capabilities and functionings is eliminated through investments in high-quality education, timely access to health services, and in general, a social policy that ensures prospects for social mobility. This is the daunting task still ahead.

References

Acedo Angulo, Blanca (ed.). 1995. *Solidaridad en Conflicto. El Funcionamiento del Pronasol en los Municipios Gobernados por la Oposición*. México: Nuevo Horizonte Editores.
Acemoglu, Daron and Robinson, James. 2006. *Economic Origins of Dictatorship and Democracy*. New York: Cambridge University Press.
Acemoglu, Daron, Johnson, Simon and Robinson, James. 2002. "Reversal of Fortune: Geography and Institutions in the Making of the Modern World Income Distribution." *The Quarterly Journal of Economics*. 117 (4): 1231–1294.
Achen, Christopher and Shively, Phillips. 1995. *Cross-Level Inference*. Chicago: Chicago University Press.
Alatas, Vivi, Banerjee, Abhijit, Hanna, Rema, Olken, Benjamin and Tobiass, Julia. 2012. "Targeting the Poor: Evidence for a Field Experiment in Indonesia." *American Economic Review*. 102 (4): 1206–1240.
Albertus, Michael. 2015. "Explaining Patterns of Redistribution Under Autocracy: The Case of Peru's Revolution from Above." *Latin American Research Review*. 50 (2): 107–134.
Albertus, Michael, Diaz-Cayeros, Alberto, Magaloni, Beatriz, and Weingast, Barry R. 2016. "Authoritarian Survival and Poverty Traps: Land Reform in Mexico." *World Development*. 77: 154–170.
Alesina, Alberto and La Ferrara, Eliana. 2000. "Participation in Heterogeneous Communities." *Quarterly Journal of Economics*. 115 (3): 847–904.
Alesina, Alberto and Rodrik, Dani. 1994. "Distributive Politics and Economic Growth." *Quarterly Journal of Economics*. 108: 465–490.
Alesina, Alberto, Baqir, Reza and Easterly, William. 1999. "Public Goods and Ethnic Divisions." *Quarterly Journal of Economics*. 114 (4): 1243–1284.
Alianza Cívica. 2006. *Observación del Proceso Electoral Federal 2006*. Mexico: Alianza Civica.
Alves, Denisard and Belluzzo, Walter. 2005. "Child Health and Infant Mortality in Brazil." Interamerican Development Bank Research Network Working Paper No. R-493. Washington, DC: IADB.

Ames, Barry. 1987. *Political Survival: Politicians and Public Policy in Latin America* Berkeley: University of California Press.
  1995. "Electoral Rules, Constituency Pressures and Pork Barrel: Bases of Voting in the Brazilian Congress." *Journal of Politics.* 57 (2): 324–343.
Anderson, G.M. and Tollison, R.D. 1991. "Congressional Influence and Patterns of New Deal Spending. 1933–1939." *Journal of Law and Economics.* 34: 161–175.
Anselin, Luc. 1988. *Spatial Econometrics, Methods and Models.* Boston: Kluwer Academic.
  2006. "Spatial Econometrics," in Mills, T.C. and Patterson, K. (eds.), *Palgrave Handbook of Econometrics: Vol. 1, Econometric Theory.* Basingstoke: Palgrave Macmillan, pp. 901–969.
Anselin, Luc, Syabri, Ibnu and Kho, Youngihn. 2004. "GeoDa: An Introduction to Spatial Data Analysis." *Spatial Analysis Laboratory.* Urbana, IL: Department of Agricultural and Consumer Economics, University of Illinois, Urbana-Champaign.
Archer, Ronald. 1990. "The Transition from Traditional to Broker Clientelism in Colombia: Political Stability and Social Unrest." Kellog Institute for International Studies, Working Paper No. 140.
Arrom, Silvia Marina. 2000. *Containing the Poor: The Mexico City Poor House, 1774–1871.* Durham: Duke University Press.
Aspe, Pedro. 1993. *Economic Transformation the Mexican Way.* Cambridge: Cambridge University Press.
Attanasio, Oazio, Battistin, Erich, Fitzimons, Emla, Mesnard, Alice and Vera-Hernández, Marcos. 2005. "How Effective Are Conditional Cash Transfers: Evidence from Colombia." Institute for Fiscal Studies, Briefing Note No. 54
Auyero, Javier. 2007. *Routine Politics and Violence in Argentina: That Gray Zone of State Power.* Cambridge: Cambridge University Press.
Bailey, John. 1994. "Centralism and Political Change in Mexico: The Case of National Solidarity," in Cornelius, Wayne, Craig, Ann and Fox, Jonathan (eds.), *Transforming State-Society Relations in Mexico: The National Solidarity Strategy* La Jolla: Center for U.S.-Mexican Studies, UCSD.
Baland, Jean-Marie and Robinson, James. 2007. "How Does Vote Buying Shape the Economy?" in Schaffer, Frederic (ed.), *Elections for Sale: The Causes and Consequences of Vote Buying.* Boulder: Lynne Rienner.
  2012. "The Political Value of Land: Political Reform and Land Prices in Chile." *American Political Science Review.* 56 (3): 601–619.
Baldwin, Peter. 1989. "The Scandinavian Origins of the Social Interpretation of the Welfare State." *Society of Comparative Studies in Society and History.* 31 (1) (January): 3–24.
  1990. *The Politics of Social Solidarity: Class Bases of the European Welfare State, 1875–1975.* Cambridge: Cambridge University Press.
Banco, de Mexico. 1996. *Informe Anual 1995.* Mexico: Banco de Mexico.
Banerjee, Abhijit. 2004. "Who Is Getting the Public Goods in India? Some Evidence and Some Speculation," in Bas, Kaushik (ed.), *India's Emerging Economic Performance and Prospects in the 1990s and Beyond.* Cambridge: MIT Press.
Banerjee, Abhijit V. and Iyer, Lakshmi. 2005. "History, Institutions and Economic Performance: The Legacy of Colonial Land Tenure Systems in India." *American Economic Review.* 95 (4) (September): 1190–1213.

Banerjee, Abhijit V. and Somanathan, Rohini. 2007. "The Political Economy of Public Goods: Some Evidence from India." *Journal of Development Economics*. 82 (2) (March): 287–314.

Banerjee, Abhijit V., Benabou, Roland and Mookherjee, Dilip (eds.). 2006. *Understanding Poverty*. Oxford: Oxford University Press.

Banfield, Edward. 1958. *The Moral Basis of a Backward Society*, New York: Free Press.

Baqir, Reza. 2002. Districting and Government Overspending. *Journal of Political Economy*. 110 (6): 1318–1354.

Bardhan, Pranab. 2005. *Scarcity, Conflicts and Cooperation*. Cambridge: MIT Press.

Bardhan, Pranab and Mookherjee, Dilip. 2005a. "Decentralizing Anti-Poverty Program Delivery in Developing Countries." *Journal of Public Economics*. April. 89.4: 675–704.

2005b. "Decentralization, Corruption and Government Accountability: An Overview," in Rose-Ackerman, Susan (ed.), *Handbook of Economic Corruption*. London: Edward Elgar.

2006. "Decentralisation and Accountability in Infrastructure Delivery in Developing Countries." *Economic Journal*. January. 116(508): 101–127.

Barham, Tania. 2011. "A Healthier Start: The Effect of Conditional Cash Transfers on Neonatal and Infant Mortality in Rural Mexico." *Journal of Development Economics*. 94: 70–85.

Baron, David P. 1991. "Majoritarian Incentives, Pork Barrel Programs, and Procedural Control." *American Journal of Political Science*. 35 (1): 57–90.

Barrientos, Armando, Niño-Zarazúa, Miguel and Maitrot, Mathilde 2010. Social Assistance in Developing Countries Database. Brooks World Poverty Institute and University of Manchester.

Bates, Robert. 1981. Markets and States in Tropical Africa Berkeley and Los Angeles: Berkeley: University of California Press.

Baum, Matthew A. and Lake, David. 2003. "The Political Economy of Growth: Democracy and Human Capital." *American Journal of Political Science*. 47 (2): 333–347.

Becerra, Lorena. 2012. *Does Everyone Have a Price? The Demand Side of Clientelism and Vote-Buying in an Emerging Democracy*. Ph.D. Dissertation. Duke University.

Becker, Sascha and Ichino, Andrea. 2002. "Estimation of Average Treatment Effects Based on Propensity Scores." *The Stata Journal*. 2 (4): 358–377.

Beer, Caroline. 2003. *Electoral Competition and Institutional Change in Mexico*. Notre Dame, IN: University of Notre Dame Press.

Behrman, J., Sengupta, P. and Todd, P. 2000. *The Achievement of Progresa in Achievement Test Scores in the First Year*. Washington, DC: IFPRI.

Bellon, M.R., Hodson, D.P., Martinez-Romero, E. Montoya, Becceril, J. and White J.W. 2004. *Geospatial Dimensions of Poverty and Food Security: A Case Study of Mexico*. Mexico, DF: International Maize and Wheat Improvement Center (CIMMYT).

Beltrán, Ulises. 1994. "La opinión. La política social del gobierno y la opinión pública," in Warman, Arturo (ed.), *La Política Social en México, 1989–1994*. Mexico: Fondo de Cultura Económica.

Bennedsen, Morten. 1998. "Vote Buying through Resource Allocation in a Government Controlled Sector." Typescript.

Bensel, Richard Franklin. 2004. *The American Ballot Box in the Mid-Nineteenth Century*. Cambridge: Cambridge University Press.

Besley, Timothy and Burgess, Robin. 2000. "Land Reform, Poverty Reduction and Growth: Evidence from India." *Quarterly Journal of Economics*. 115 (2): 389–430.
  2002. "The Political Economy of Government Responsiveness: Theory and Evidence." *Quarterly Journal of Economics*. 117 (4): 1415–1451.
Besley, Timothy and Coate, Stephen. 2003. "Centralized Versus Decentralized Provision of Local Public Goods: A Political Economy Approach." *Journal of Public Economics*. 87: 2611–2637.
Besley, Timothy and Ghatak, Maitreesh. 2006. "Public Goods and Economic Development," in Banerjee, Abhijit, Benabou, Roland and Mookherjee, Dilip (eds.), *Understanding Poverty*. New York: Oxford University Press, pp. 285–302.
Besley, Timothy, and Kudamatsu, Masayuki. 2006. "Health and Democracy." *The American Economic Review*. 96(2): 313–318.
Besley, Timothy and Prat, Andrea. 2001. "Handcuffs for the Grabbing Hand? Media Capture and Government Accountability." *American Economic Review*. 96 (3) (June): 720–736.
Bigman, David and Fofack, Hippolyte. 2000. "Geographic Targeting for Poverty Alleviation: An Introduction of the Special Issue." *World Bank Economic Review*. 14 (1): 129–146.
Bird, Richard. 1995. "Decentralizing Infrastructure: For Good or Ill?" in Estache, Wntonio (ed.), *Decentralizing Infrastructure: Advantages and Limitations*. World Bank Discussion Paper No. 290. Washington, DC: World Bank.
Blaug, Mark. 1963. "The Myth of the Old Poor Law and the Making of the New." *The Journal of Economic History*. 23: 151–184.
Block, Fred and Somers, Margaret. 2003. "In the Shadow of Speenhamland: Social Policy and the Old Poor Law." *Politics and Society*. 31: 283–323.
Bloom, David E., Canning, David and Sevilla, Jaypee. 2003. "Geography and Poverty Traps." *Journal of Economic Growth*. 8 (4) (December): 355–378.
Blum, Roberto and Diaz-Cayeros, Alberto. 2002. "Rentier States and Geography in Mexico's Development." Inter-American Development Bank Latin American Research Network Working Paper No. R-443. New York: Inter-American Development Bank.
Bobadilla, José Luis and Langer, Ana. 1990. "La mortalidad infantil en México: un fenómeno en transición." *Revista Mexicana de Sociología*. 52 (1): 111–131.
Boix, Carles. 2003. *Democracy and Redistribution*. Cambridge: Cambridge University Press.
Boltvinik, J. 1999. "Poverty Measurement Methods – An Overview." *SEPED Series on Poverty Reduction*. New York: UNDP.
Borja Tamayo, Arturo (ed.). 2001. *Para Evaluar al TLCAN*. Mexico City: Miguel Angel Porrua.
Boyer, George. 2002. "English Poor Laws." EH.Net Encyclopedia, edited by Robert Whaples. http://eh.net/encyclopedia/article/boyer.poor.laws.england . Accessed May 7, 2002.
Bradbury, John and Mark Crain. 2001. "Legislative Organization and Government Spending, Cross-Country Evidence." *Journal of Public Economics*. 82: 309–325.
Brady, Henry and Collier, David. 2004. *Rethinking Social Inquiry. Diverse Tools, Shared Standards*. Lanham: Rowman and Littlefield.

Brass, William. 1975. *Methods for Estimating Fertility and Mortality from Limited and Defective Data*. Chapell Hill: Carolina Population Center, Laboratories for Population Statistics.
Brown, David and Hunter, Wendy. 1999. "Democracy and Social Spending in Latin America, 1980–1992." *American Political Science Review*. 93 (4): 779–790.
Bruhn, Kathleen. 1996. "Social Spending and Political Support: The 'Lessons' of the National Solidarity Program in Mexico." *Comparative Politics*. 26 (January): 151–177.
Brusco, Valeria, Nazareno, Marcelo and Stokes, Susan. 2004. "Vote Buying in Argentina." *Latin American Research Review*. 39 (2): 66–88.
Bryce, J., Terreri, N., Victoria, C., Mason, E., Daelmans, B., Bhutta, Z.A., Bustreo, F., Songane, F., Salama, P. and Wardlaw, T. 2006. "Countdown to 2015: Tracking Intervention Coverage for Child Survival." *The Lancet*. 368 (9541): 1067–1076.
Bueno de Mesquita, Bruce and Root, Hilton L. 2000 "When Bad Economics Is Good Politics," in Bueno de Mesquita, Bruce and Root, Hilton L. (eds.), *Governing for Prosperity*. New Haven: Yale University Press, pp. 1–16.
Bueno de Mesquita, Bruce, Morrow, James D., Sieverson, Randolph and Smith, Alastair. 2000. "Political Institutions, Political Survival, and Policy Success," in Bueno de Mesquita, Bruce and Root, Hilton L. (eds.), *Governing for Prosperity*. New Haven: Yale University Press, pp. 59–84.
Bueno de Mesquita, Bruce, Smith, Alastair, Siverson, Randolph, M. and Morrow, James D. 2003. *The Logic of Political Survival*. Cambridge: MIT Press.
Burgess, Katrina and Levitsky, Steven. 2003. "Explaining Populist Party Adaptation in Latin America: Environmental and Organizational Determinants of Party Change in Argentina, Mexico, Peru, and Venezuela." *Comparative Political Studies*. 36 (8): 881–911.
Cabrero, Enrique. 1998. *Las Politicas Decentralizadoras en Mexico (1983–1993)*. Mexico: CIDE / M.A. Porrua.
Calvo, Ernesto and Escolar, Marcelo. 2003. "The Local Voter: A Geographically Weighted Approach to Ecological Inference." *American Journal of Political Science*. 47 (1): 189–204.
Calvo, Ernesto and Murillo, M. Victoria. 2004. "Who Delivers? Partisan Clients in the Argentine Electoral Market." *American Journal of Political Science*. 48 (4): 742–757.
   2012. "When Parties Meet Voters: Partisan Networks and Distributive Expectations in Argentina and Chile." *Comparative Political Studies*. 0010414012463882.
Camp, Roderic Ai. 2007. *Politics in Mexico: The Democratic Consolidation*. Oxford: Oxford University Press.
Campello, Daniela. 2013. *Globalization adn Democracy: The Politics of Market Discipline in Latin America*. Cambridge: Cambridge University Press.
Cantú, Francisco. 2005. "El Impacto Electoral en Progresa-Oportunidades." Mexico: ITAM, BA Thesis.
Carpenter, Daniel P. 2001. *The Forging of Bureaucratic Autonomy: Reputations, Networks, and Policy Innovation in Executive Agencies, 1862–1928*. Princeton University Press.
Castañeda, Jorge. 2000. *Perpetuating Power*. New York: New Press.

Chandler, Dewitt Samuel. 1991. *Social Assistance and Bureaucratic Politics: The Montepíos of Colonial Mexico, 1767–1821*. University of New Mexico Press.

Chang, Eric and Golden, Miriam. 2007. "Electoral Systems, District Magnitude and Corruption." *British Journal of Political Science*. 37 (1): 115–137.

Chang, Eric, Golden, Miriam, Hill, Seth J. 2010. "Legislative Malfeasance and Political Accountability." *World Politics*. 62 (2): 177–220.

Charles Seymour. 1915. *Electoral Reform in England and Wales*. New Haven. Yale University Press.

Chattopadhyay, Raghabendra and Duflo, Esther. 2001. "Women as Policymakers: Evidence from an India-Wide Randomized Policy Experiment." NBER Working Paper No. 8615.

Chen, Jowei. 2013. "Voter Partisanship and the Effect of Distributive Spending on Political Participation." *American Journal of Political Science*. 57: 200–217.

Chhibber, Pradeep and Nooruddin, Irfan. 2004. "Do Party Systems Count? The Number of Parties and Government Performance in the Indian States." *Comparative Political Studies*. 37 (2): 152–187.

Chong, Alberto, Ana De la O, Dean Karlan, and Leonard Wantchekon. 2015. "Does Corruption Information Inspire the Fight or Quash the Hope? A Field Experiment in Mexico on Voter Turnout, Choice, and Party Identification." *The Journal of Politics*. 77 (1): 55–71.

Cleary, Matthew. 2002. "Do Parties Enforce Electoral Accountability in Mexico?" Paper Delivered at the 2002 Annual Meeting of the American Political Science Association, Boston, August 29–September 1.

  2003. "Competencia electoral, influencia ciudadana y desempeño del gobierno en los municipios mexicanos." *Política y Gobierno*. 10 (1): 183–217.

  2004. "Electoral Competition, Participation and the Quality of Government in Mexico." Paper Delivered at the 2004 Annual Meeting of the American Political Science Association (Chicago, IL, September 2–5).

  2006. "Explaining the Left's Resurgence." *Journal of Democracy*. 17 (4): 35–49.

Coady, David, Grosh, Margaret and Hoddinott, John. 2004. *Targeting of Transfers in Developing Countries: Review of Lessons and Experience*. Washington, DC: World Bank.

Coale, Ansley and Demeny, Paul. 1966. *Regional Model Life Tables and Stable Populations*. Princeton: Princeton University Press.

Coatsworth, John Henry. 1976. *Growth against Development: The Economic Impact of Railroads in Porfirian Mexico*. Mexico: Sep Setentas.

Coetzee, J.M. 2007. "Excerpt from 'Diary of a Bad Year'." *New York Review of Books*. 54 (12): 20–23.

Comisión de Desarrollo Social. 1998. *Instrumentos de Distribución de los Recursos del Ramo 33*. Comisión de Desarrollo Social de la Cámara de Diputados, LVII Legislatura. Mexico: Cámara de Diputados.

CONAPO (Consejo Nacional de Población). 1993. *Indice de Marginación, 1990*. México: CONAPO.

  1993. *Indicadores Socioeconómicos e Indice de Marginación Municipal, 1990*. Mexico: CONAPO-CNA.

  2000. *Indices de Desarrollo Humano, 2000: Anexo Metodológico*. México: CONAPO.

References

Consejo Consultivo del Programa Nacional de Solidaridad. 1994. *El Programa Nacional de Solidaridad*. Mexico: Fondo de Cultura Económica.

Coplamar. 1982. *Necesidades Esenciales de México*. México: Siglo XXI.

Cornelius, Wayne, Craig, Ann and Fox, Jonathan (eds.). 1994. *Transforming State-Society Relations in Mexico: The National Solidarity Strategy*. La Jolla: Center for U.S.-Mexican Studies, UCSD.

Cornelius, Wayne, Eisenstadt, Todd and Hindley, Jane (eds.). 1999. *Subnational Politics and Democratization in Mexico*. San Diego: Center for U.S.-Mexican Studies: UCSD.

Cornelius, Wayne. 1975. *Poverty and Politics of the Migrant Poor in Mexico City* Stanford: Stanford University Press.

   2004. "Mobilized Voting in the 2000 Elections: The Changing Efficacy of Vote Buying and Coercion in Mexican Electoral Politics," in Domínguez, Jorge and Lawson, Chapell (eds.), *Mexico's Pivotal Democratic Election*. Stanford: Stanford University Press.

Cortés Cázeres, Fernando et al., 2005. "Evolución y Características de la Pobreza en México en la Última Década del Siglo XX," in Székeli, Miguel (ed.), *Números que mueven al mundo: la medición de la pobreza en México*. Mexico: SEDESOL/CIDE/Anuies/M.A. Porrúa.

Courchene, Thomas and Diaz-Cayeros, Alberto. 2000. "Transfers and the Nature of the Mexican Federation," in Giugale, Marcelo and Webb, Steven B. (eds.), *Achievements and Challenges of Fiscal Decentralization. Lessons from Mexico*. Washington, DC: World Bank.

Cox, Gary. 1997. *Making Votes Count*. Cambridge: Cambridge University Press.

   2005. *The Efficient Secret: The Cabinet and the Development of Political Parties in Victorian England*. Cambridge: Cambridge University Press.

   2009. "Swing Voters, Core Voters and Distributive Politics," in Shapiro, Ian, Stokes, Susan, Elisabeth, Wood and Kirshner, Alexander S. (eds.), *Political Representation*. Cambridge: Cambridge University Press.

Cox, Gary and McCubbins, Mathew D. 1986. "Electoral Politics as a Redistributive Game." *Journal of Politics*. 48 (May): 370–389.

Cox, Gary and Thies, Michael. 2000. "How Much Does Money Matter? 'Buying' Vote in Japan, 1967–1990." *Comparative Political Studies*. 33 (1): 37–57.

Cox, Gary, McCubbins, Mathew D. and Sullivan, Terry. 1984. "Policy Choice as an Electoral Investment." *Social Choice and Welfare*. 1: 231–242.

Dahlberg, Matz and Johansson, Eva. 2002. "On the Vote-Purchasing Behavior of Incumbent Governments." *American Political Science Review*. 96 (1): 27–40

Dasgupta, Partha. 1993. *An Inquiry into Well Being and Destitution*. Oxford: Clarendon Press.

Dayton-Johnson, Jeff. 2000. "The Determinants of Collective Action on the Commons: A Model With Evidence for Mexico." *Journal of Development Economics*. 62(1): 181–208.

De Ferranti, David, Perry, Guillermo E., Ferreira, Fancisco H.G. and Walton, Michael. 2004. *Inequality in Latin America: Breaking with History?* Washington, DC: World Bank.

De Janvry, Alain. 2006. "Conditional Cash Transfer Programs in the Bigger Picture of Social Policy: Where Do They Fit? How Can They Be Made to Be More Effective?"

http://info.worldbank.org/etools/iccto6/DOCS/English/Day1/Alain_CCT_keynote_AM.pdf. Accessed July 19, 2007. Keynote Address to the Third International Conference on Conditional Cash Transfers, Istanbul, Turkey, June 26–30.

De Janvry, Alain and Sadoulet, Elisabeth. 2000. "Growth, Poverty and Inequality in Latin America: A Causal Analysis, 1970–1994." *Review of Income and Wealth.* 46 (3): 267–287.

De Janvry, Alain, Gordillo, Gustavo, Platteau, Jean-Phillipe and Sadoulet, Elisabeth. 2002. *Access to Land, Rural Poverty and Public Action.* Oxford: Oxford University Press.

De la Brière, Bénédicte and Rawlings, Laura. 2006. "Examining Conditional Cash Transfer Programs: A Role for Increased Social Inclusion?" Social Protection Discussion Paper No. 0603. Washington, DC: World Bank.

De La O, Ana. 2013. "Do Conditional Cash Transfers Affect Electoral Behavior? Evidence from a Randomized Experiment in Mexico." *American Journal of Political Science.* 57.1: 1–14.

2015. *Crafting Policies to End Poverty in Latin America: The Quiet Transformation.* Cambridge: Cambridge University Press.

De La, O. and L. Ana. 2013. "Do conditional cash transfers affect electoral behavior? Evidence from a randomized experiment in Mexico." *American Journal of Political Science.* 57 (1): 1–14.

De Remes, Alan. 1998. "Gobiernos yuxtapuestos en México: hacia un marco analítico para el estudio de las elecciones municipales." *Política y Gobierno.* 6 (1): 225–153.

De Tocqueville, Alexis. 1997 [1835]. *Memoir on Pauperism.* Tr. Seymour Drescher. London: Civitas.

De Vries, Jan and Wan der Woude, Ad. 1997. *The First Modern Economy: Success, Failure and Perseverance of the Dutch Economy, 1500–1815.* Cambridge: Cambridge University Press.

Deaton, Angus. 1997. *The Analysis of Household Surveys.* Washington, DC: World Bank.

2010. "Instruments, Randomization, and Learning about Development." *Journal of Economic Literature.* 48 (2): 424–455.

2013. *The Great Escape: Health, Wealth, and the Origins of Inequality.* Princeton University Press.

Diaz-Cayeros, Alberto. 2006. *Federalism, Fiscal Authority and Centralization in Latin America.* Cambridge: Cambridge University Press.

2008. "Electoral Risk and Redistributive Politics in Mexico and the United States." *Studies in International Comparative Development.* 43 (2): 129–150.

Diaz-Cayeros, Alberto, and Beatriz Magaloni. "The Politics of Public Spending–Part II. The Programa Nacional de Solidaridad (PRONASOL) in Mexico." *Background Papers for the World Bank World Development Report 2004* 28013 (2003).

Diaz-Cayeros, Alberto and Magaloni, Beatriz. 2009. "Aiding Latin America's Poor." *Journal of Democracy.* 20 (4): 36–49.

Díaz-Cayeros, Alberto, Beatriz Magaloni and Alexander Ruiz-Euler. 2014. "Traditional Governance, Citizen Engagement, and Local Public Goods: Evidence from Mexico." *World Development.* 53: 80–93.

Díaz-Cayeros, Alberto, Federico Estévez, and Beatriz Magaloni. 2009. "Welfare Benefits, Canvassing and Campaign Handouts in the 2006 Presidential Race." Domínguez, Jorge I., Chappell H. Lawson, and Alejandro Moreno. *Consolidating Mexico's democracy: the 2006 presidential campaign in comparative perspective.* Johns Hopkins University Press.

Diaz-Cayeros, Alberto, González, Jose Antonio and Rojas, Fernando. 2006. "Mexico's Decentralization at a Cross-Roads," in Srinivasan, T.N. and Wallack, Jessica Seddon (eds.), *Federalism, Economic Reform, and Globalization*. Cambridge: Cambridge University Press.

Diaz-Cayeros, Alberto, Magaloni, Beatriz and Weingast, Barry. 2001. "Democratization and the Economy in Mexico: Equilibrium (PRI) Hegemony and Its Demise." Typescript. Stanford University.

Dion, Michelle. 2000. "La Economía Política del Gasto Social. El Programa Nacional de Solidaridad, 1988–1994." *Estudios Sociológicos*. 18 (53): 329–362.

2010. *Workers and Welfare: Compartive Institutional Change in Twentieth Century Mexico*. Pittsburgh: University of Pittsburgh Press.

Dixit, Avinash and Londregan, John. 1996. "The Determinants of Success of Special Interests in Redistributive Politics." *Journal of Politics*. 58 (November): 1132–1155.

Domínguez, Jorge and Lawson, Chapell (eds.). 2004. *Mexico's Pivotal Democratic Election*. Stanford: Stanford University Press.

Domínguez, Jorge and McCann, James. 1996. *Democratizing Mexico*. Baltimore: Johns Hopkins University Press.

Domínguez, Jorge and Poiré, Alejandro (eds.). 1999. *Toward Mexico's Democratization*. New York: Routledge.

Dornbusch, Rudiger and Werner, Alejandro. 1994. "Mexico: Stabilization, Reform, and No Growth." *Brookings Papers on Economic Activity*. 25: 253–316. Washington, DC: Economic Studies Program, The Brookings Institution.

Dresser, Denise. 1991. *Neopopulist Solutions to Neoliberal Problems: Mexico's National Solidarity Program*. Current Issue Brief Series, No. 3. La Jolla: Center for U.S.-Mexican Studies, University of California, San Diego.

1994a. "Bringing the Poor Back In: National Solidarity as a Strategy of Regime Legitimation," in Cornelius, Wayne, Craig, Ann and Fox, Jonathan (eds.), *Transforming State-Society Relations in Mexico: The National Solidarity Strategy* La Jolla: Center for U.S.-Mexican Studies, UCSD.

1994b. "Pronasol y Política: Combate a la Pobreza como Fórmula de Gobernabilidad," in Vélez, Félix (ed.), *La Pobreza en México*. México: Fondo de Cultura Económica.

Duflo, Esther. 2006. "Field Experiments in Development Economics," in Blundell, Richard et al. (eds.), *Advances in Economics and Econometrics: Theory and Appplications*. Ninth World Congress. Cambridge: Cambridge University Press.

Easterly, William. 2002. *The Elusive Quest for Growth*. Cambridge: MIT Press

Eisenstadt, S.N. and Lemarchand, René (eds.). 1981. Political Clientelism, Patronage and Development. Sage Studies in Contemporary Political Sociology. 3. Thousand Oaks: Sage Publications.

Emminghaus. A. 1870. *Das Armenwesen un die Armen Gesetzgebung in Europaishen Staaten*. Berlin: Verlag Von FA. Herbig. Some chapters are translated in Eastwick, E.B. 1873. *Poor Relief in Different Parts of Europe*. London: Edward Stanford.

Epstein, David and O'Halloran, Sharyn. 1999. *Delegating Powers: A Transaction Cost Politics Approach to Policy Making under Separate Powers*. Cambridge: Cambridge University Press.

Escobal, Javier and Torero, Maximo. 2003. "Adverse Geography and Differences in Welfare in Peru." Working Papers, UNU-WIDER Research Paper No. DP2003/73. Helsinki, Finland: UNU-WIDER.

Esping-Andersen, Gosta. 1990. *The Three Worlds of Welfare Capitalism*. Princeton: Princeton University Press.

Esquivel, Gerardo. 2000. "Geography and Economic Development in Mexico." Inter-American Development Bank Latin American Research Network Working Paper No. R-389. New York: Inter-American Development Bank.

Esquivel, Gerardo and Larrain, Felipe B. 2002. "The Impact of G-3 Exchange Rate Volatility on Developing Countries." G-24 Discussion Papers 16. Geneva: United Nations Conference on Trade and Development.

Estévez, Federico and Magaloni, Beatriz. 1998. "Legislative Parties and Their Constituencies in the Budget Battle of 1997." *Political Science Working Paper No. 2000–01*. Mexico: ITAM.

Estévez, Federico, Díaz-Cayeros, Alberto and Magaloni, Beatriz. 2008. "A House Divided against Itself," in Friedman, Edward and Wong, Joseph (eds.), *Political Transitions in Dominant Party Systems: Learning to Lose*. New York: Routledge.

Fagen, Richard and Tuohy, William. 1972. *Power and Privilege in a Mexican City*. Stanford: Stanford University Press.

Faguet, Jean-Paul. 2004. "Does Decentralization Increase Responsiveness to Local Needs? Evidence from Bolivia." *Journal of Public Economics*. 88: 867–894.

Falleti, Tulia G. 2005. "A Sequential Theory of Decentralization: Latin American Cases in Comparative Perspective." *American Political Science Review*. 99 (3): 327–346.

Fama, Eugene and French, Kenneth. 1996. "Multifactor Explanations of Asset Pricing Anomalies." *Journal of Finance*. 51: 55–86. A good textbook discussion is Bodie, Zvi, Kane, Alex and Marcus, Alan. 2001. *Investments*. Fifth Edition. Boston: Mc-Graw-Hill.

Fearon, James. 1999. "Why Ethnic Politics and Pork Tend to Go Together." Paper Presented at a MacArthur Foundation-Sponsored Conference on Ethnic Politics and Democratic Stability held at Wilder House, University of Chicago, May 21–23. Working Paper.

Fearon, James and Laitin, David. 2003. "Ethnicity, Insurgency, and Civil War." *American Political Science Review*. 97 (1) (February): 75–90.

Ferejohn, John. 1974. *Pork Barrel Politics*. Stanford: Stanford University Press.

  1986. "Incumbent performance and electoral control." *Public Choice*. 50 (1): 5–25.

Ferraz, Claudio, and Finan, Frederico. 2008. Exposing corrupt politicians: the effects of Brazil's publicly released audits on electoral outcomes. *Quarterly Journal of Economics*. 123 (3): 703.

Finan, Frederico and Schechter, Laura. 2012. "Vote-Buying and Reciprocity." *Econometrica*. 80 (2): 863–882.

Fiorina, Morris. 1981. *Retrospective Voting in American National Elections*. New Haven, CT: Yale University Press.

Fiszbein, Ariel. 2004. Beyond Truncated Welfare States: Quo Vadis Latin America? Draft Note. Washington, DC: World Bank.

Flamand, Laura. 2004. *The Vertical Dimension of Government: Democratization and Federalism in Mexico*. PhD Dissertation. Rochester, NY: Unversity of Rochester Department of Political Science.

Fleck, Robert K. 1999. "The Value of the Vote: A Model and Test of the Effects of Turnout on Distributive Policy." *Economic Inquiry*. 37 (4): 609–623.

  2001a. "Inter-Party Competition, Intra-Party Competition, and Distributive Policy: A Model and Test using New Deal Data." *Public Choice*. 108: 77–100.

  2001b. "Population, Land, Economic Conditions, and the Allocation of New Deal Spending." *Explorations in Economic History*. 38: 396–304.

Florescano, Enrique. 1995. *Breve Historia de la Sequia en Mexico*. Jalapa: Universidad Veracruzana.

Fogel, Robert William. 2004. *The Escape from Human Suffering and Premature Death, 1700–2100: Europe, America, and the Third World*. Cambridge: Cambridge University Press.

Foster, Andrew D. and Rosenzweig, Mark D. 2004. "Democratization and the Distribution of Local Public Goods in a Poor Rural Economy." Typescript. Brown University.

Fotheringham, A.S., Brunsdon, C. and Charlton, M. 2000. *Quantitative Geography: Perspectives on Spatial Data*. London: Sage.

Fox, Jonathan. 1994. "The Difficult Transition from Clientelism to Citizenship: Lessons from Mexico." *World Politics*. 46: 151–184.

Francois, Marie Eileen. 2006. *A Culture of Everyday Credit: Housekeeping, Pawnbroking, and Governance in Mexico City, 1750-1920*. University of Nebraska Press.

Frankel, Jeffrey and Romer, David. 1999. "Does Trade Cause Growth?" *American Economic Review*. 89 (3) (June): 379–399.

Fried, Biran. 2012. "Distributive Politics and Conditional Cash Transfers: The Case of Brazil's Bolsa Familia." *World Development*. 40: 1042–1053

Fundar. 2006. *Monitoreo de Programas Sociales en Contextos Electorales*. Mexico: FUNDAR.

Gakidou, Emmanuela et al., 2006. "Assessing the Effect fo the 2001–06 Mexican Health Reform: An Interim Report Card." *The Lancet*. 368: 1920–1935.

Galasso, Emanuela and Ravallion, Martin. 2001. "Decentralized Targeting of an Anti-Poverty Program." Typescript. Washington, DC: World Bank.

Galiani, Sebastian, Gertler, Paul and Schargrodsky, Ernesto. 2005. "Water for Life: The Impact of the Privatization of Water Services on Child Mortality." *Journal of Political Economy*. 113 (1): 83–120.

Gallup-IMPO. 1991. Gallup Poll – Mexico (Survey financed by Televisa).

Gallup, John L., Gaviria, Alejandro and Lora, Eduardo. 2003. *Is Geography Destiny?* Washington, DC: Interamerican Development Bank.

Gallup, John L., Sachs, Jeffrey and Mellinger, Andrew. 2001. "Geography and Economic Development." Center for International Development at Harvard University Working Paper No. 1. Cambridge, MA: Harvard University.

Gans-Morse, Jordan, Mazzuca, Sebastian and Nichter, Simeon. 2014. "Varieties of Clientelism: Machine Politics During Elections." *American Journal of Political Science*. 58(2): 415–432.

Geddes, Barbara. 1994. *Politician's Dilemma: Building State Capacity in Latin America* Berkeley: University of California Press.

Gerring, John, Thacker, Strom, C. and Moreno, Carola. 2005. "Centripetal Democratic Governance: A Theory and Global Inquiry." *American Political Science Review*. 99 (4): 567–582.

Gerring, John, Bond, Philip, Barndt, William and Moreno, Carola. 2005. "Democracy and Growth: A Historical Perspective." *World Politics*. 57 (3): 323–364.

Gershberg, Alec Ian. 1994. "Distributing Resources in the Education Sector: Solidarity's Escuela Digna Program," in Cornelius, Wayne, Craig, Ann and Fox, Jonathan (eds.), *Transforming State-Society Relations in Mexico: The National Solidarity Strategy*. La Jolla: Center for U.S.-Mexican Studies, UCSD.

Gertler, Paul. 2004. "Do Conditional Cash Transfers Improve Child Health? Evidence from PROGRESA's Control Randomized Experiment." *American Economic Review*. 94 (2): 336–341.

Gibson, Edward. 1996. *Class and Conservative Parties: Argentina in Comparative Perspective*. Baltimore: Johns Hopkins University Press.

Gil-Diaz, Francisco and Carstens, Agustin. 1996. "One Year of Solitude: Some Pilgrim Tales About Mexico's 1994–1995 Crisis." *American Economic Review*. 2: 164–169.

Gingerich, Daniel. 2013. "Can Institutions Cure Clientelism? Assessing the Impact of the Australian Ballot in Brazil." Typescript. University of Virginia.

Gingerich, Daniel W., and Luis Fernando Medina. 2013. "The Endurance and Eclipse of the Controlled Vote: A Formal Model of Vote Brokerage under the Secret Ballot." *Economics & Politics*. 25 (3): 453–480.

Giraudy, A. 2007. "The Distributive Politics of Emergency Employment Programs in Argentina (1993–2002)." *Latin American Research Review*. 42 (2): 33–55.

Giugale, Marcelo and Webb, Steven B. 2000. *Achievements and Challenges of Fiscal Decentralization. Lessons from Mexico*. Washington, DC: World Bank.

Giugale, Marcelo, Lafourcade, Olivier and Nguyen, Vinh H. 2001. *Mexico. A Comprehensive Development Agenda for the New Era*. Washington, DC: World Bank.

Golden, Miriam. 2003. "Electoral Connections: The Effects of the Personal Vote, on Political Patronage, Bureaucracy and Legislation in Post-War Italy." *British Journal of Political Science*. 33 (April): 189–212.

2004. "International Economic Sources of Regime Change: How European Economic Integration Undermined Italy's Postwar Party System." *Comparative Politics Studies*. 37 (December): 1238–1274.

Golden, Miriam and Chang, Eric. 2001. "Competitive Corruption: Factional Conflict and Political Malfeasance in Postwar Italian Christian Democracy." *World Politics*. 53 (July): 588–622.

Golden, Miriam and Picci, Lucio. 2008. "Pork Barrel Politics in Postwar Italy, 1953–1994." *American Journal of Political Science*. 52 (2): 268–289.

Golden, Miriam, Chang, Eric and Hill, Seth. 2010. "Legislative Malfeasance and Political Accountability." *World Politics*. 62 (2) 177–220.

Gómez de León, José. 1988. "Análisis Multivariado de la Mortalidad Infantil en México: Un Ejemplo del Uso de Modelos Log-lineales para Estimar Modelos de Riesgos Proporcionales," in Bronfman, Mario and Gómez de León, José (eds.), *La Mortalidad en México: Niveles, Tendencias y Determiantes*. Mexico: El Colegio de México, pp. 333–367.

Gómez, López Marcela and Pineda Antúnez, Sandra. 1999. El Reparto Municipal del Pronasol: Criterios de Asignación en Aguascalientes y Michoacán. BA Thesis, ITAM, Mexico.

Gordon, Linda. 2000. *Pitied But Not Entitled: Single Mothers and the History of Welfare, 1890–1935*. New York: Free Press.

Green, Kenneth. 2007. *Why Dominant Parties Lose: Mexico's Democratization in Comparative Perspective*. Cambridge: Cambridge University Press.

Green, Kenneth and Lawson, Chappell. 2012. "Self-Enforcing Clientelism: The Politics of Reciprocity." Typescript. Harvard University.

Green, Tina. 2005. "Do Social Transfer Programs Affect Voter Behavior? Evidence from Progresa in Mexico, 1997–2000." Typescript. University of California, Berkeley.

Guasti, Laura. 1981. "Clientelism in Decline: A Peruvian Regional Study," in Eisenstadt, S.N. and Lemarchand, René (eds.), *Political Clientelism, Patronage and*

Development. Sage Studies in Contemporary Political Sociology, Vol. 3. Thousand Oaks: Sage Publications.
Guy, Donna J. 2001. Introduction to The Rise of the Welfare State in Latin America. *The Americas*. 58 (1) (July): 1–6.
  2009. *Women Build the Welfare State: Performing Charity and Creating Rights in Argentina, 1880–1955*. Durham: Duke University Press.
Habyarimana, James, Humphreys, Macarthan, Posner, Daniel and Weinstein, Jeremy. 2007. "Why Does Ethnic Diversity Undermine Public Goods Provision?" *American Political Science Review*. 101 (4): 709–725.
  2009. *Coethnicity: Diversity and Dilemmas of Collective Action*. New York: Russell Sage Foundation.
Haggard, Stephan and Kaufman, Robert. 1995. *The Political Economy of Democratic Transitions*. Princeton, NJ: Princeton University Press.
  2008. *Development, Democracy and Welfare States*. Princeton: Princeton University Press.
Hall, Robert and Charles Jones. 1999. "Why Do Some Countries Produce So Much More Output per Worker than Others?" *Quarterly Journal of Economics*. 114 (1) (February): 83–116.
Hansen, R.D. 1971. *Mexican Economic Development: The Roots of Rapid Growth*. Washington, DC: National Planning Association.
Hartmann, Michael. 1991. "A Parametric Model for Census Based Estimation of Child Mortality." *Journal of Official Statistics. Statistics Sweden*. 7: 45–55.
Harvard Initiative for Public Health. 2006. Mexico Health Metrics 2005 Report. Harvard University: Initiative for Global Health.
Hawkins, Kirk, Rosas, Guillermo and Johnson, Michael E. 2011. "The Misiones of the Chávez Government," in Smilde, David and Venezuela, Daniel Hellinger, *Bolivarian Democracy: Participation, Politics and Culture under Chavez*. North Carolina: Duke University Press.
Heckman, James. 1996. "Randomization as an Instrumental Variable." *Review of Economics and Statistics*. 77 (2): 336–341.
Heckman, James and Navarro-Lozano, Salvador. 2004. "Using Matching, Instrumental Variables, and Control Functions to Estimate Economic Choice Models." *Review of Economics and Statistics*. 86.1: 30–57.
Hicken, Allen. 2007a. "How Do Rules and Institutions Encourage Vote Buying?" in Schaffer, Frederic (ed.), *Elections for Sale: The Causes and Consequences of Vote Buying*. Boulder: Lynne Rienner.
  2007b. "How Effective Are Institutional Reforms?" in Schaffer, Frederic (ed.), *Elections for Sale: The Causes and Consequences of Vote Buying*. Boulder: Lynne Rienner.
  2011. "Clientelism." *Annual Review of Political Science*. 14: 289–310.
Hill, Kenneth, Pande, Rohini, Mahy, Mary and Jones, Gareth. 1999. "Trends in Child Mortality in the Developing World: 1960 to 1996." (KH-98.1)
Himmelfarb, Gertrude. 1997. *Introduction to Alexis de Tocqueville's Memoir on Pauperism*. London: Civitas.
Hirschleifer, Jack and Riley, John. 1992. *The Analytics of Uncertainty and Information*. Cambridge: Cambridge University Press.
Hiskey, Jonathan. 2003. "Demand Based Development and Local Electoral Environments in Mexico." *Comparative Politics*. 36 (1): 41–60.

Hiskey, Jonathan and Bowler, Shaun. 2005. "Local Context and Democratization in Mexico." *American Journal of Political Science*. 49 (1): 57–71.

Hiskey, Jonathan and Canache, Damarys. 2005. "The Demise of One-Party Politics in Mexican Municipal Elections." *British Journal of Political Science*. 35: 257–284.

Hiskey, Jonathan Thomas. 1999. "Does Democracy Matter?: Electoral Competition and Local Development in Mexico." PhD diss., JT Hiskey.

Ho, Daniel E., Imai, Kosuke, King, Gary and Stuart, Elizabeth A. 2007. "Matching as Nonparametric Preprocessing for Reducing Model Dependence in Parametric Causal Inference." *Political Analysis*. 15: 199–236.

Horiuchi, Yusaku and Saito, Jun. 2009. "Rain, Election, and Money: The Impact of Voter Turnout on Distributive Policy Outcomes." Paper Presented at the 2007 Annual Meeting of the Midwest Political Science Association, Revised in 2009. Draft.

Hsieh, Chang-Tai, Miguel, Edward, Ortega, Daniel and Rodriguez, Francisco. 2011. "The Price of Political Opposition: Evidence from Venezuela's Maisanta." *American Economic Journal: Applied Economics*. 3 (2): 196–214.

Huber, Evelyn and Stephens, John. 2001. *Development and Crisis of the Welfare State: Parties and Policies in Global Markets*. Chicago: University of Chicago Press.

Huber, John and Shipan, Charles. 2002. *Deliberate Discretion: The Institutional Foundations of Bureaucratic Autonomy*. Cambridge: Cambridge University Press.

Von Humboldt, Alexander. 1811. *Political Essay on the Kingdom of New Spain*. Vol. 1. I. New York: Riley.

Hunter, Wendy. 2007. "The Normalization of an Anomaly: The Worker's Party in Brazil. *World Politics*. 59 (3): 440–475.

2010. *The Transformation of the Worker's Party in Brazil, 1989–2009*. Cambridge: Cambridge University Press.

Hunter, Wendy and Power, J. Timothy. 2007. "Rewarding Lula: Executive Power, Social Policy, and the Brazilian Elections of 2006." *Latin American Politics and Society*. 49 (1): 1–30.

Hunter, Wendy and Sugiyama, Natasha Borges. 2009. "Democracy and Social Policy: Advancing Basic Needs, Preserving Privileged Interests." *Latin American Politics and Society*. 51 (2): 29–58.

Imai, Kosuke. 2005. "Do Get-Out-the-Vote Calls Reduce Turnout? The Importance of Statistical Methods for Field Experiments." *American Political Science Review*. 99 (2): 283–300.

Imbens, Guido W. 2003. "Sensitivity to Exogeneity Assumptions in Program Evaluation." *The American Economic Review, Papers and Proceedings*. 96(2): 126–132.

2010. "Better LATE Than Nothing: Some Comments on Deaton (2009) and Heckman and Urzua (2009)." *Journal of Economic Literature*. 48 (2): 399–423.

INEGI (Instituto Nacional de Estadística, Geografía e Informática). 1996. *La Mortalidad Infantil en México, 1990*. México: INEGI.

2000. *La Mortalidad Infantil en México*. México: INEGI.

Irwin, Douglas and Marko Tervio. 2000. "Does Trade Raise Income? Evidence from the Twentieth Century." NBER Working Paper 7745.

Iversen, Torben. 2005. *Capitalism, Democracy and Welfare*. New York: Cambridge University Press.

Jalan, J. and Ravallion, Martin. 2002. "Geographic Poverty Traps? A Micro Model of Consumption Growth in Rural China." *Journal of Applied Econometrics*. 17 (4): 329–346.

References

Kahl, Sigrun. 2005. "The Religious Roots of Modern Poverty Policy: Catholic, Lutheran, and Reformed Protestant Traditions Compared." *Archives Européennes de Sociologie (European Journal of Sociology).* 46 (1): 91–126.

2009. "Religious Doctrines and Poor Relief: A Different Causal Path," in Van Kersbergen, Kees and Manow, Philip (eds.), *Religion, Class Coalitions and Welfare States.* New York: Cambridge University Press.

Kalyvas, Stathis N. 1996. *The Rise of Christian Democracy in Europe.* Cornell University Press.

Kasara, Kimuli. 2007. "Tax Me If You Can: Ethnic Geography, Democracy, and the Taxation of Agriculture in Africa." *American Political Science Review.* 101 (1): 159.

Katz, Jonathan and King, Gary. 1999. "A Statistical Model for Multiparty Electoral Data." *American Political Science Review.* 93 (1): 15–32.

Kaufman, Robert and Segura-Ubiergo, Alex. 2001. "Globalization, Domestic Politics and Social Spending in Latin America: A Time Series Cross-Section Analysis, 1973–1977." *World Politics.* 53 (July): 553–587.

Kaufman, Robert and Trejo, Guillermo. 1997. "Regionalism, Regime Transformation and PRONASOL: The Politics of the National Solidarity Programme in Four Mexican States." *Journal of Latin American Studies.* 29: 717–745.

Keefer, Phillip. 2007. "Democracy, Credibility and Policy Choices in Young Democracies." *American Journal of Political Science.* 51 (4): 804–821.

Keefer, Philip and Vlaicu, Razvan. 2008. "Democracy, Credibility and Clientelism." *Journal of Law, Economics and Organization.* 24 (2): 371–406.

Keefer, Philip, and Stuti Khemani. 2014. "Mass Media and Public Education: The Effects of Access to Community Radio in Benin." *Journal of Development Economics.* 109: 57–72.

Kelly, Morgan and O'Grada, Cormac. 2010. The Poor Law of Old England: Institutional Innovation and Demographic Regimes. *Journal of Interdisciplinary History.* 41 (3) (Winter): 339–366.

Kennedy, Peter. 1998. *A Guide to Econometrics.* Cambridge: MIT Press.

Khemani, Stuti. 2004. "Political Cycles in a Developing Economy: Effect of Elections on the Indian States." *Journal of Development Economics.* 73: 125–154.

2007. "Party Politics and Fiscal Discipline a Federation: Evidence from the States in India." *Comparative Political Studies.* 40 (6): 691–712.

Khwaja, Asim. 2007. "Can Good Projects Succeed in Bad Communities?" *Journal of Public Economics.* 93: 899–916.

King, Gary. 1997. *A Solution to the Ecological Inference Problem.* Princeton: Princeton University Press.

King, Gary, Keohane, Robert and Verba, Sydney. 1994. *Designing Social Inquiry: Scientific Inference in Qualitative Research.* Princeton: Princeton University Press.

King, Gary, Tomz, Michael and Wittenberg, Jason. 2000. "Making the Most of Statistical Analyses: Improving Interpretation and Presentation." *American Journal of Political Science.* 44 (2): 347–361.

Kitschelt, Herbert. 2000. "Linkages between Citizens and Politicians in Democratic Politics." *Comparative Political Studies.* 33 (6/7):845–879.

2011. "Clientelistic Linkage Strategies: A Descriptive Exploration." Paper Prepared for the Workshop on Democratic Accountability Strategies, Duke University.

Kitschelt, Herbert, and Daniel M. Kselman. 2013. "Economic Development, Democratic Experience, and Political Parties' Linkage Strategies." *Comparative Political Studies.* 46 (11): 1453–1484.

Kitschelt, Herbert and Wilkinson, Steven. 2007. *Patrons, Clients and Policies: Patterns of Democratic Accountability and Political Competition.* Cambridge: Cambridge University Press.

Klesner, Joseph. 1996. "Realineación of Desalineación? Consecuencias de la Crisis y la Reestructuración Economica para el Sistema Partidiario Mexicano," in Lorena Cook, Maria, Middlebrook, Kevin and Molinar, Juan (eds.): *Las dimensiones políticas de la reestructuración económica.* México: Cal y Arena.

2000. "The 2000 Mexican Presidential and Congressional Elections: Pre-Election Report." *Center for Strategic and International Studies, Western Hemisphere Election Study Series*, Vol. 18, Study 1. Washington, DC: CSIS.

Kohli, Atul (ed). 2001. *The Success of India's Democracy.* Cambridge: Cambridge University Press.

Kudamatsu, Masayuki. 2012. "Has Democratization Reduced Infant Mortality in Sub-Saharan Africa? Evidence from Micro Data." *Journal of the European Economic Association.* 10 (6): 1294–1317.

Kuran, Timur. 2001. "The Provision of Public Goods under Islamic Law: Origins, Contributions, and Limitations of the Waqf System." *Law and Society Review.* 35 (4): 841–897.

Kurtz, Marcus. 2004. *Free Market Democracy and the Chilean and Mexican Countryside.* Cambridge: Cambridge University Press.

Laakso, Markku and Taagepera, Rein. 1979. "Effective Number of Parties: A Measure with Application to West Europe." *Comparative Political Studies.* 12: 3–27.

Lake, David and Baum, Matthew. 2001. "The Invisible Hand of Democracy: Political Control and the Provision of Public Services." *Comparative Political Studies.* 34 (6): 587–621.

Lande, Carl H., Schmidt, Steffen W., Guasti, Laura, Landé, Carl H., and Scott, J. 1977. *Friends, Followers and Factions: A Reader in Political Clientelism.* Berkeley: University of California Press.

Langston, Joy. 2001. "Why Rules Matter: Changes in Candidate Selection in Mexico's PRI, 1988–2000." *Journal of Latin American Studies.* 33: 485–512.

2011. "Governors and 'Their' Deputies: New Legislative Principals in Mexico." *Legislative Studies Quarterly.* 35 (2): 235.

Larreguy, Horacio Alejandro. 2012. "The Monitoring Role of Clientelistic Networks: Evidence from Communal Lands in Mexico." Typescript. Department of Economics, MIT.

Lemarchand, Rene. 1972. "Political Clientelism and Ethnicity in Tropical Africa: Competing Solidarities in Nation Building." *American Political Science Review.* 66 (1): 68–90.

Lemarchand, Rene and Legg, Keith. 1972. "Political Clientelism and Development: A Preliminary Analysis." *Comparative Politics.* 4 (2): 149–178.

Levitsky, Steven. 2003. *Transforming Labor-Based Parties in Latin America: Argentine Peronism in Comparative Perspective.* Cambridge: Cambridge University Press.

Levitsky, Steven, and Lucan A. Way. 2010. "Why Democracy Needs a Level Playing Field." *Journal of Democracy.* 21 (1): 57–68.

Levitsky, Steven, and Maria Victoria Murillo. 2008. "Argentina: From Kirchner to Kirchner." *Journal of Democracy.* 19 (2): 1630.

Levitt, Steven and James Snyder. 1995. "Political Parties and the Distribution of Federal Outlays." *American Journal of Political Science.* 39 (4): 958–980.

Levy, Daniel C. and Bruhn, Kathleen. 2001. *Mexico: The Struggle for Democratic Development*. Berkeley: University of California Press.

Levy, Santiago. 1991. "Poverty Alleviation in Mexico." *World Bank Policy, Research, and External Affairs Working Papers No. WPS 679*. Washington, DC: World Bank.

1994. "La Pobreza en México," in Vélez, Félix (ed.), *La Pobreza en México*. México: Fondo de Cultura Económica.

1998. "Análisis Metodológico de la Distribución de los Recursos en el Ramo33," in *Comisión de Desarrollo Social Instrumentos de Distribución de los Recursos del Ramo 33*. México: Cámara de Diputados.

2006. *Progress against Poverty: Sustaining Mexico's Progresa-Oportunidades Program*. Washington, DC: Brookings Institution.

2010. *Good Intentions, Bad Outcomes: Social Policy, Informality, and Economic Growth in Mexico*. Washington, DC: Brookings Institution Press.

Levy, Santiago and Rodriguez, Evelyn. 2005. *Sin Herencia de Pobreza*. Mexico: Planeta.

Lindbeck, Assar and Weibull, Jorgen. 1987. "Balanced Budget Redistribution as the Outcome of Political Competition." *Public Choice*. 52 (3): 273–297.

Lindberg, Staffan and Morrison, Minion. 2008. "Are African Voters Really Ethnic or Clientelistic? Survey Evidence from Ghana." *Political Science Quarterly*, 123(1): 95–122.

Lindert, Peter H. 1998. "Poor Relief before the Welfare State: Britain versus the Continent, 1780–1880." *European Review of Economic Studies*. 2: 101–140.

2004. *Growing Public: Social Spending and Economic Growth Since the Eighteenth Century, Volume I: The Story*. New York: Cambridge University Press.

Lindert, Kathy, Skoufias, Emmanuel, and Shapiro, Joseph. 2006. "Redistributing Income to the Poor and the Rich: Public Transfers in Latin America and the Caribbean." *Social Safety Nets Primer Series*.

Lizzeri, Alessandro and Persico, Nicola. 2001. "The Provision of Public Goods under Alternative Electoral Incentives." *American Economic Review*. 91 (1): 225–239.

Londoño, Juan Luis and Székely, Miguel. 2000. "Persistent Poverty and Excess Inequality: Latin America, 1970–1995." *Journal of Applied Economics*. 3 (1): 93–134.

Londregan, John. 2006. "Political Income Redistribution." Chapter 5 in Weingast, Barry and Wittman, Donald. *The Oxford Handbook of Political Economy*. Oxford: Oxford University Press.

2007. *Legislative Institutions and Ideology in Chile*. Cambridge: Cambridge University Press.

Lopez-Cordova, Ernesto J. and Meissner, Christopher M. 2005. "The Globalization of Trade and Democracy, 1870–2000." NBER Working Paper No. 11117, February.

Los Angeles Times. 1991. Poll 258, *Mexico-Political and Economic Issues*. (Collected by Belden-Rusonello September 11 to October 2, 1991).

Lozano, Rafael, Soliz, Patricia, Gakidou, Emmanuela, Abbott-Klafter, Jesse, Feehan, Dennis M., Vidal, Cecilia, Ortiz, Juan Pablo and Murray, Christopher J. L. 2006. "Benchmarking of Performance of Mexican States with Effective Coverage." *The Lancet*. 368: 1729–1741.

Lujambio, Alonso. 2000. *El poder compartido: un ensayo sobre la democratización mexicana*. Mexico City: Editorial Océano.

Lupu, Noam. 2013. "Party Brands and Partisanship: Theory with Evidence from a Survey Experiment in Argentina." *American Journal of Political Science*. 57(1): 49–64.

Lustig, Nora. 1994. "Solidarity as a Strategy of Poverty Alleviation," in Cornelius, Wayne, Craig, Ann and Fox, Jonathan (eds.), *Transforming State-Society Relations in Mexico: The National Solidarity Strategy*. La Jolla: Center for U.S.-Mexican Studies, UCSD.
  1995. *Coping with Austerity. Poverty and Inequality in Latin America*. Washington, DC: Brookings Institution.
Madrid, Raul. 2012. *The Rise of Ethnic Politics in Latin America*. Cambridge: Cambridge University Press.
Magaloni, Beatriz. 2006. *Voting for Autocracy: Hegemonic Party Survival and Its Demise in Mexico*. Cambridge: Cambridge University Press.
  2010. "The Game of Electoral Fraud and the Ousting of Authoritarian Rule." *American Journal of Political Science*. 54 (3): 751–765.
Magaloni, Beatriz and Poiré, Alejandro. 2004. "Strategic Coordination in the Mexico 2000 Presidential Race," in Dominguez, J.I., Lawson, C. (eds.), *Mexico's Pivotal Democratic Elections: Candidates, Voters and the Presidential Campaign of 2000*. Palo Alto, CA: Stanford University Press.
Magaloni, Beatriz, Diaz-Cayeros, Alberto and Estévez, Federico. 2007. "Clientelism and Portfolio Diversification: A Model of Electoral Investment with Applications to Mexico," in Kitschelt, Herbert and Wilkinson, Steven (eds.), *Patrons, Clients and Policies: Patterns of Democratic Accountability and Political Competition*. Cambridge: Cambridge University Press.
Magar, Eric and Romero, Vidal. 2006. "Changing Patterns of Governance in Mexican States: What Do They Tell Us about Future Directions of National Politics? A report prepared for the World Bank." Mexico, ITAM.
Mainwaring, Scott. 1999. *Rethinking Party Systems in the Third Wave of Democratization: The Case of Brazil*. Stanford: Stanford University Press
  2012. "From Representative Democracy to Participatory Competitive Authoritarianism: Hugo Chavez and Venezuelan Politics." *Perspectives on Politics*. 10 (4): 955–967.
Marcos, Subcomandante. 2001 [1994]. "Who Should Ask for Pardon and Who Can Grant It?" in Ponce de León, Juana (ed.), *Our Word Is Our Weapon. Selected Writings. Subcomandante Insurgente Marcos*. New York: Seven Stories Press.
Mares, Isabela. 2004. *The Politics of Social Risk: Business and Welfare State Development*. New York: Cambridge University Press.
Mares, Isabela and Matthew E. Carnes. 2009. "Social Policy in Developing Countries." *Annual Review of Political Science*. 12 (June): 93–113.
Markowitz, Harry. 1952. "Portfolio Selection." *Journal of Finance*. 7: 77–91.
McCubbins, Mathew D., Noll, Roger G. and Weingast, Barry R. 1987. "Administrative Procedures as Instruments of Political Control." *Journal of Law, Economics, and Organization*. 3 (2): 243.
McGuire, James. 2010. *Wealth, Health and Democracy in East Asia and Latin America*. Cambridge: Cambridge University Press.
  2013. "Conditional Cash Transfers in Bolivia: Origins, Impact, Universality." Paper Presented at the 2013 Annual Meeting of the International Studies Association, San Francisco, April 3–6.
McMillan, John and Pablo Zoido. 2004. "How to Subvert Democracy: Montesinos in Peru." *Journal of Economic Perspectives*. 18 (4): 69–92.

Mebane, Walter. 2013. "Election Forensics: The Meanings of Precinct Vote Counts' Second Digits." Typescript. University of Virginia.
Medellin, Rodrigo. 1974. "La Dinamica del Distanciamiento Economico y Social en Mexico," in Miguel Wionczek (ed.), *La Sociedad Mexicana: Presente y Futuro*. Mexico: Fondo de Cultura Economica.
Medina, Luis Fernando and Stokes, Susan. 2006. "Monopoly and Monitoring: An Approach to Political Clientelism," in Herbert Kitschelt and Steven Wilkinson (eds.), *Patrons, Clients, and Policies*. Cambridge: Cambridge University Press.
Meltzer, Allan and Scott F. Richard. 1981. "A Rational Theory of the Size of Government." *The Journal of Political Economy*. 89 (5): 914–927.
Mesa-Lago, Carmelo. 1978. *Social Security in Latin America: Pressure Groups, Stratification and Inequality*. Pittsburgh: University of Pittsburgh Press.
Mesa-Lago, Carmelo and Bertranou, Fabio. 1998. *Manual de economía de la seguridad social en América Latina*. Centro Latinoamericano de Economia Humana. Montevideo: Claeh.
Middlebrook, Kevin. 2004. *Dilemmas of Political Change in Mexico*. London: Institute of Latin American Studies.
Middlebrook, Kevin and Zepeda, Eduardo. 2003. *Confronting Development: Assessing Mexico's Economic and Social Policy Challenges*. Stanford: Stanford University Press.
Miguel, Edward. 2004. "Tribe or Nation? Nation Building and Public Goods in Kenya versus Tanzania." *World Politics*. 56.03: 328–362.
Miguel, Edward and Gugerty, Mary Kay. 2005. "Ethnic Diversity, Social Sanctions, and Public Goods in Kenya." *Journal of Public Economics*. 89: 2325–2368.
Milesi-Ferreti, Gian-Maria, Perotti, Roberto and Rostagno, Massimo. 2002. "Electoral Systems and Public Spending." *Quarterly Journal of Economics*. 609–657.
Miller, Grant. 2008. "Women's Suffrage, Political Responsiveness, and Child Survival in American History." *The Quarterly Journal of Economics*. 123 (3): 1287–1327.
Milner, Helen V. and Kubota, Keiko. 2005. "Why the Move to Free Trade? Democracy and Trade Policy in the Developing Countries." *International Organization*. 59: 107–143.
Mina Valdez, Alejandro. 1988. "La Medición Indirecta de la Mortalidad Infantil en los Primeros Años de Vida en México," in Bronfman, Mario and Gómez de León, José (eds.), *La Mortalidad en México: Niveles, Tendencias y Determiantes*. Mexico: El Colegio de México, pp. 273–306.
Moe, T.M. 1990. "The Politics of Structural Choice: Toward a Theory of Public Bureaucracy," in Williamson, Oliver (ed.), *Organization Theory: From Chester Barnard to the Present and Beyond*. Oxford: Oxford Univesity Press, pp. 116–153.
Mogollón, Olivia. 2002. "De la discreción a las fórmulas: mecanismos de distribución de recursos decentralizados para alivio a la pobreza." Tesis de Maestría. Instituto Tecnológico Autónomo de México.
Molinar, Juan. 1991. *El Tiempo de la Legitimidad. Elecciones, Democracia y Autoritarismo en México* México: Cal y Arena.
Molinar, Juan and Weldon, Jeffrey. 1994. "Electoral Determiants and Consequences of National Solidarity," in Cornelius, Wayne, Craig, Ann and Fox, Jonathan (eds.), *Transforming State-Society Relations in Mexico: The National Solidarity Strategy* La Jolla: Center for U.S.-Mexican Studies, UCSD.
Montesquieu, Charles de Secondat, Baron de. 1914 [1752]. Nugent, Thomas. Trans. *The Spirit of Laws*. London: G. Bell & Sons, Ltd.

Moran, P.A.P. 1950. "Notes on Continuous Stochastic Phenomena." *Biometrika.* 37: 17–23.
Morgan, Jana. 2011. *Bankrupt Representation and Party System Collapse.* University Park: Pennsylvania State University Press
Morgenstern, Scott and Potthoff, Richard. 2005. "The Components of Elections: District Heterogeneity, District-Time Effects, and Volatility." *Electoral Studies.* 24: 17–40.
Mukherjee, C., White, H. and Wuyts, M. 1998. *Econometrics and Data Analysis for Developing Countries.* London: Routledge.
Nahmad, Salomón, Tania Carrasco, and Sergio Sarmiento. 1999. "Acercamiento etnográfico y cultural sobre el impacto del programa Progresa en doce comunidades de seis estados de la República." *Gómez J. y R. Loyola [comps.], Alivio a la pobreza: Análisis del programa de educación, salud y alimentación.* México: Centro de Investigaciones y Estudios Superiores en Antropología social.
Navia, Patricio and Zweifel, Thomas D. 2003. "Democracy, Dictatorship and Infant Mortality Revisted." *Journal of Democracy.* 14 (3): 90–103.
Nichter, Simeon. 2008. "Vote Buying or Turnout Buying? Machine Politics and the Secret Ballot."*American Political Science Review.* 102 (February): 15–28.
    2009. "Declared Choice: Citizens's Strategies and Dual Commitment." Problems Paper Prepared for Presentation at the Annual Meeting of the American Political Science Association in Toronto, Ontario, September 3–6.
Nichter, Simeon Charaka. 2010. "Politics and Poverty: Electoral Clientelism in Latin America." University of California, Berkeley, Ph.D. Dissertation.
O'Gorman, Frank. 2001. "Patronage and the Reform of the State in England, 1700–1860," in Piattoni, Simona (ed.), *Clientelism, Interests, and Democratic Representation: The European Experience in Historical and Comparative Perspective.* Cambridge: Cambridge University Press, pp. 54–76.
Olken, Benjamin. 2006. "Corruption and the Costs of Redistribution: Micro Evidence from Indonesia." *Journal of Public Economics.* 90: 853–870.
    2010. "Direct Democracy and Local Public Goods: Evidence from a Field Experiment in Indonesia." *American Political Science Review.* 104 (02): 243–267.
Olson, Mancur. 1993. "Dictatorship, Democracy, and Development." *American Political Science Review.* 87.03: 567–576.
O'Neill, Kathleen. 2005. *Decentralizing the State: Elections, Parties, and Local Power in the Andes.* Cambridge: Cambridge University Press.
Openshaw, S. 1984. "The Modifiable Areal Unit Problem." *Concepts and Techniques in Modern Geography.* 38: 41.
Oppenheimer, Andreas. 1996. *Bordering on Chaos: Guerrillas, Stockbrokers, Politicians, and Mexico's Road to Prosperity.* Boston: Little, Brown & Company.
Ordóñez, Carlos. 1994. Política y pobreza: Análisis de los criterios de inversión del PRONASOL. BA thesis in Social Sciences, ITAM, Mexico City.
Ortiz Hernán, Sergio. 1994. *Caminos y transportes en México: una aproximación socioeconómica: fines de la colonia y principios de la vida independiente.* Mexico: FCE.
Ozbudun, Ergun. 1981. "Turkey: The Politics of Clientelism," in Eisenstadt, S.N. and Lemarchand, René (eds.), *Political Clientelism, Patronage and Development.* Sage Studies in Contemporary Political Sociology. Vol. 3: Thousand Oaks. Sage Publications.

Palliccia, G.M. 1906. "The Relief of the Poor in Italy." *Annals of the American Academy of Political and Social Science.* 28 (September): 113–118.
Pande, Rohini. 2003. "Can Mandated Political Representation Increase Policy Influence for Disadvantaged Minorities? Theory and Evidence from India." *The American Economic Review.* 93 (4): 1132–1151.
Paxson, Christina and Schady, Norbert. 2002. "The Allocation and Impact of Social Funds: Spending on School Infrastructure in Peru." *World Bank Economic Review.* 16 (2): 297–319.
Pérez-Liñal, Anibal. 2007. *Presidential Impeachment and the New Political Instability in Latin America.* Cambridge: Cambridge University Press
Persson, Torsten and Tabellini, Guido. 1999. "Alfred Marshall Lecture on The Size and Scope of Government: Comparative Politics with Rational Politicians." *European Economic Review.* 43: 699–735.
  2003. *The Economic Effects of Constitutions: What Do the Data Say?* Cambridge, MA: MIT Press.
Persson, Torsten, Roland, Gerard and Tabellini, Guido. 2000. "Comparative Politics and Public Finance." *Journal of Political Economy.* 108 (61): 1121–1161.
Peza, Juan de D. 1881. *La Beneficiencia en Mexico.* Mexico: Imprenta de Francisco Diaz de Leon.
Piattoni, Simona. 2001. *Clientelism, Interests and Democratic Representation* Cambridge: Cambridge University Press.
  2005a. *Il Clientelismo: L'Italia in Prosppetiva Comparata.* Roma: Caroccio.
  2005b. "Tipi di clientelismo." Typescript.
Pierson, Paul (ed.). 2001. *The New Politics of the Welfare State.* New York: Oxford University Press.
Piven, Frances Fox and Cloward, Richard A. 1993. *Regulating the Poor: The Functions of Public Welfare.* New York: Vintage.
Platteau, Jean-Paul. 2004. "Monitoring Elite Capture in Community-Driven Development." *Journal of Development Studies.* 35 (2): 223–246.
PNUD. 2003. *Informe Sobre el Desarrollo Humano en México 2002.* México: PNUD.
  2007. "Informe sobre la Encuesta Nacional sobre la Protección de los Programas Sociales (ENAPP 2006)." Mexico.
Poiré, Alejandro. 2001. "Do Electoral Institutions Affect Party Discipline?, or: Nominations Rule! Comparative Evidence on the Impact of Nomination Procedures on Party Discipline." ITAM Working Papers on Political Science No. WPPS2001-03.
Poiré, Alejandro and Estrada, Luis. 2007. "Taught to Protest, Learning to Lose." *Journal of Democracy.* 18 (1): 73–87.
Polo, Michele. 1998. "Electoral competition and Political Rents." Typescript. Milan: IGIER and Bocconi University.
Pontusson, Jonas. 2005. *Inequality and Prosperity: Social Europe vs. Liberal America.* Ithaca: Cornell University Press.
Posner, Daniel. 2005. *Institutions and Ethnic Politics in Africa.* Cambridge: Cambridge University Press.
Posner, Daniel and Kramon, Eric. 2013. "Who Benefits from Distributive Politics? How the Outcome One Studies Affects the Answer One Gets." *Perspectives on Politics.* 11 (2): 361–474.

Pribble, Jennifer. 2011. "Worlds Apart: Social Policy Regimes in Latin America." *Studies in Comparative International Development*. 46 (2) :191–216.
Pritchett, Lant. 2005. "A Lecture on the Political Economy of Targeted Safety Nets." World Bank Social Protection Discussion Paper Series No.0501. Washington, DC: World Bank.
Przeworski, Adam. 2004. "Democracy and Economic Development," in Mansfield, Edward D. and Sisson, Richard (eds.), *The Evolution of Political Knowledge*. Columbus: Ohio State University Press.
  2007. "Is the Science of Comparative Politics Possible?" in Boix, Carles and Stokes, Susan C. (eds.), *Oxford Handbook of Comparative Politics*. New York: Oxford University Press.
Przeworski, Adam and Sprague, John. 1986. *Paper Stones*. Chicago: Chicago University Press.
Przeworski, Adam, Alvarez, Michael E., Cheibub, Jose Antonio and Limongi, Fernando. 2000. *Democracy and Development*. Cambridge: Cambridge University Press.
Putnam, Robert. 1993. *Making Democracy Work: Civic Traditions in Modern Italy*. Princeton: Princeton University Press.
Ravallion, Martin. 2001. "Growth, Inequality and Poverty: Looking beyond Averages." *World Development*. 29 (11): 1803–1815.
Ravallion, Martin and Datt, Gaurav. 2002. "Why Has Economic Growth Been More Pro-Poor in Some States of India than Others?" *Journal of Development Economics*. 68: 381–400.
Ravaillon, Martin and Wodon, Quentin. 1998. "Evaluating a Targeted Social Program When Placement Is Decentralized." Typescript. World Bank.
Rawlings, Laura B. and Rubio, Gloria. 2003. *Evaluación del Impacto de los Programas de Transferencias Condicionadas en Efectivo*. Cuadernos de Desarrollo Humano. 10. México: Secretaría de Desarrollo Social.
Rawlings, Laura B. and Schady, Norbert. 2002. Impact Evaluation of Social Funds. An Introduction." *World Bank Economic Review*. 16 (2): 213–217.
Rawlings. Laura B., Sherburne-Benz, Lynne and Van Domelen, Julie. 2004. *Evaluating Social Funds: A Cross-Country Analysis of Community Investments*. Washington, DC: World Bank.
Reinikka, Ritva and Svensson, Jakob. 2004. "Local Capture: Evidence from a Central Government Transfer Program in Uganda." *Quarterly Journal of Economics*. 119 (2): 679–705.
Reinikka, Ritva, amd Svensson, Jakob. 2005. "Fighting Corruption to Improve Schooling: Evidence from a Newspaper Campaign in Uganda." *Journal of the European Economic Association*. 3 (2–3): 259–267.
Reveles, Jose. 2012. *Las Historias Mas Negras de Narco Corrupcion e Impunidad de Mexico*. Mexico: Random House Mondadori (De Bolsillo).
Rijpma, Auke. 2011. "Estimating and Explaining Public Service Provision by Religious Organizations in the Late-Medieval Low Countries." Typescript.
Roberts, Robert E. 1973. "Modernization and Infant Mortality in Mexico." *Economic Development and Cultural Change*. 21 (4): 655–669.
Robinson, James and Torvik, Ragnar. 2002. "White Elephants." CEPR Discussion Paper No. 3459, July.

Robinson, James and Verdier, Thierry. 2002. "The Political Economy of Clientelism." Paper Presented at the Conference The Political Economy of Clientelism, Stanford University, May.
Rocha Menocal, Alina. 2001. "Do Old Habits Die Hard? A Statistical Exploration of the Politisation of Progresa, Mexico's Latest Federal Poverty-Alleviation Programme, Under the Zedillo Administration." *Journal of Latin American Studies*. 33: 513–538.
 2005. "Less Political and More Pro-Poor? The Evolution of Social Welfare Spending in Mexico in a Context of Democratisation and Decentralization." Nord-Sud Aktuell. Special Edition: Fighting Poverty.
Rodríguez, Francisco and Rodrik, Dani. 2000. "Trade Policy and Economic Growth: A Skeptic's Guide to the Cross-National Evidence." *NBER Macroeconomics Annual*. 15: 261–338.
Rodríguez, Victoria. 1997. *Decentralization in Mexico. From Reforma Municipal to Solidaridad to Nuevo Federalismo*. New York: Westview Press.
Rodríguez, Victoria and Ward, Peter (eds.). 1995. *Opposition Government in Mexico*. Albuquerque: University of New Mexico Press.
Rojas, Carlos. 1994a. *El Programa Nacional de Solidaridad*. México: Fondo de Cultura Económica.
 1994b. "Solidaridad," in Warman, Arturo (ed.), *La Política Social en México, 1989–1994*. Mexico: Fondo de Cultura Económica.
Rosenbaum, P.R. and Rubin, D.B. 1983. "The Central Role of the Propensity Score in Observational Studies for Causal Effects." *Biometrika*. 70: 41–55.
Ross, Michael. 2006. "Is Democracy Good for the Poor?" *American Journal of Political Science*. 50 (4): 860–874.
Roy, A.D. 1952. "Safety First and the Holding of Assets." *Econometrica*. 20 (3): 431–449.
Rozevitch, Simon and Avi, Weiss. 1993. "Beneficiaries from Federal Transfers to Muncipalities: The Case of Israel." *Public Choice*.
Rubin, D.B. 2006. *Matched Sampling for Causal Effects*. New York: Cambridge University Press.
Sachs, Jeffrey. 2005. *The End of Poverty*. New York: Penguin Press.
Sachs, Jeffrey, Tornell, Aaron and Velasco, Andres. 1996. "The Mexican Peso Crisis: Sudden Death or Death Foretold?" *Journal of international economics*. 41 (3): 265–283.
Salinas de Gortari, Carlos. 1982. *Political Participation, Public Investment, and Support for the System: A Comparative Study of Rural Communities in Mexico*. La Jolla: Center for U.S.-Mexican Studies, University of California, San Diego.
 2000. *México: un paso difícil a la modernidad*. Mexico: Plaza & Janés.
Samuels, David J. 2002. "Pork Barreling Is Not Credit Claiming or Advertising: Campaign Finance and the Sources of the Personal Vote in Brazil." *Journal of Politics*. 64 (3): 845–863.
Samuels, David. 2006. "Sources of mass partisanship in Brazil." *Latin American Politics and Society*. 48.2: 1–27.
Schady, Norbert R. 2000. "The Political Economy of Expenditures by the Peruvian Social Fund (FONCODES), 1991–95." *American Political Science Review*. 94 (2): 289–304.

Schaffer, Frederic Charles. 2006. *Elections for Sale: The Causes and Consequences of Vote Buying.* Boulder: Lynne Rienner.

Schaffer, Frederic Charles and Schedler, Andreas. 2007. "What Is Vote Buying?" in Schaffer, Frederic (ed.), *Elections for Sale: The Causes and Consequences of Vote Buying.* Boulder: Lynne Rienner.

Schedler, Andreas. 2002. "My Vote? Not for Sale: How Mexican Citizens View Electoral Clientelism." Typescript. CIDE.

Scheiner, Ethan. 2005. "Pipelines of Pork: Japanese Politics and a Model of Local Opposition Party Failure." *Comparative Political Studies.* 38 (7): 799–823.

Scott, James. 1972a. *Comparative Political Corruption.* Englewood Cliffs: Prentice Hall.

1972b. "Patron-Client politics and Political Change in Southeast Asia." *American Political Science Review.* 66 (1): 91–113.

Scott, John. 1998. "Ramo 33: descentralización y focalización," in Cámara de Diputados (ed.), *Instrumentos de Distribución de los Recursos del Ramo 33.* Comisión de Desarrollo Social de la Cámara de Diputados, LVII Legislatura. Mexico: Cámara de Diputados.

2009. "Gasto Público y Desarrollo Humano en México: Análisis de Incidencia y Equidad." Documento de Trabajo para el Informe de Desarrollo Humano de México 2010, PNUD México.

Seawright, Jason. 2012. *Party System Collapse.* Stanford: Stanford University Press

Secretaría de Salud. 2006. *La Mortalidad en México, 2000–2004 "Muertes Evitables: magnitud, distribución y tendencias."* México: Secretaría de Salud.

Secretary of State for Foreign Affairs. 1875. *Poor Laws in Foreign Countries: Reports Communicated to the Local Government Board by Her Majesty's Secretary of State for Foreign Affairs.* London: George Eyre and William Spottiswoode.

Seddon Wallack, J., A. Gaviria, U. Panizza and E. Stein. 2000. "Political Particularism Around the World." Mimeo, IADB and Stanford University

Sedesol (Secretaría de Desarrollo Social). 1994. Hechos en Solidaridad. CD-ROM.

2005. "Presentación sobre la medición del desarrollo 2000–2002," in Székeli, Miguel (ed.), *Números que mueven al mundo: la medición de la pobreza en México.* Mexico: SEDESOL/CIDE/Anuies/M.A. Porrúa.

2006. "Comentarios al Estudio 'Monitoreo de Programas Sociales en Contextos Electorales' por lo que se refiere al Fondo de Aportaciones para la Infraestructura Social (FAIS)." Typescript. Sedesol.

Sen, Amartya. 1981. *Poverty and Famines: An Essay on Entitlement and Deprivation.* Oxford: Oxford University Press.

1999. *Development as Freedom.* New York: Anchor Books.

Sepúlveda, Jaime, Bustreo, F., Tapia, R., Rivera, J., Lozano, R., Oláiz, G., Partida, V., García-García, L. and Valdespino, J. 2006. "Improvement of Child Survival in Mexico: The Diagonal Approach." *The Lancet.* 368 (9551): 2017–2027.

Sharpe, W. 1964. "Capital Asset Prices: A Theory of Market Equilibrium under Conditions of Risk." *Journal of Finance.* 19: 425–442.

Shefter, Martin. 1994. *Political Parties and the State: The American Historical Experience.* Princeton: Princeton University Press

Skocpol, Theda. 1992. *Protecting Soldiers and Mothers: The Political Origins of Social Policy in the United States.* Cambridge, MA: Belknap/Harvard University Press.

Skoufias, Emmanuel. 2001. "PROGRESA and Its Impacts on the Human Capital and Welfare of Households in Rural Mexico: A Synthesis of the Results and and Evaluation by IFPRI." Washington, DC: IFPRI.

Skoufias, Emmanuel and McClafferty, Bonnie. 2001. *Is Progresa Working? Summary of the Results of an Evaluation by IFPRI*. Washington, DC: International Food Research Institute.

Skoufias, Emmanuel, Davis, B. and Behrman, Jere. 1999. *Final Report: An Evaluation of the Selection of Beneficiary Households in the Education, Health and Nutrition Program (Progresa) in Mexico*. Washington, DC: International Food Research Institute.

Smith, Peter H. 1979. *Labyrinths of Power: Political Recruitment in 20th Century Mexico*. Princeton: Princeton University Press.

Snyder, James M. 1989. "Election Goals and the Allocation of Campaign Resources." *Econometrica*. 57 (3): 637–660.

Soares, Fábio Veras, Ribas, Rafael Perez, and Osório, Rafael Guerreiro. 2010. "Evaluating the Impact of Brazil's Bolsa Familia: Cash Transfer Programs in Comparative Perspective." *Latin American Research Review*. 45 (2): 173–190.

Stokes, Donald E. 1965. "A Variance Components Model of Political Effects." *Mathematical Applications in Political Science*. 1.1: 61–85.

Stasavage, David. 2005. "Democracy and Education Spending in Africa." *American Journal of Political Science*. 49.2: 343–358.

Stokes, Susan. 2001. *Mandantes and Democracy: Neoliberalism by Surprise in Latin America*. Cambridge: Cambridge University Press.

2005. "Perverse Accountability: A Formal Model of Machine Politics with Evidence from Argentina." *American Political Science Review*. 99 (3): 315–325.

2007. "Political Clientelism," in Boix, Carles and Stokes, Susan (eds.), *Comparative Politics Handbook of Political Science*. Oxford: Oxford University Press.

Stokes, Susan and Cleary, Mathew. 2006. *Democracy and the Culture of Skepticism: Political Trust in Argentina and Mexico*. New York: Russell Sage Foundation Series on Trust.

Stokes, Susan, Dunning, Thad, Nazareno, Marcelo and Brusco, Valeria. 2013. *Brokers, Voters, and Clientelism: The Puzzle of Distributive Politics*. Cambridge: Cambridge University Press.

Stratmann, Thomas and Bauer, Martin. 2002. "Plurality Rule, Proportional Representation, and the German Bundestag: How Incentives to Pork-Barrel Differ Across Electoral Systems." *American Journal of Political Science*. 46 (3): 506–514.

Strömberg, David. 2001. *Radio's Impact on Public Spending*. Stockholm: Institute for International Economic Studies.

2002. *Optimal Campaigning in Presidential Elections: The Probability of Being Florida*. Stockholm: Institute for International Economic Studies.

Szekeli, Miguel. 1998. *The Economics of Poverty, Inequality and Wealth Accumulation in Mexico*. New York: St. Martin's Press.

2005. *Números que mueven al mundo: la medición de la pobreza en México*. Mexico: SEDESOL/CIDE/Anuies/M.A. Porrúa.

Szwarcberg, Mariela. 2012. "Uncertainty, Political Clientelism, and Voter Turnout in Latin America: Why Parties Conduct Rallies in Argentina." *Comparative Politics*. 45 (1): 88–106.

Takahashi, Yuriko. 2006. "Neoliberal Manipulation (or Politization) of Social Spending in Latin America: Evidence from Mexico." Typescript. Cornell University Press.

Tanck de Estrada, Dorothy. 2005. *Atlas Ilustrado de los Pueblos de Indios: Nueva Espana, 1800*. Mexico: El Colegio de Mexico.

Tarrow, Sidney. 2006. "Space and Comparative Politics." *APSA-CP Newsletter*. 17 (1) (Winter): 1–4.

Tendler, Judith. 1997. *Good Governance in the Tropics*. Baltimore: Johns Hopkins University Press.

Terry Karl. 2000. "Economic Inequality and Democratic Instability." *Journal of Democracy*. 11 (1) (January): 149–156.

Tomz, Michael, Wittenberg, Jason and King, Gary. 2001. *CLARIFY: Software for Interpreting and Presenting Statistical Results. Version 2.0*. Cambridge, MA: Harvard University. http://gking.harvard.edu. Accessed June 1, 2001.

Trejo, Guillermo. 2009. "Religious Competition and Ethnic Mobilization in Latin America: Why the Catholic Church Promotes Indigenous Movements in Mexico." *American Political Science Review*. 103 (3): 323–342.

2012. *Popular Movements in Autocracies: Religion, Repression, and Indigenous Collective Action in Mexico*. Cambridge: Cambridge University Press.

Trejo, Guillermo and Jones, Claudio. 1998. "Political Dilemmas of Welfare Reform: Poverty and Inequality in Mexico," in Kaufman Purcell, Susan and Rubio, Luis (eds.), *Mexico under Zedillo*. Boulder: Lynne Rienner.

Tsai, Lilly. 2007. "Solidary Groups, Informal Accountability, and Local Public Goods Provision in Rural China." *American Political Science Review*. 101 (2): 355–372.

Tucker, Joshua. 2006. *Regional Economic Voting: Russia, Poland, Hungary, Slovakia, and the Czech Republic, 1990–1999*. Cambridge: Cambridge University Press.

Tufte, Edward. 1978. *The Political Control of the Economy*. Princeton: Princeton University Press.

UNDP. 2011. "Ejercicio Apreciación Sustantiva Mi Familia Progresa." Guatemala: United Nations Development Programme.

UNICEF. 2004. "The State of the World's Children 2004. Girls, Education and Development." UNICEF, New York.

2007. "Monitoring the Situation of Women and Children." www.childinfo.org/ Accessed July 9, 2007.

United Nations. 1983. *Manual X: Indirect Techniques for Demographic Estimation*. ST/ESA/SER.A/81. New York: United Nations.

Valencia Lomeli, Enrique. 2008. "Conditional Cash Transfers as Social Policy in Latin America: An Assessment of Their Contributions and Limitations." *Annual Review of Sociology*. 34: 475–499.

Van de Walle, Dominique and Nead, Kimberly (eds.). 1995. *Public Spending and the Poor: Theory and Evidence*. Baltimore: Johns Hopkins University Press.

Van Kersbergen, Kees and Manow, Philip (eds.). 2009. *Religion, Class Coalitions and Welfare States*. New York: Cambridge University Press.

Van Leewen, Marco H.D. 1994. "Logic of Charity: Poor Relief in Preindustrial Europe." *Journal of Interdisciplinary History*. 24.4 (Spring): 589–613.

2009. "'Giving in the Golden Age' Presentation of a New Research Project." Paper for the Fourth Flemish-Dutch Conference on the Economic and Social History of the Low Countries before 1850, Leiden, January 29–30.

Vilalta y Perdomo, Carlos Javier. 2006. "El Mecanismo Causal del Voto de Oposicion a una Obra Vial: Una Exploracion Espacial y Sociologica." EGAP Working Paper No. 2006–11. Mexico: Tecnológico de Monterrey, Campus Ciudad de México.

Villamil, Antonio. 1877. *Memoria histórica del Nacional Monte de Piedad*. Mexico: I. Escalante.

Villareal, Andres. 2002. "Political Competition and Violence in Mexico: Hierarchical Social Control in Local Patronage Structures." *American Sociological Review*. 67 (4) (August): 477–498.

2004. "The Social Ecology of Rural Violence: Land Scarcity, the Organization of Agricultural Production, and the Presence of the State." *American Journal of Sociology*. 110 (2) (September): 313–348.

Wallis, John Joseph. 1984. "The Birth of the Old Federalism: Financing the New Deal." *Journal of Economic History*. 44: 139–159.

1987. Employment, Politics and Economic Recovery during the Great Depression." *The Review of Econmics and Statistics*. 59: 516–520.

1998. "The Political Economy of New Deal Spending Revisited, Again: With and without Nevada." *Explorations in Economic History*. 35: 140–170.

Walsh-Sanderson, Susan 1984. *Land Reform in Mexico: 1910–1980*. Orlando: Academic Press.

Wantchekon, Leonard. 2004. "Clientelism and Voting Behavior: Evidence from a Field Experiment in Benin." *World Politics*. 55 (3): 399–422.

Ward, Hugh and John, Peter. 1999. "Targeting Benefits for Electoral Gain: Constituency Marginality and the Distribution of Grants to English Local Authorities." *Political Studies*. 47 (1): 32–52.

Ward, Peter. 1986. *Políticas Sociales de Bienestar Social en México, 1970–1989*. México: Nueva Imagen.

Ward, Peter M. and Rodriguez, Victoria E. 1999. "New Federalism and State Government in Mexico: Bringing the States Back In." A.S.-Mexican Policy Report No. 9. University of Texas at Austin.

Warner, Carolyn. 2001. "Mass Parties and Clientelism in France and Italy," in Piattoni, Simona (ed.), *Clientelism, Interests and Democratic Representation*. Cambridge: Cambridge University Press.

Weingast, Barry R. 1995. "The Economic Role of Political Institutions: Market Preserving Federalism and Economic Development." *Journal of Law, Economics and Organization*. 11 (1): 1–31.

Weingast, Barry R., Shepsle, Kenneth A. and Johnsen, Christopher. 1981. "The Political Economy of Benefits and Costs: A Neoclassical Approach to Distributive Politics." *Journal of Political Economy*. 89 (4): 642–664.

Weinstein, Jeremy. 2006. *Inside Rebellion: The Political Economy of Rebel Organization* Cambridge: Cambridge University Press.

Weitz-Shapiro, Rebecca. 2012. "What Wins Votes: Why Some Politicians Opt Out of Clientelism." *American Journal of Political Science*. 56 (3): 568–583.

2014. *Curbing Clientelism in Argentina: Politics, Poverty, and Social Policy*. Cambridge: Cambridge University Press.

Werner, Alejandro. 1995. "The Currency Risk Premium in Mexico: A Closer Look at Interest Rate Differentials." Unpublished manuscript. International Monetary Fund.

Weyland, Kurt. 2004. *The Politics of Market Reform in Fragile Democracies: Argentina, Brazil, Peru and Venezuela*. Princeton: Princeton University Press.

Weyland, Kurt, Madrid, Raul and Hunter, Wendy. 2010. *Leftist Governments in Latin America: Successes and Shortcomings*. Cambridge: Cambridge University Press.

Wilkie, James. 1978. *La Revolución Mexicana (1910–1976): Gasto Federal y Cambio Social*. Mexico, DF: Fondo de Cultura Económica.

Wilkinson, Steven. 2004. *Votes and Violence*. Cambridge: Cambridge University Press.

Wise, Paul. 2003. "The Anatomy of a Disparity in Infant Mortality." *Annual Review of Public Health*. 24: 341–362.

Wodon, Quentin. 1999. "Government Programs and Poverty in Mexico." Report No. 19214-ME. Washington, DC: World Bank.

2001. "Government Programs and Poverty," in Giugale, Marcelo, Lafourcade, Olivier and Nguyen, Vinh (eds.), *Mexico. A Comprehensive Development Agenda for the New Era*. Washington, DC: World Bank.

Wood, Elisabeth. 2000. *Forging Democracy from Below*. Cambridge: Cambridge University Press.

World Bank. 2004a. *World Development Report 2005: A Better Investment Climate for Everyone*. Oxford: Oxford University Press.

2004b. *World Development Report: Making Public Services Work for the Poor*. Oxford: Oxford University Press.

2005. *Poverty in Mexico: An Assessment of Conditions, Trends and Government Strategy*. Mexico: World Bank.

2007. *World Development Report 2008: Agriculture for Development*. Oxford: Oxford University Press.

Wright, Gavin. 1974. "The Political Economy of New Deal Spending: An Econometric Analysis." *The Review of Economics and Statistics*. 56 (1): 30–38.

Yamada, Gustavo and Castro, Juan Francisco. 2007. "Poverty, and Social Polices in Peru." Universidad del Pacifico, Documento de Discusion DD/07/06

Young L. 1994. "Paupers, Property, and Place: A Geographical Analysis of the English, Irish, and Scottish Poor Laws in the Mid-19th Century." *Environment and Planning D: Society and Space*. 12 (3): 325–340.

Zarazaga, Rodrigo. 2011. "Vote-Buying and Asymmetric Information: A Model with Applications to Argentina." APSA 2011 Annual Meeting Paper.

Zhurakvskaya, Ekaterina V. 2000. "Incentives to Provide Local Public Goods: Fiscal Federalism, Russian Style." *Journal of Public Economics*. 76 (3) (June): 337–376.

Zucco, Cesar. 2010. "Poor Voters vs. Poor Places: Persisting Patterns and Changes in Brazilian Electoral Patterns." Typescript. Yale Program on Democracy.

2013. "When Payouts Pay Off: Conditional Cash Transfers and Voting Behavior in Brazil 2002–10." *American Journal of Political Science*. 57 (4): 810–822.

Zweifel, Thomas D. and Navia, Patricio. 2000. "Democracy, Dictatorship, and Infant Mortality." *Journal of Democracy*. 11 (2): 99–119.

Index

accountability, 115, 120–124, 125n6, 125n8, 125–126, 135, 135n31
Agency, 185
Aguascalientes, 133n25
Alianza Cívica, 165
Alms, 195
Aportaciones, 114
Argentina, 26, 33, 36–38, 50n7, 68, 187, 187n10
Asistencialista, 117, 195, 196n23
Australian ballot, 187

Beneficence, 194–195
Bentzul, Enrique, 15n8, 14–16, 16n9, 186
Blindaje Electoral, 165
Bolivia, 26, 33, 40–42
Bolsa Familia, 26, 29, 38–40
Brazil, 26, 29, 33, 38–40, 50n7, 124, 125n8, 186
Britain, 185–186, 190
Bucharest, 194n21
bureaucracy, 49

cacique, 15–16
Calderón, Felipe, 164, 174
Canada, 189
Catholic, 191, 193, 195
CCT, 186, 200
Ceará, 124
Chamber of Deputies, 163
Chávez, Hugo, 26, 33, 35–36
Chiapas, 14, 16–17, 115–116, 120, 133n25, 136, 144, 148, 152

Chile, 26, 29, 33, 38n3, 50n7, 187, 187n10
Church, 191, 192n14, 195
Clientelism, ix, 5, 8–9, 12–14, 17, 20–22, 26, 32, 34, 40, 44, 67, 67n1, 69–71, 73, 79, 81, 83–84, 88n3, 88–90, 96, 98–99, 101–103, 106, 108, 111–112, 115, 118, 127, 152, 154–156, 160–161, 165–166, 170, 180–183, 184n5, 185n6, 184–189, 191, 196, 216, 224, 231
Colom, Alvaro, 30, 42
Colombia, 8n4, 26, 29, 33, 39n3
Commitment, 201
CONAPO, 53n10, 98, 128n16
Conditional Cash Transfer, 4, 14–16, 18, 20
conditional party loyalty, 21, 75, 89–91, 97, 100–101, 103, 111, 160
CONEVAL, 46, 46n2, 51, 53n10
core voter, 2, 10n6, 9–12, 17, 21, 34, 40, 49, 63, 68–71, 72n3, 77n6, 78n7, 72–85, 87, 89–92, 97n9, 94–104, 106, 108–109, 111–112, 131, 135, 160, 180–181, 202
Correa, Rafael, 26, 33
Corruption, 184–185, 187–188, 202
Counterfactual, 189
Cox, 10
Cuba, 29

Dasgupta, Partha, 2
De Tocqueville, Alexis, 191, 193n19, 193–194, 196
decentralization, 6, 19, 22, 40, 114n2, 114–118, 125n6, 125–127, 157, 183, 186n7, 186–187, 196n24, 201–202

233

democracy, 1, 25, 28, 30–31, 36, 39–40, 42, 187
diarrhea, 119
Discretion, 186, 186n7, 188
discretionary, 7–9, 20–21
Dominican Republic, 29

Ecuador, 26, 29, 33, 35
Ejidos, 187
El Salvador, 29
Elections, 118, 185, 188
electricity, 2–3, 5, 22
Elizabethan Acts, 191
endogeneity, 122, 122n2, 126, 130
England, 193n17, 190–194, 194n19, 196, 196n24, 198, 201
Entitlements, 113, 189, 192, 196–198, 201, 203
ethnolinguistic fractionalization ELF, 123

Familias en Acción, 8n4
FDSM, 61, 113–114, 114n2, 132–133, 134n29, 138
Federal District, 164
Federal Electoral Institute IFE, 163
Federalism, 116
FISM, 4, 18–19, 61n15, 61–62, 113–115, 120, 122, 133, 134n29, 138, 140–142, 145, 148, 153, 157, 160–161, 169–170, 173, 188
Florence, 194
Fondos Municipales, 61n14
formula-based, 7, 18
Formulas, 114–116
Fox, Vicente, 49, 117, 163–166, 172, 174, 179
France, 191
Fujimori, Alberto, 26, 33–36
Fundar, 165

Gallup, 161n1
GIS, 57n12
governance, 1
Governors, 116
Guadalupe Tepeyac, 17
Guanajuato, 133n25
Guatemala, 26, 29–30, 35, 42
Guerrero, 116, 120, 144, 148

Haiti, 29
Hidalgo, 133n25, 148

Honduras, 29
Hospital, 195
Human Development Index, 53, 128n16
Humboldt, Alexander von, 195

IMR, 18–19, 147n1, 147n2, 150n4, 151n7, 153n10, 154n11, 145–157
IMSS, 47, 48n4, 50, 153n10, 164
Indonesia, 8n4
INEGI, 46n3, 128n16, 133, 150–152
infant mortality, 2, 18, 22, 117
INFONAVIT, 48
instrumental variable, 122n2, 130, 132n23, 133n27, 132–134, 138
ISSSTE, 48, 50, 153n10

Jamaica, 29

Kirchner, Nestor, 37
Kirschner, Cristina, 37
Kuran, Timur, 193n18

Labastida, Francisco, 163, 174
leakage, 120, 125
Levy, Santiago, 117, 117n7, 186
Liconsa, 51n8
Lopez Obrador, Andres Manuel, 63, 164–165, 174, 178
Lula da Silva, Luiz Inacio, 29, 38

Machine politics, 185, 196
Madrazo, Roberto, 174
Malthus, Thomas Robert, 192n15, 192n16
Marcos, *Subcomandante*, 3, 17, 19, 115
McCubbins, 10
Mesa, Carlos, 40
Ministry of Social Development, 87
Monte de Piedad, 194, 194n20
Montesquieu, 45
Morales, Evo, 26, 40–42
Municipal, 113, 113n1, 116, 120–121, 124, 125n8, 125–126, 128–130, 132–133, 133n27, 135, 136n32
municipalities, 4, 19, 21, 45, 53, 56–58, 60–63, 70, 88n2, 88–90, 97n9, 93–98, 100–106, 107n10, 107–110, 112, 118, 137–138, 138n36, 140–141, 144, 147, 151n7, 151–152, 157

Nayarit, 133n25
Netherlands, 192–193, 193n17

Index

New Spain, 194–195
Nicaragua, 29

Oaxaca, 6, 120, 137, 148
Oportunidades, 4–6, 18, 26, 29, 38, 49–51, 61–62, 117, 145, 148, 160–162, 164n4, 164–166, 169–170, 172–175, 178–179, 201–203

PAN, 4, 62–63, 97n9, 113, 116, 158, 163–166, 169, 174–175, 177, 179
PASSPA, 117
patron-client, 17
Peru, 26, 28, 33–35
Peso Crisis, 46, 188
Petra, 158
Polanyi, Karl, 190–191
Poor Laws, 190–192, 192n15, 192n16, 193n19, 196, 199, 201
pork-barrel politics, 8
portfolio, 9, 21
Portugal, 194
Poverty, 1, 3–6, 13, 17, 19, 21, 45–46, 46n2, 49–51, 53, 53n9, 53n10, 57n12, 56–58, 62, 67, 86–88, 90, 96–99, 101–102, 108, 112, 115–118, 117n7, 118, 122, 124, 132–133, 137, 145, 149, 152, 153n10, 155n11, 157, 192n15, 193n17, 193n18, 194n19, 194n20, 187–195, 196n23, 196–200, 202
PRD, 62–63, 97n9, 113, 116, 158, 164–165, 177–179
PRI, 4–6, 19, 21, 49, 62–63, 68, 86–89, 91n6, 91–97, 97n9, 99–106, 108–109, 111–113, 115–118, 120, 131, 135, 157–158, 163, 165–166, 168–170, 174, 177, 179, 186–187
Procampo, 50, 50n6, 51n8, 164
Programmatic, 184–185, 199, 202
Progresa, 4, 18–19, 26, 29, 42, 49–50, 58, 61, 61n16, 114n2, 114–115, 117–118, 145, 147–148, 151–152, 154, 156–157, 160–164, 166, 169–170, 173–175, 177–179, 203, 207
Pronasol, 3–5, 17–19, 21, 49, 59, 60n13, 60–62, 70, 88n2, 88n3, 89n4, 85–90, 90n5, 91n6, 91–92, 97n9, 96–104, 106, 107n10, 107–108, 111n11, 113n1, 111–114, 116, 118, 120, 122, 128n18, 131n21, 131–132, 132n23, 134n29, 138, 138n36, 141–142, 145, 147–148, 152–153, 157, 161n2, 160–162, 167–169, 173
propensity score, 173, 173n14, 175, 175n17
Protestant, 191
Puebla, 49n5, 120, 133n25, 152

railroad, 131
Redistribution, 116
rent-seeking, 1, 6
Revenue-sharing, 116
reversibility, 7
Rural, 3–4, 6, 46, 49, 51, 61, 61n16, 88, 97–98, 116, 120, 144, 147

Salinas, Carlos, 3, 49n5, 86–88, 96, 105, 108, 116
San Juan Chamula, 14–16
San Luis Potosí, 120, 133n25
Sánchez de Lozada, Gonzalo, 40–41
Sedesol, 87, 165
Seguro Popular, 164, 164n4, 165n5, 180
Sen, Amartya, 2
sewage, 3
Skocpol, Theda, 196
social insurance, 25
Social policy, 186–187, 191, 193n17, 197
Social protection, 186, 190n12, 190n13, 188–191, 195–201
Sonora, 133n25
Spain, 192, 195–196
Speenhamland, 190–192
Subsecretario de Egresos, 117
Sweden, 189
swing voter, 10, 12, 17, 40, 70–73, 75, 78n7, 77–79, 81–82, 82n10, 84, 87, 96, 111, 180

Tamaulipas, 133n25
Tequio, 137, 137n34
Tzotzil, 15

UNDP, 53, 165
United States, 186, 196n24, 196–197

VAT, 116n6
Venezuela, 26, 29, 33, 35
Venice, 194

Voters, 7, 9–14, 17, 20n14, 19–22, 31, 34n1, 34–36, 38, 48, 62, 64, 69, 77n6, 78n7, 79–80, 66–81, 83–89, 95, 97, 99–101, 103, 108–109, 111–112, 116, 118, 121, 124, 126n12, 126–127, 131, 159–161, 163, 165–167, 174, 178–181, 184–188, 201

wages, 48, 98, 146, 153
Waqf, 193n18
water, 1–3, 5, 7, 22

welfare state, 5, 22, 25–27, 30, 44, 183, 188–190, 190n12, 192–193, 193n17, 198n26, 197–201
World Bank, 5n2, 50, 119, 149, 150n4, 225

Zapatista, 3–4, 17, 115, 144
Zapotec, 6
Zedillo, Ernesto, 4, 13, 62, 115–116, 134n29, 162–163, 169
Zinacantán, 15n8, 16n9

Other Books in the Series (*continued from page iii*)

Carles Boix, *Political Order and Inequality: Their Foundations and Their Consequences for Human Welfare*
Carles Boix, *Political Parties, Growth, and Equality: Conservative and Social Democratic Economic Strategies in the World Economy*
Catherine Boone, *Merchant Capital and the Roots of State Power in Senegal, 1930-1985*
Continued after the Index
Catherine Boone, *Political Topographies of the African State: Territorial Authority and Institutional Change*
Catherine Boone, *Property and Political Order in Africa: Land Rights and the Structure of Politics*
Michael Bratton, Robert Mattes, and E. Gyimah-Boadi, *Public Opinion, Democracy, and Market Reform in Africa*
Michael Bratton and Nicolas van de Walle, *Democratic Experiments in Africa: Regime Transitions in Comparative Perspective*
Valerie Bunce, *Leaving Socialism and Leaving the State: The End of Yugoslavia, the Soviet Union, and Czechoslovakia*
Daniele Caramani, *The Nationalization of Politics: The Formation of National Electorates and Party Systems in Europe*
John M. Carey, *Legislative Voting and Accountability*
Kanchan Chandra, *Why Ethnic Parties Succeed: Patronage and Ethnic Headcounts in India*
Eric C. C. Chang, Mark Andreas Kayser, Drew A. Linzer, and Ronald Rogowski, *Electoral Systems and the Balance of Consumer-Producer Power*
José Antonio Cheibub, *Presidentialism, Parliamentarism, and Democracy*
Ruth Berins Collier, *Paths toward Democracy: The Working Class and Elites in Western Europe and South America*
Pepper D. Culpepper, *Quiet Politics and Business Power: Corporate Control in Europe and Japan*
Rafaela M. Dancygier, *Immigration and Conflict in Europe*
Christian Davenport, *State Repression and the Domestic Democratic Peace*
Donatella della Porta, *Social Movements, Political Violence, and the State*
Alberto Diaz-Cayeros, *Federalism, Fiscal Authority, and Centralization in Latin America*
Jesse Driscoll, *Warlords and Coalition Politics in Post-Soviet States*
Thad Dunning, *Crude Democracy: Natural Resource Wealth and Political Regimes*
Gerald Easter, *Reconstructing the State: Personal Networks and Elite Identity*
Margarita Estevez-Abe, *Welfare and Capitalism in Postwar Japan: Party, Bureaucracy, and Business*
Henry Farrell, *The Political Economy of Trust: Institutions, Interests, and Inter-Firm Cooperation in Italy and Germany*
Karen E. Ferree, *Framing the Race in South Africa: The Political Origins of Racial Census Elections*
M. Steven Fish, *Democracy Derailed in Russia: The Failure of Open Politics*
Robert F. Franzese, *Macroeconomic Policies of Developed Democracies*
Roberto Franzosi, *The Puzzle of Strikes: Class and State Strategies in Postwar Italy*

Timothy Frye, *Building States and Markets After Communism: The Perils of Polarized Democracy*
Geoffrey Garrett, *Partisan Politics in the Global Economy*
Scott Gehlbach, *Representation through Taxation: Revenue, Politics, and Development in Postcommunist States*
Edward L. Gibson, *Boundary Control: Subnational Authoritarianism in Federal Democracies*
Jane R. Gingrich, *Making Markets in the Welfare State: The Politics of Varying Market Reforms*
Miriam Golden, *Heroic Defeats: The Politics of Job Loss*
Jeff Goodwin, *No Other Way Out: States and Revolutionary Movements*
Merilee Serrill Grindle, *Changing the State*
Anna Grzymala-Busse, *Rebuilding Leviathan: Party Competition and State Exploitation in Post-Communist Democracies*
Anna Grzymala-Busse, *Redeeming the Communist Past: The Regeneration of Communist Parties in East Central Europe*
Frances Hagopian, *Traditional Politics and Regime Change in Brazil*
Henry E. Hale, *The Foundations of Ethnic Politics: Separatism of States and Nations in Eurasia and the World*
Mark Hallerberg, Rolf Ranier Strauch, Jürgen von Hagen, *Fiscal Governance in Europe*
Stephen E. Hanson, *Post-Imperial Democracies: Ideology and Party Formation in Third Republic France, Weimar Germany, and Post-Soviet Russia*
Silja Häusermann, *The Politics of Welfare State Reform in Continental Europe: Modernization in Hard Times*
Michael Hechter, *Alien Rule*
Gretchen Helmke, *Courts Under Constraints: Judges, Generals, and Presidents in Argentina*
Yoshiko Herrera, *Imagined Economies: The Sources of Russian Regionalism*
J. Rogers Hollingsworth and Robert Boyer, eds., *Contemporary Capitalism: The Embeddedness of Institutions*
John D. Huber and Charles R. Shipan, *Deliberate Discretion? The Institutional Foundations of Bureaucratic Autonomy*
Ellen Immergut, *Health Politics: Interests and Institutions in Western Europe*
Torben Iversen, *Capitalism, Democracy, and Welfare*
Torben Iversen, *Contested Economic Institutions*
Torben Iversen, Jonas Pontusson, and David Soskice, eds., *Unions, Employers, and Central Banks: Macroeconomic Coordination and Institutional Change in Social Market Economies*
Thomas Janoski and Alexander M. Hicks, eds., *The Comparative Political Economy of the Welfare State*
Joseph Jupille, *Procedural Politics: Issues, Influence, and Institutional Choice in the European Union*
Stathis Kalyvas, *The Logic of Violence in Civil War*
David C. Kang, *Crony Capitalism: Corruption and Capitalism in South Korea and the Philippines*
Stephen B. Kaplan, *Globalization and Austerity Politics in Latin America*
Junko Kato, *Regressive Taxation and the Welfare State*
Orit Kedar, *Voting for Policy, Not Parties: How Voters Compensate for Power Sharing*

Robert O. Keohane and Helen B. Milner, eds., *Internationalization and Domestic Politics*
Herbert Kitschelt, *The Transformation of European Social Democracy*
Herbert Kitschelt, Kirk A. Hawkins, Juan Pablo Luna, Guillermo Rosas, and Elizabeth J. Zechmeister, *Latin American Party Systems*
Herbert Kitschelt, Peter Lange, Gary Marks, and John D. Stephens, eds., *Continuity and Change in Contemporary Capitalism*
Herbert Kitschelt, Zdenka Mansfeldova, Radek Markowski, and Gabor Toka, *Post-Communist Party Systems*
David Knoke, Franz Urban Pappi, Jeffrey Broadbent, and Yutaka Tsujinaka, eds., *Comparing Policy Networks*
Allan Kornberg and Harold D. Clarke, *Citizens and Community: Political Support in a Representative Democracy*
Amie Kreppel, *The European Parliament and the Supranational Party System*
David D. Laitin, *Language Repertoires and State Construction in Africa*
Fabrice E. Lehoucq and Ivan Molina, *Stuffing the Ballot Box: Fraud, Electoral Reform, and Democratization in Costa Rica*
Mark Irving Lichbach and Alan S. Zuckerman, eds., *Comparative Politics: Rationality, Culture, and Structure, 2nd edition*
Evan Lieberman, *Race and Regionalism in the Politics of Taxation in Brazil and South Africa*
Richard M. Locke, *Promoting Labor Standards in a Global Economy: The Promise and Limits of Private Power*
Pauline Jones Luong, *Institutional Change and Political Continuity in Post-Soviet Central Asia*
Pauline Jones Luong and Erika Weinthal, *Oil Is Not a Curse: Ownership Structure and Institutions in Soviet Successor States*
Julia Lynch, *Age in the Welfare State: The Origins of Social Spending on Pensioners, Workers, and Children*
Doug McAdam, John McCarthy, and Mayer Zald, eds., *ComparativePerspectives on Social Movements*
Lauren M. MacLean, *Informal Institutions and Citizenship in Rural Africa: Risk and Reciprocity in Ghana and Côte d'Ivoire*
Beatriz Magaloni, *Voting for Autocracy: Hegemonic Party Survival and its Demise in Mexico*
James Mahoney, *Colonialism and Postcolonial Development: Spanish America in Comparative Perspective*
James Mahoney and Dietrich Rueschemeyer, eds., *Comparative Historical Analysis in the Social Sciences*
Scott Mainwaring and Matthew Soberg Shugart, eds., *Presidentialism and Democracy in Latin America*
Isabela Mares, *From Open Secrets to Secret Voting: Democratic Electoral Reforms and Voter Autonomy*
Isabela Mares, *The Politics of Social Risk: Business and Welfare State Development*
Isabela Mares, *Taxation, Wage Bargaining, and Unemployment*
Cathie Jo Martin and Duane Swank, *The Political Construction of Business Interests: Coordination, Growth, and Equality*
Anthony W. Marx, *Making Race, Making Nations: A Comparison of South Africa, the United States, and Brazil*

Bonnie M. Meguid, *Party Competition between Unequals: Strategies and Electoral Fortunes in Western Europe*
Joel S. Migdal, *State in Society: Studying How States and Societies Constitute One Another*
Joel S. Migdal, Atul Kohli, and Vivienne Shue, eds., *State Power and Social Forces: Domination and Transformation in the Third World*
Scott Morgenstern and Benito Nacif, eds., *Legislative Politics in Latin America*
Kevin M. Morrison, *Nontaxation and Representation: The Fiscal Foundations of Political Stability*
Layna Mosley, *Global Capital and National Governments*
Layna Mosley, *Labor Rights and Multinational Production*
Wolfgang C. Müller and Kaare Strøm, *Policy, Office, or Votes?*
Maria Victoria Murillo, *Political Competition, Partisanship, and Policy Making in Latin American Public Utilities*
Maria Victoria Murillo, *Labor Unions, Partisan Coalitions, and Market Reforms in Latin America*
Monika Nalepa, *Skeletons in the Closet: Transitional Justice in Post-Communist Europe*
Ton Notermans, *Money, Markets, and the State: Social Democratic Economic Policies since 1918*
Eleonora Pasotti, *Political Branding in Cities: The Decline of Machine Politics in Bogotá, Naples, and Chicago*
Aníbal Pérez-Liñán, *Presidential Impeachment and the New Political Instability in Latin America*
Roger D. Petersen, *Understanding Ethnic Violence: Fear, Hatred, and Resentment in Twentieth-Century Eastern Europe*
Roger D. Petersen, *Western Intervention in the Balkans: The Strategic Use of Emotion in Conflict*
Simona Piattoni, ed., *Clientelism, Interests, and Democratic Representation*
Paul Pierson, *Dismantling the Welfare State?: Reagan, Thatcher, and the Politics of Retrenchment*
Marino Regini, *Uncertain Boundaries: The Social and Political Construction of European Economies*
Kenneth M. Roberts, *Changing Course in Latin America: Party Systems in the Neoliberal Era*
Marc Howard Ross, *Cultural Contestation in Ethnic Conflict*
Ben Ross Schneider, *Hierarchical Capitalism in Latin America: Business, Labor, and the Challenges of Equitable Development*
Lyle Scruggs, *Sustaining Abundance: Environmental Performance in Industrial Democracies*
Jefferey M. Sellers, *Governing from Below: Urban Regions and the Global Economy*
Yossi Shain and Juan Linz, eds., *Interim Governments and Democratic Transitions*
Beverly Silver, *Forces of Labor: Workers' Movements and Globalization since 1870*
Prerna Singh, *How Solidarity Works for Welfare: Subnationalism and Social Development in India*
Theda Skocpol, *Social Revolutions in the Modern World*
Dan Slater, *Ordering Power: Contentious Politics and Authoritarian Leviathans in Southeast Asia*

Regina Smyth, *Candidate Strategies and Electoral Competition in the Russian Federation: Democracy Without Foundation*
Richard Snyder, *Politics after Neoliberalism: Reregulation in Mexico*
David Stark and László Bruszt, *Postsocialist Pathways: Transforming Politics and Property in East Central Europe*
Sven Steinmo, *The Evolution of Modern States: Sweden, Japan, and the United States*
Sven Steinmo, Kathleen Thelen, and Frank Longstreth, eds., *Structuring Politics: Historical Institutionalism in Comparative Analysis*
Susan C. Stokes, *Mandates and Democracy: Neoliberalism by Surprise in Latin America*
Susan C. Stokes, ed., *Public Support for Market Reforms in New Democracies*
Susan C. Stokes, Thad Hall, Marcelo Nazareno, and Valeria Brusco, *Brokers, Voters, and Clientelism: The Puzzle of Distributive Politics*
Duane Swank, *Global Capital, Political Institutions, and Policy Change in Developed Welfare States*
Sidney Tarrow, *Power in Movement: Social Movements and Contentious Politics, Revised and Updated 3rd Edition*
Tariq Thachil, *Elite Parties, Poor Voters: How Social Services Win Votes in India*
Kathleen Thelen, *How Institutions Evolve: The Political Economy of Skills in Germany, Britain, the United States, and Japan*
Kathleen Thelen, *Varieties of Liberalization and the New Politics of Social Solidarity*
Charles Tilly, *Trust and Rule*
Daniel Treisman, *The Architecture of Government: Rethinking Political Decentralization*
Guillermo Trejo, *Popular Movements in Autocracies: Religion, Repression, and Indigenous Collective Action in Mexico*
Lily Lee Tsai, *Accountability without Democracy: How Solidary Groups Provide Public Goods in Rural China*
Joshua Tucker, *Regional Economic Voting: Russia, Poland, Hungary, Slovakia and the Czech Republic, 1990-1999*
Ashutosh Varshney, *Democracy, Development, and the Countryside*
Jeremy M. Weinstein, *Inside Rebellion: The Politics of Insurgent Violence*
Stephen I. Wilkinson, *Votes and Violence: Electoral Competition and Ethnic Riots in India*
Jason Wittenberg, *Crucibles of Political Loyalty: Church Institutions and Electoral Continuity in Hungary*
Elisabeth J. Wood, *Forging Democracy from Below: Insurgent Transitions in South Africa and El Salvador*
Elisabeth J. Wood, *Insurgent Collective Action and Civil War in El Salvador*

Printed in Poland
by Amazon Fulfillment
Poland Sp. z o.o., Wrocław